The Field Trip Book

Study Travel Experiences in Social Studies

The Field Trip Book

Study Travel Experiences in Social Studies

Ronald V. Morris
Ball State University

Information Age Publishing, Inc.
Charlotte, North Carolina • www.infoagepub.com

Library of Congress Cataloging-in-Publication Data

Morris, Ronald V.
  The field trip book : study travel experiences in social studies / Ronald
V. Morris.
    p. cm.
  Includes bibliographical references.
  ISBN 978-1-61735-076-4 (paperback) — ISBN 978-1-61735-077-1 (hardcover) —
ISBN 978-1-61735-078-8 (e-book)
  1. Social sciences—Study and teaching (Elementary)—United States. 2.
Social sciences—Study and teaching (Middle school)—United States. 3.
School field trips—United States. I. Title.
  LB1584.M77 2010
  372.83'044—dc22

                                                                2010027129

Printed in the United States of America

CONTENTS

ACKNOWLEDGMENTS

This book is in honor of Wendy Jolliff: my sister in bad times and in good times. Skiing, hiking, traveling, and all sorts of adventures are fun with you around. You always do the most amazing things, and I am glad you are my friend.

I would like to thank the following people for their contributions to this book. Barbara Johnson introduced me to the town of Hope. I would like to thank Link Luddington of the Indiana Department of Natural Resources for letting me visit the Lanier House even when it was closed. I thank Jean McNeely for introducing me to the state of Texas and letting me tag along to Antietam National Battlefield, Gettysburg National Military Park, and Washington, D. C. I would like to thank Martha L. V. Morris for proofreading this manuscript, earlier drafts, and articles. I would also like to thank John Stacier of Historic Madison, Inc. for opening several closed houses in the off-season. I would like to thank the teachers, staff, administration, and students in Crawfordsville for letting me write about their encounters with the Amish. I would like to thank my former students at Mary Bryan Elementary School, who were very gracious as I dragged them across the state of Indiana.

I would like to thank the publishers of *Canadian Social Studies* and *The Social Studies* for allowing articles to be reprinted in this volume.

CHAPTER 1

THE ECONOMY
OF THE FIELD TRIP

When students engage in study travel experiences they leave the school grounds to gather information about their world. Students may have formal assignments or engage in experiences that allow them to gather information through enactive experiences. They may also conduct inquiry activities in the field connected with their classroom studies. In study travel situations, students always have definite academic purposes in their travel supported by teacher goals and objectives. Students remember ideas, events, and feelings they experience on field trips years after the event is over (Alleman, Knighton, & Brophy, 2007; Knapp, 2007, 2000; Falk & Dierking, 2002). They need to see the importance of curricula being transferable to their future lives outside school.

It is because students participate as citizens in a community that the student must go into the community and learn from its members. A citizen cannot be insulated from his or her community, thus all of his or her learning cannot occur within the walls of the school classroom. Students meet the people of the community who are engaged in commerce or politics and see them in their infinite variety. By looking at differences and commonalities of the people in their communities, students can see a comparative slice of their world. They learn about their communities by acting in the present within their communities. Students see the people and the physical connection they have with the land. The purpose of the

The Field Trip Book: Study Travel Experiences in Social Studies
pp. 1–6
Copyright © 2010 by Information Age Publishing
All rights of reproduction in any form reserved.

study travel experience is to help students examine the breadth and depth of the social studies curriculum (Noel & Colopy, 2006; Morris, 2006). The focus of the study travel experience is on helping students become good citizens who can live in a globally interconnected world, and teachers need to help students see how social studies is both important and relevant to their lives in the community (Brophy & Alleman, 2009, 2006; Alleman, Knighton, & Brophy, 2007). Students need to know the stories of multiple people, whether they inhabit the land simultaneously or at various times (Pascal & Bertram, 2009; Banks, 2001). Social studies by definition provides an interdisciplinary curriculum (National Council for the Social Studies [NCSS], 1994), and students get many opportunities through the open-ended experience of a field trip to frame questions themselves in an integrated curriculum (Holloway & Chiodo, 2009; Schuitema, Veuglelers, Rijlaarsdam, & ten Darn, 2009; Kozak & Bretherick, 2002). Therefore, social studies education must help the students define how they connect as citizens in their communities, and social studies teachers should talk about citizenship and commitment as the essential qualities necessary to perpetuate a democratic system of government for future generations (Mitchell & Parker, 2008; Parker, 2006). Through travel experiences, students understand the geographic scale of the land, the economic might of the people, and the rich cultural context and the deep historical connection of societal practices. Students are charged with maintaining and upholding their community through their commitment and actions within the community. Students pull in a vast array of sensory experiences connected to community.

The field trip calls educators to deliberation; every action, thought, word, and gesture must be premeditated, deliberative, and purposeful. The cost of the field trip is relatively high compared to sitting in a classroom, in terms of logistics, labor, and resources. The two greatest quantities that must be dealt with are time and space. Time from the classroom must be accounted for, and time can be lost to weather, ill-prepared sites, poor lunch facilities, and inconvenient restrooms. Space can be daunting because of distance, traffic and obstructions, and navigation. Because of these factors, planning and executing a field trip requires detailed planning and constant monitoring. Time and distance from the classroom can be justified by the long days, distinctive experiences, quality and quantity of information gathered, and strengthening of the community. Resources can be provided from schools, community, and parents, and the teacher's labor must include dedicated and thorough planning. After rigorous planning, the serendipitous moments and unexpected discoveries may be celebrated by those prepared to recognize them.

Teachers continue to be buffeted by a flurry of salvos of pedantic falderal between proponents of history- or social studies-based instruction.

Adherents of each camp claim to have the true holy grail of the core curriculum. Members of each camp claim the other is missing the point and that the influence of the other is hurting children by limiting their education. Yet, looking in schools and classrooms, it is hard to see any evidence of either camp holding sway. There is neither vigorous, enlightened historical inquiry nor is there healthy, robust social studies inquiry. Instead, there is silence on the part of students that passes for good discipline, and there are lectures by teachers at the front of the classroom that pass for quality education.

It would be exciting to walk down the hallway in an elementary school and see either vigorous, enlightened historical inquiry or healthy, robust social studies inquiry. It would be just plain amazing to walk down an elementary hallway and see both. Unfortunately, at this point it would be amazing to see either, because in light of high-stakes testing of reading and math, economics, history, geography, and social studies instruction have been pushed out of the elementary school curriculum. Oh, it is still possible to see it now and then on a Friday afternoon after the fire drill, but for all practical purposes learning about the contributions of people is no longer an important part of American public education. While educators argue over whether to teach students history or social studies, nothing is happening to excite students about either, and learning about people has faded into the mists of time.

In those few places where states test social studies to meet state standards, learning about people consists of memorizing lists to be repeated in a high-stakes trivia game. Students repeat information found in highlighted sections from the text as reinterpreted by the questions at the end of the chapter. This is not the insightful examination of controversial issues to inform citizens or enlighten public policy debate that either historians or educators would like to see. This is merely another mind-numbing exercise that students describe as busy work. More testing is not by itself the answer, but a détente or de-escalation of student testing proliferation is needed.

What of those college students who have been tested so many times and here proved they are adequate to be teachers? Students eager to become teachers come to methods classes dreading to learn about social studies because it was so poorly taught, or they did not have it in school. Every professor of college methods and every elementary school social studies teacher hears the same lines over and over:

I never liked social studies, because it was just a bunch of dates.

I never understood why this stuff was important until now.

We never had social studies until [fourth, fifth, or] sixth grade.

We never did anything except read from the textbook.

If a student did not learn about social studies in elementary school, it is very difficult to make up lost time in college. When a student learns a passion for people and their contributions, he or she thinks about the people and the decisions they faced and resolved. Some students find learning about people fascinating; they are inspired by the hopes, dreams, and the challenges people faced.

Students remember few things that they did in school. They cannot recall interesting people, wonderful events, and stimulating analysis of content, nor can they remember what they did to learn about social studies. They cannot remember making a difference in their community, doing service learning, conducting inquiry, being in plays, participating in simulations, working with primary sources, or examining artifacts unless they got the experience of doing it. Although the students remembered the field trips, too often the memories are few, confused, and detached from meaning. If students got a field trip experience, and if it had educational value, it consisted basically of more of the same types of experiences they had already received in school. The teacher or docent talked in a different place, but either way adults talked and students listened. With all of this in mind, how can educators set up field trips wherein students take ownership, wherein students do the investigating, and wherein students connect with their community and world as members of a democracy?

Students need to see the connection between their lives in the community today and the lives in the future and in the past. By looking at multiple aspects of their communities, students find connections through a variety of disciplines or an integrated curriculum (Van Kannel-Ray & Newlin-Haus, 2009; Roessing, 2007). By working with an integrated curriculum, students can look at themes that cut across anthropology, economics, history, geography, sociology, and psychology. They see that they make decisions today that will inform their future, just as people in the past made decisions that shaped the present. The integrated curriculum that links social science disciplines to past and present connects students to the site where people have interacted.

When students go on-site, the events, interactions, and controversy flood them and they in turn take this flood of information and sensation and turn it into meaningful commentary. Students sort their empiricism to determine between the historical, the modern, and the interaction between those two when they experience a site. An integrated curriculum provides more potential for inquiry projects that students use to practice democratic skills and that students use to learn about social studies content (Rovegno & Gregg, 2007; Kornfeld & Leyden, 2005; Schuchat, 2005). Students interpret the site by evaluating it; through studied analysis and by providing additional information, they create a synthesis that deepens their understanding of events. Insightful investigation and critical commentary are the virtues a citizen needs as he or she enters into living in a community.

The economy of the field trip is not paid in easy access or preparation for the teacher, and it is not inexpensive when compared to sitting in a classroom. It is economical however, when students find deep meaning from investigations they conduct on-site or in conjunction with the site. The economics are in the prospective yield of the investment into the site—the results of the students when they produce knowledge from the site. The students learn about democracy, integrative curriculum, citizenship, empathy, and community. When students investigate the site, they must invest in the trip and the research question or experience they are trying to examine; the proceeds from student investment out-produce the investments of school or teacher.

All of this is to say that the student becomes a producer of knowledge. The student must produce new knowledge, insights, thoughts, and feelings about a site, subject, or experience. They may create this new knowledge by meeting people, exploring a new site, or reinterpreting a familiar site to produce new insights. The time in the field may be just a part of their learning or it can be long-term, but regardless of the duration the time in the field captures the imagination and stirs the soul of the individual to investigate further. They are not passive receptors; they are active.

CHAPTER 2

TEACHER SUCCESS WITH STUDY TRAVEL LOGISTICS

INTRODUCTION

Study travel experiences are like a box of chocolates: You never really know what you are going to get until you have made the commitment. There are many advantages to making study travel experiences, however. These advantages include both valuable site resources and outstanding interpretations. The disadvantages of study travel experiences include the disorientation of a new site, poor staff resources, poorly exhibited resources at the site, and negligible interpretation. All of this is to say that anything that could be a plus for taking a study travel experience could also be a detriment. Educators need to have a good understanding of the site before they take their students to that site; they need to also communicate clearly to the staff at the site what they hope the students will get from the site and how the staff can help the group leader meet the goals for taking the trip.

Each study travel experience needs a major theme for students to explore (Cartwright, Aronson, Stacey, & Winbush, 2001). In the following example, the theme is stated as a question for exploration: "What tensions existed between the industrial age and the environment?" As students visit sites, they explore this theme through viewing a frontier fort breaking into the wilderness, the home of a working family, the home of a

The Field Trip Book: Study Travel Experiences in Social Studies
pp. 7–33

captain of industry, factories and retail space, the rejection of technology by a religious group, the home and private gardens of a naturalist, and a public park. The sites may come from a variety of places and periods of time. The information that students learn from their travels may confirm or disconfirm the ideas they have about the theme. By selecting a theme, students build facts, concepts, and generalizations about each site and find connections between the sites.

To find a theme, the teacher must look at a variety of possible places to go for study travel experiences. In order to find what places are available to visit, the teacher should use tourism websites to locate special events, daily programs, and available hours. Some sites have specified hours and days when they are open, and other sites reserve some days specifically for groups. Do not just consider big museums when looking for themes; usually smaller museums are more flexible and accommodating, to the point of designing custom programs for groups. Both large and small sites have advantages; plan to visit a mixture of both. Some sites to consider visiting for study travel experiences include the following: county museums, courthouses, historic homes, libraries, both light and heavy industry sites, battlefields, military posts, mines, monuments, national parks, postal facilities, private collections, state parks, trails, universities, utilities, and transportation routes and hubs for such modes of travel as autos, boats, airplanes, and trains.

After checking the location on the Internet and determining what might be available to see, make a pre-visit trip to inspect the site. Of course, the group leader will examine the site for intellectual rigor and determine what there is for students to see and do. It is important to evaluate all museum programs because many sites offer programming that could be done just as effectively in classrooms at the school. If they can be done in school, they should be done there, and the valuable field trip resource should be saved for something else. Although some student programs are very entertaining, there may be no new ideas generated from them. Make certain that students see the big ideas, issues, and conflicts of the time and place that are addressed in any program that is selected for a field trip. Try to determine the most important ideas the site can interpret. What will the students do at this site? How will they learn? What themes are present? Are the staff members capable of providing interpretation or will the teacher need to do most of the interpretive work at this site? Can the students explore the site or will they need an assignment to focus them on the site?

While the teacher is on site, compare the cost and distance to the value of the interpretation; if the site is favorably reviewed, make the reservations either while still on the site or by phone shortly thereafter. Tell the site personnel what the goals and objectives for the group are and how this site can best help the group to reach them. The site personnel will be both surprised and pleased that you have thought about this.

Next, check the restrooms; the larger the group the longer it will take for logistics, and an inadequate restroom can stop a trip in its tracks. Next, check for either food service or areas for eating sack lunches; if students will spend the night, make sure to see that site, too. It is important to anticipate potential problems with the sites, the food service, and the lodging (Collins & Redcross, 2005; Mawdsley, 1999). The leader needs to be familiar with the various spaces so that when the group arrives at the site, the leader can immediately direct people to the proper areas.

The guidelines provided for overnight field trips can obviously be adapted for a one-day or a half-day field trip. If a teacher can comprehend and execute an overnight field trip, they can scale it back easily. It is much more difficult to go the other way, however, by extrapolating an overnight field trip from a half-day or one-day field trip.

ONE YEAR AHEAD

It is best, from a logistical perspective, to plan study travel experiences one year in advance. This long-range planning enables the dates to be approved by the administration; provides time to alert the cafeteria and request sack lunches; informs the nurse when the group will be gone; allows time to make reservations and complete connections, especially when large or highly scheduled sites are being considered; and permits adequate time to schedule transportation. Long-range planning allows the teacher to construct a detailed plan, develop themes, look for logical progressions, examine connections between sites, and keep the study travel experiences from being haphazard or merely afterthoughts. Certainly study travel experiences can also be spontaneous and should erupt from student investigations, but in this instance these study travel experiences are the ones the teacher knows ahead of time that the class will take. Spontaneous study travel experiences are more likely to be close to the school and involve smaller numbers of students, and thus may not require such large-scale planning. Another benefit of planning field trips a year in advance is that during the first weeks of the school year parents and students can receive a list of the school study travel experiences that are already scheduled (Figure 2.1). The list in the box includes the title and the year; after stating the name of the field trip, which is usually the destination, the month and the day or days of the field trip are then given, and finally the grade level is noted in parenthesis (Figure 2.2). Busy parents really appreciate this scheduling tool that informs them of upcoming

---

Field Trip Dates to Remember
School Year Date

August:
27–28   Northeastern Indiana Study Travel Experiences (4)
September:
8   Oldfields (4)
10   Lafayette Study Travel Experience (5)
24–25   Corydon, Louisville, Clarksville, Jeffersonville, and New Albany
                Study Travel Experience (4)
October:
1   National Road Study Travel Experience (5)
November:
1   Pioneer Woodworking Tools Field Experience (4)
12   Johnson County Field Experience (5)
December:
1   Behind the Scenes at the Indianapolis Museum of Art (5)
5   Christmas at Conner Prairie (4)
January:
9   Alpine Electronics Study Travel Experience (5)
11   Allied Metal Products Study Travel Experience (4)
February:
1   Wave Tek (5)
4   Indianapolis in the Hoosier State Study Travel Experience (4)
11   Indianapolis in the Nation and the World Study Travel Experi-
                ence (5)
March:
4   Crawfordsville Study Travel Experience (4)
11   Madison Study Travel Experiences (5)
April:
7   L & E Engineering (4)
8   Conner Prairie (5)
May:
5–7   Lincoln, New Harmony, and Angel Mounds Study Travel Expe-
                rience (4)
27–28   Vincennes Study Travel Experience (5)

Figure 2.1.   Example annual schedule.

Field Trip Dates to Remember
Year

Month

Date: Trip name (grade level going)

Figure 2.2.   Annual schedule template.

events in their child's life. They can then do long-range planning for their family and thus minimize many scheduling conflicts.

The long lead-time will allow time to determine if the parent group or local foundation will support students who do not have the means to afford the trip. Parent groups, civic groups, and local foundations should coordinate fund raising efforts. Some teachers like the idea of fund raising to provide for students who do not have the finances to participate in a study travel experience. However, the teacher's time is too valuable to spend it involved in fund raising. In the time it takes to sell fruitcakes, light bulbs, sausages, fertilizer, or lawn ornaments, a teacher could have done something educationally challenging and important. Many teachers spend hours of their lives fretting over nickels and dimes when the rate of return just does not merit the time invested.

At the beginning of the year fill out all of the bus forms for the year and send a copy of the itinerary and trip papers to the bus driver prior to the trip. Make sure to take road maps showing all of the destinations when traveling and check with the bus driver the morning of the trip to see that he or she really knows where the group is going. Watch the driver at any crucial points to make sure they know the destination of the group; under no circumstances should the teacher presume that the bus driver knows where they are going. On the other hand, once the group gets a reputation for being good to work with, bus drivers come out of the woodwork to work with the group; once a good relationship develops, group leaders can request and get the same bus drivers year after year. A great bus driver really helps make a trip go smoothly, because he or she can be trusted to know the way and he or she knows what to expect and how the trips work.

ONE MONTH AHEAD

Send home the parent permission form one month prior to the trip and request that it be returned two weeks prior to the trip. Most families do not make commitments a month in advance, so there should be few conflicts. A month is a short enough span of time that parents can remember the event, but it is not so far away that they forget it. The two weeks for the return of the permission slip gives the teacher time to plan and make last minute group arrangements. The notice at the beginning of the year helps families that make long-range plans, and the one-month notice helps parents to make timely decisions. On the day of the trip, take the phone numbers of the students' parents as well as necessary medical information, including lists of any food allergies within the group.

One month prior to the study travel experience, send out a parent informational letter (Figure 2.3); this helps communicate to parents the

123 School Drive
City, State, Zip+4
(Area Code) Phone Number
Email Address
January 1, 20XX

Dear Parents,

The Clio Historians will be exploring Montgomery County to find out about glacial action and the culture of Crawfordsville, Indiana, on Saturday, March 5, 20XX. We will leave at 8:00 a.m. for two nature preserves, which demonstrate the power of the glaciers. We will be outdoors most of the morning. Plan to send waterproof boots or a change of shoes and socks. Have your child dress for the weather and expect some long hikes. Those who are afraid of heights are cautioned about this stop; there are some breathtaking views. We will stop for lunch at a fast food restaurant in Crawfordsville before visiting the Old Jail Museum, Lane Place, and the Ben Hur Museum. We will return to Clio Elementary School by 7:00 p.m. Each child will need a $10.00 non-refundable deposit to reserve a space on this trip.

Sincerely,

Dr. Ronald Vaughan Morris
Manager of the Clio Historians

- -

My child, _____, may travel with the Clio Historians to Montgomery County.

_____   _____
Parent's signature   Date

PLEASE RETURN THIS FORM AND THE NON-REFUNDABLE DEPOSIT TO DR. RONALD VAUGHAN MORRIS BY FEBRUARY 25, 20XX.

Figure 2.3.   Example field trip permission slip.

events of the class and alerts them of any special needs for that day. Start with content information; tell who will go, where the students will go, and what they will learn. Inform them of the day, month, date, and year of the trip; include the departure and anticipated return times. Explain if the students need special clothing for exploring the environment or if they will engage in a specific physical activity. Describe the lunch arrangement and any costs associated with the trip. Add a tear-and-return section at the bottom of the letter stating the date, location, the child's name, and name of the school or class. Have a line for the parent to sign and date, and at the bottom of the sheet include where and when to return the information. Information needs to be returned two weeks prior to the trip to allow for final arrangements to be made. Collect the fees or deposit and state that this holds a place on the trip for the child; this fee is non-refundable because even if the child is sick the expenses still have been contracted. If there is money left over after all expenses for the trip have been met, as much money as possible will be returned to the students; thus, neither the teacher nor the school will be required to subsidize the trip.

The teacher gives the students and the parents a packing guide for overnight trips; this lists the personal items they need to bring and tells why each item is important. The teacher also needs to alert both students and parents of the potential hazards of plants, weather, and the planned activity (Figure 2.4). Announce that the trip will go forward regardless of the weather, so appropriate weather gear will be needed.

Parents often pack for the students and the students do not know what they have brought; thus, labeling items is crucial to returning lost articles. Place a disclaimer in the information letter stating that student possessions are ultimately their own responsibility. Suggest that parents provide soft luggage since hard baggage does not pack under a bus seat easily. To prevent the teacher from rolling fifty sleeping bags, parents need to teach their child to roll their sleeping bag prior to the trip. Many students own sleeping bags that are not very warm, because they were designed for slumber parties in heated homes; therefore, the student may need an extra blanket.

Suggest both good and poor bus activities; good activities promote quiet interaction with peers. Students need to interact and learn while the bus is in motion, so board games, cards, books, and maps are encouraged. Poor bus items are noisy, isolating, or provide a potential for loss. Items that tend to isolate individuals, such as headphones, are discouraged because students need to learn and practice how to talk and listen to one another. High levels of sound for prolonged periods of time can cause hearing damage so interactions during transportation need to be times when people can work together or trade information. For long charter

- Each person must be responsible for his or her own property.
- All items should be labeled. Put all clothing in a soft bag or pillow case and tie the opening.
- Put your pillow and an extra blanket inside your sleeping bag, then roll and tie it tightly and neatly so it will not come apart.
- Do not bring hard suitcases or overnight cases because we have no room for them.
- Wear jeans or slacks if you are allergic to plants.
- Dress for the weather.
- Wear walking shoes or heavy-soled shoes.
- No sandals or open toes are allowed.
- Bring rain gear and one complete change of clothing.
- Bring a washcloth, towel, soap, toothbrush, toothpaste, and a comb or brush.
- Students are encouraged to bring maps of Indiana, books, games, crossword puzzles, and other diversions to share with the other students on the bus trip.
- No radios, musical instruments, beeping games, or alarm clocks, please.
- No candy or food that will invite animals into the cabins.
- We will not be stopping for souvenirs or snacks.
- Extra money is not needed on the trip.
- Bring cameras only if you are willing to be responsible for them.

Figure 2.4.   Prototype necessities list.

bus trips there is usually a video player; the teacher can use such equipment to enrich the ride by showing content videos that supplement the interpretation provided at the destination.

Students can bring water, but they cannot take it into most sites because of the danger to artifacts and structures. Despite a society based on instant gratification, students can wait until the next meal before eating; candy, drinks, and food are not necessary because the students are well feed at regular meals. Food products invite insects, rodents, and mammal pests, and they can also make a mess. Someone needs to clean up every food accident and just one overturned drink can run the whole length of a bus. It is suggested that such food and drink items be left at home. Encourage the students not to bring lunch boxes on the trip because these must be monitored for the rest of the day.

The students' deposits cover all of their expenses so there is no need for additional money. Such additional money on trips is a needless headache because of the potential for loss or theft. Additional money also tends to divide the group into *haves* and *have-nots*. Without additional money, the group does not need to stop for snacks or souvenirs; in practice, there is a rejection of both recreational eating and denying an endorsement of commercialism. Students do not need to constantly forage on snacks between meals when they travel. Educators need to expose students to new ideas and experiences rather than encourage souvenir hunting and shopping at every gift shop on the trip; American children already know how to shop. Further shopping takes time away from the site. Museum managers calculate how much the average person will spend in their shop because the shop is the revenue-producing area of the museum. Parents really do appreciate this "no additional money" policy; they feel it acutely if they do not have money to send with their child, especially if all the other kids have additional money. It also keeps the total cost of the field trip relatively low, since the trip is one price with no add-ons or extra fees.

Students need a list of field trip rules at the same time they get the parent permission form (Figure 2.5); the rules are held to a minimum and cover five areas. Food and drinks are mentioned to protect against huge messes; sleep during the trip is not optional because the students need to be well-rested in order to learn. Safety issues and supervision are noted in two additional rules, which describe the reputation of the group so that they may return to the site the following year. The last area is an acknowledgement that the adults are all volunteers and the experience must be fun for them too or they will not come back (Giacalone, 2003). This might be the single most important rule, since everyone is giving up time to be there; it is expected that everyone will work to make this a pleasant experience. Good volunteers are hard to find; it is easier to keep the good ones than to recruit new ones each time.

It is important to determine the social goal of the trip. If it is to build community among the students, fewer parents will be needed, but if the goal is cross-generational education, then more parents can be taken (Patton, 2006; DeSteno, 2000). Check to make sure that the school district does not have a policy about too many parents going, thus making it into a parent trip rather than a student trip. In addition, since one central person fills out all of the forms, one central person needs to hear about all of

1. No food or drinks are allowed on the bus.
2. When the lights go out at night, it is time to go to sleep.
3. No one may leave the cabin without permission from the cabin leader.
4. We must leave the camp cleaner than we found it.
5. Cooperate with your group leader and bus driver.
6. Wherever you go, take a friend.
7. We will be on state property for most of the trip. It is our responsibility to protect and care for it.

Figure 2.5.   Prototype field trip rules.

the problems. The group leader must lead and assert their authority in order for parents and students to take responsibility; the group leader does not do all of the thinking for the entire group, however.

Just as a good teacher knows how to stretch a student without letting them fail, the group leader must make excellent decisions in selecting volunteers who can perform outstanding service. The volunteer may be out of his or her element or may even need assistance doing new things. The group leader never wants to put well-meaning volunteers behind the wheel to shuttle students around. Even well-intentioned drivers can be held liable for traffic accidents; therefore, it is important to help good people by not putting them in a place where they could fail. Put lots of effort and thought into getting good volunteers to accompany the students on the trip; do not assume that this will just happen. Find volunteers who can remember the needs of the group in addition to the needs of their own children. Poor volunteers load the whole trip as dead weight.

Just like the three bears' porridge, volunteers come in three flavors: those who seem to have no idea what the students are doing, those who want to control them too tightly, and those who are just right. Most volunteers want to help but do not know how; the letter in Figure 2.6 will help communicate clear expectations of how they can help. The letter helps to set the tone for their role on the expedition. Because volunteers do not usually have an educational background, the group leader may need to help them think about safety and then give them a long leash. It is important for the group leader to talk with the volunteers about how important it is that the students hear the same rules from all of the adults and how the rules remain the same on every field trip taken by school bus. The volunteers need to look for safety issues and become conscious of the press of time and its relationship to learning on the site. Most volunteers would figure out all of these things in two or three trips, but this letter helps them to understand their jobs faster.

As students get on the bus, it is easy for volunteers to individually ask if they have everything they need. This insures that students do not leave their possession in the car or on the curb. All other adults need to help students push belongings under their seats; this will give the students a lot more room on the trip and make the trip more comfortable. Volunteers can also write the students' names on their lunch bags as they get on the bus. By taking charge early, the volunteers immediately know that they are assisting the group leader to make the trip a success.

Teachers want students to talk and ask questions about the site; therefore, teachers do not want all the adults sitting together and all of the students sitting separately on the bus or at meals. Parent volunteers need to be available to talk with students and to provide supervision rather than

THANK YOU FOR VOLUNTEERING TO WORK WITH THE CLIO HISTORIANS

How to help:
I. Study/Travel Experiences
  A. Know where to find each one of your group members at any given time.
    1. You do not need to stay with them every second during tours or hikes, but you do need to know what they are doing, especially during non-tour times.
  B. Share the rules with the students.
    1. No food or drinks on the bus.
    2. Cooperate with your group leader and bus driver.
    3. Wherever you go, take a friend.
    4. We will be on state and private property; it is our responsibility to protect and care for it.
  C. Bus safety
    1. Sit flat.
    2. Pick a seat and stay in it.
    3. Use a low voice.
  D. Share the information about each site, which is in your packet, with the students while on the bus.
  E. While moving people, watch the intersections, parking lots, and streets.
  F. Help the students to stay attentive to the site or guide since we are here to learn.
  G. Make sure that the students thank the guides.
  H. We do not stop at gift shops due to time constraints and out of monetary consideration to parents.
  I. Fast food
    1. Adults order first.
    2. Know what you want to order.
    3. Have your money in your hand when you order.
    4. Center your drink when you pick up your tray.
    5. Only one trip to the counter.
  J. Share any problems with Dr. Morris.
  K. Enjoy the students and the trip.
II. Spending the Night
  A. Bring an alarm clock.
  B. Loading the bus
    1. Ask the students if they have
      a. Lunch
      b. Sleeping bag
      c. Clothes
    2. Students carry on their possessions and place them under their seat.
  C. Share these additional rules with the students.
    1. When the lights go out at night, it is time to go to sleep.
    2. No one may leave the cabin without permission from the cabin leader.
    3. We need to leave the camp cleaner than we found it.
  D. Unloading the bus
    1. The students pull their possessions from under their seats and place them on their seats.
    2. The students may exit empty-handed and their possessions will be handed to them from the back door of the bus.
    3. No student may leave until the entire bus is empty.

Figure 2.6.   Prototype volunteers letter.

all clustering together in one particular spot away from the students. While this interaction or supervision is important on the bus, it becomes crucial in restaurants and during informal times when no particular program is occurring and the students could scatter. During these unstructured times the volunteers need to provide coverage that provides a safety net but is not smothering. The volunteers need additional information about the site so they can share it with inquisitive students. In addition, volunteers need to get correct information so that they will be informed in case a student asks them a question. Some resources that volunteers find helpful include photocopies from Web sites and books of background information concerning each stop as well as all informative papers concerning the students, such as schedules. Volunteers need to have access to and give out the correct information.

Docents play favorites; if they like a group or if a group has a good reputation, the docents go above and beyond the call of duty to make the tour extra special for them. This may include letting the ropes down in a room, letting students touch artifacts, showing part of the site not normally on the tour, or donating material to the group. There is every advantage to making a good impression on a docent; if these people are happy, then everybody is happy. Three senior volunteers staff one well-known house museum, and they seem to think the property is their personal fief; on one trip they met the students with scowls and hostile glances. The students got a very curt and perfunctory tour, so the teacher dreaded returning the second year. This time, the docents remembered the group and the scowls were not as obvious, but the tour was still perfunctory until the last room in the house, where the students asked about the large iron cooking stove. The docent explained how it worked and in the process revealed how she had cooked on a stove similar to it as a young person. The students followed up on this statement with questions of their own and the docent was hooked; she told the students that a burning corn cob was just enough fuel for cooking one egg and many other stories. The students left the house with a new friend, and every following year the group was met with smiles and friendly tours. The moral of the story is to always applaud and thank the docents at the end of each tour.

The fast food policies may sound harsh at first, but they will help smooth the next student trip through the land of burgers and fries. First, select a very common chain restaurant where a majority of the students have had previous experience eating. Even if it is not their favorite or the leader's favorite, the importance of finding something that is a common experience diminishes the potential for complaining about the food selection. Select a chain that can be counted on for fast service; with a group every minute counts, and even one minute per child adds up to a long lunch break. Adults go first in fast food lines, because they do not tend to eat very fast compared to students, who tend to bolt their food in ten minutes. The students are ready to continue this habit, because they regularly eat this rapidly at school; every student knows that the faster they eat, the faster they get to go out and play. Adults, however, who try this with their "older" digestive systems feel uncomfortable for the rest of the day. In spite of being served last, the students are still finished with lunch first. Students do not wait patiently for adults to finish their food; they are on a study travel experience, they are eager to go and explore even more.

The students need to know what they want to order before they step up to the counter; they also need to have their money out so that they do not make people behind them wait as they fish quarters out of their pockets. Try to leave one cash register open for other patrons in the restaurant so that it does not feel as though the group is taking over the restaurant. Children rarely get to carry trays in fast food restaurants; their parents usually do it for them. Because the food items are of different weights and shapes from the school lunches, food tends to slide without the little compartments to secure the meal on the trays. Big soft drinks tip and slide very easily when they are on the edge of the tray. The students need to order everything they want in one trip, otherwise the group will eat and wait all afternoon as people keep going back to the counter for one more thing. While the students are in line, one adult watches the crowd, and when the first adult finishes his or her lunch, he or she exchanges places with the adult watching the line. The adults watch for the occasional spill, help students find food item prices, and sometimes help with math and change. Finally, at the end of the line they thank the restaurant staff for helping the group. Students need to sit at individual tables; do not let them move all of the tables together. The difference in the noise level is amazing; students seated in groups of two or four are like regular restaurant patrons, but when they are seated at long tables they become a restless mob. Before the group leaves, make sure everyone has cleaned up his or her area and discarded all trash.

Students, volunteers, parents, bus drivers, and teachers all need a schedule to help keep them on track (Figure 2.7). Start with the title of the trip, but do not put any dates on this sheet; it will be easy to pull this letter out and use it in subsequent years with just a few changes. The schedule needs to list the gathering, arrival, departure, and return times. The group leader needs to list not only the names of the stops, the times of arrival and departure, but he or she should also include food arrangements and notes for the bus drivers. Build in plenty of time to see the site, but also watch to see when students are ready to leave. The teacher puts a

Tour of Northern Indiana

Saturday
  7:00 a.m.   Pack and load the bus at Clio
  7:30 a.m.   Depart for Fort Wayne
  10:00 a.m.   Louis A. Warren Lincoln Library and Museum
  11:15 a.m.   Depart
  11:30 a.m.   SACK LUNCH
  12:00 p.m.   Historic Fort Wayne
  1:30 p.m.   Depart (I-69 & U.S. 20)
  2:15 p.m.   National Automobile and Truck Museum of the United States
  3:15 p.m.   Auburn-Cord-Duesenberg Museum
  4:30 p.m.   Depart
  5:30 p.m.   Supper
  6:00 p.m.   Menno-Hof
  7:30 p.m.   Depart
  9:00 p.m.   Chain O'Lakes Group Camp Ground
  10:00 p.m.   Lights out

Sunday
  6:00 a.m.   Rise/Pack the bus
  6:30 a.m.   Breakfast
  7:00 a.m.   Depart
  8:00 a.m.   Gene Straton-Porter Home and Garden Tour
  9:30 a.m.   Depart (U.S. 6 & U.S. 31)
  11:00 a.m.   Copshaholm
  12:30 p.m.   Lunch
  1:00 p.m.   Depart
  1:15 p.m.   Studebaker National Museum
  1:45 p.m.   Depart
  5:00 p.m.   Arrive at Clio

Figure 2.7.   Prototype schedule.

lot of time and effort into getting the group to the site; so be sure to use the time completely.

SETUP CREWS

For special jobs like camping, the group needs volunteer help in the form of a setup crew. For example, a tent setup crew of two volunteers gets a free camping weekend when they set up the tents and pack up the tents the next day; they have no child supervision obligations. When the group does not need to spend time setting up or taking down tents, they will be able to travel later in the day as well as have an earlier morning departure time. On a school field experience, camping is not an end in itself; it is a means to help students see sites inexpensively, so leave camping skills and crafts to the Boy and Girl Scouts. Usually, when camping with a group it is not worth trying to cook; eat a fast food breakfast instead. Even though it is more expensive to eat elsewhere, the setup, cooking, tear-down, and cleanup time is not worth the extra time required to cook. The decision is based upon three factors: the age of the students, number of students, and experience of the students. There may be good leadership and group goals that encourage a teacher to camp with students. If so, consider teaching and practicing camp skills prior to leaving school and increase the number of skilled adults to help students with the camp tasks.

Some trips are in such remote areas that no food service is available, but there are full kitchens in group campgrounds that have cabins. Another helpful setup crew is an advanced shopping crew. See Figure 2.8, which is a sample shopping list to give to a volunteer who will shop prior to the trip. These menus are popular with students, easy to prepare and clean up after preparation, and can easily be adjusted for varying numbers of students. They require ingredients that are flexible so that the unused ingredients can be stored from trip to trip. It is important to make sure the students are well fed, especially at breakfast; if an army marches on its stomach, so do the students on a study travel experience. There are two major reasons to feed students well. First, the day will be physically active, and the students need the food for energy. The major reason is that the students will be mentally active all day and they need food to stay alert. Do not try to cut costs by skimping on food; this strategy will only come back to haunt the group later with other problems, including fatigue, lack of attention, or low morale.

Another setup crew is the very valuable kitchen crew, and presented in Figure 2.9 are kitchen tools packaged for the volunteer cooks. Crew members need to travel in their own vehicle, cook dinner, spend the night, cook breakfast, and clean up afterward. For this service, the volunteers get a free weekend in a state park with no child supervision duties. Having separate kitchen crews means that the travel group is not tied to the cleanup of the kitchen when they depart the next morning; they can, therefore, get an earlier start on their activities. After the evening meal the kitchen crew also prepares the lunch for the next day and packs it in coolers. Former students in late high school and in college make great assistants, because they know the program from their own previous experiences.

Pack the food in cardboard boxes, because they are sturdier than bags, which tend to fall open, split, or spill from the vibrations of a moving

I.   Saturday lunch: Sack
II.   Saturday supper for 50:
    A.   Spaghetti and meat sauce, tossed salad, garlic bread, lemonade
        1.   2 large boxes of spaghetti
        2.   One big Styrofoam of hamburger
        3.   5 big jars of spaghetti sauce
    B.   Salad
        1.   3 heads of lettuce
        2.   1 bottle of bacon bits
        3.   2 pounds of baby carrots
        4.   2 boxes of croutons
    C.   Garlic bread
        1.   6 loaves of bread
        2.   3 bottles of squeeze margarine
        3.   Garlic
    D.   4 cans of lemonade
III. Sunday breakfast:
    A.   2 large boxes of pancake mix
        1.   Butter
        2.   2 large bottles of syrup
    B.   7 large cans of orange juice
    C.   3 gallons of milk
    D.   1 can of Pam
IV.   Sunday lunch:
    A.   Ham and cheese sandwiches
    B.   Chips
    C.   Twinkies
    D.   Lemonade

Figure 2.8.   Prototype menu.

school bus. These boxes can be discarded when they are empty, or left-over items from the trip can be brought back to the school and stored in the same boxes until the next trip. Plastic storage boxes can also be used; for the return trip they can be nested or filled with student luggage. Regardless of the method of storage, try to pack all of the items by type or meal in each box, then label the outside of the box by listing the inventory with a marker if cardboard is used or securely taping a paper sign if a plastic box is used. Try to pack as many boxes as possible on the floor of the bus so the vibrations do not jiggle them out of the seats. At the end of the trip clean and inspect all kitchen tools for wear and pack these items with an inventory on top of the boxes so that they are all ready for the next trip.

Most good campground kitchens have all of the needed kitchen tools, but just in case something is missing, it is helpful to have it available. Trash bags can be used for trash and as instant raincoats and windbreak-

I. Ice
    A. Coolers
II. Kitchen tools
    A. Can openers
    B. Food scraper
    C. Large sharp knife
    D. 2 small sharp knives
    E. 2 metal pancake turners
    F. Potholders
    G. Emery cloth
    H. Paint scraper
    I. Tongs
    J. Cookie sheets
    K. Pots for
        1. Spaghetti
        2. Meat
        3. Lemonade
        4. Orange juice
    L. Spaghetti server
    M. 2 big spoons
III. Cleanup
    A. Towels
    B. Wash cloth
    C. Dish soap
IV. Consumables
    A. Trash bags
    B. Plastic knives
    C. Plastic forks
V. Serving pieces
    A. Pepper
    B. Salt
    C. Salad bowl
    D. Ladle
    E. Coffee
    F. Plastic milk jugs
VI. First aid kit
VII. Emergency numbers

Figure 2.9. Prototype cooking supplies.

ers, but they also can contain the clothes of a sick child and provide an outfit for the sick child to wear home. Take lots of extra old towels on the trip for dishes, hot pads, and cleanup. Most group camp kitchens have griddles, so use the emery cloth and the paint scraper for cleaning the griddles. The coffee is intended to make the cooks and bus driver happy, but the cookie sheets are for the preparation of the garlic bread. The lem-

Gas	$75
Kitchen	$60 × 2 = $120
Camp fee	$1.25 per person × 2
Entrance fee to Lincoln State Park	$.50 per person
Food	$7.00 per person
New Harmony fee	$2.00 per person

Figure 2.10.   Individual and group expense summary.

Historic Fort Wayne:	$2.00 child, $3.00 adult
National Automobile and Truck Museum of the United States:	$1.00 child, $2.00 adult
Auburn-Cord-Duesenburg Museum:	$1.00 child, $20 tour guide
Menno-Hof:	$60 over 30 + $1.50 per child
Chain O'Lakes gate fee:	$.50 per person
Chain O'Lakes camp fee:	$.50 per person
Gene Straton-Porter Home:	$1.00 per person
Copshaholm:	$2.50 child, $4.00 adult
Studebaker National Museum:	$.50 per person

Figure 2.11.   Individual and group expense summary.

onade and orange juice pots are for the mixing of drink crystals or con-
centrates, but remember to save the milk jugs from breakfast and reuse
them for the lemonade for lunch. The lunch ham sandwiches, the lemonade, and the breakfast orange juice are mixed and made the night before
by the cooking crew for a faster departure the next morning. The bus and
each historic site will have a first aid kit, but it is a good idea to send
another one with the kitchen crew.

It is important to make trips as economical as possible in order to allow
as many students as possible to participate. The trip must not lose money,
so the trick of managing field trips is how to make money with the least
possible amount of profit. The group leader will use an expense summary
sheet (Figure 2.10) to help manage the expenses of the trip. This sheet
allows the group leader to determine the expenses by showing the name
of the site and the per-person fees for adults and children (Figure 2.11).
There is also a space to include flat group fees; these fees become pro-

gressively smaller the more students share costs on the field trip. As tempting as it may seem to enlarge the group in order to lower the cost per person, there are tradeoffs in logistics for a group that gets too large. It then becomes important to determine prior to the trip all of the possible contingencies in which money would be needed, how much money is needed per person, and how much each person contributes. To help people become economically astute, when the students get on the bus they are given their lunch money from their deposit. The students then must be responsible for staying within a budget and making decisions on how they spend their food allotment.

THE DAY OF THE TRIP

Greet every parent and child by name as they arrive and make one last restroom stop before loading the bus. Leave the school at the appointed time and then throw away the itinerary, because it has served its purpose. All the planning the group leader has performed has liberated the group to be flexible now rather than confining it to a rigid course of events. The leader who created this trip knows when the students are learning and when they are not. Students raise questions and their interests peak through study travel experience trips, and they need to explore their interests. The first question every docent asks is, "How much time do you have?" The reply needs to be, "We are here to learn and we will take as much time as you will give us." Do not be afraid to pull the plug on a bad docent or a poor experience and have other options of sites to visit in case of inclement weather or changing student interest. Of course, take a cell phone and have the telephone numbers for all of the sites in case the group is moving faster or slower than planned. Once the field trip starts relax and enjoy it; all of the plans will either pay off or they will not, but when the bus leaves the school, there is no reason to worry about it.

Carry a clipboard with the roster of students, destination site telephone numbers, maps, agenda (including extra copies), and parent contact numbers. This is the same information that the group members, docents, volunteers, bus driver, and the group leader refer to all day. Bring tissues, paper towels, bleach, and rubber gloves for taking universal precautions if human liquids are present on the bus. Carry the money, checks, and purchase orders on your person at all times; do not put them in anything that could be put down or put aside. The money or valuables will probably not be stolen, but there are so many items on the bus that become jumbled in the excitement of the trip that one does not want to go digging for methods of payment as the members of the group watch.

WHAT TO DO WHILE ON THE ROAD

The group leader might wish to provide the students with an assignment to help students focus on the world going past their school bus window. The example of an urban trip offered in Figure 2.12 is a good way to help students become more observant of what is going on in the world around them. This is particularly valuable in getting students talking about what they are seeing on their trip if it is a trip they have made many times before. Students fill the assignment out as they move; the teacher helps them by pointing out many interesting places on the route. Many students will not have talked about the buildings and highways, even though they have gone past them many times. The teacher may wish to introduce the students to the interstate system by helping students to determine the cities they would come to if they selected a particular exit ramp. The teacher helps the students to see the different distinctive buildings on the skyline, including businesses, monuments, churches, government buildings, transportation hubs, medical facilities, residences, and social clubs. The building materials, architectural style used, and how the buildings fit into

---

Name:

1.   Where are you starting?
2.   What is the name of the interstate?
3.   If you went south on this interstate, to what city would you come?
4.   In which direction does I-465 go?
5.   If you go west on I-70, to which city would you come?
6.   What is the name of the train station?
7.   What is the name of the company that first produced insulin?
8.   What is the name of the Marion County government building?
9.   What is the name of the tallest building in the state?
10. Which direction does the statue on the top of Monument Circle face?
11. If you go east on I-70, to which city would you come?
12. What is the name of the type of architecture used in the Morris-Butler Home?
13. What is the name of the type of architecture used in the Central Avenue United Methodist Church?
14. What car did the Stutz Automobile Company make?
15. What is the name of the building that looks as though it has a pyramid on top of it?
16. On what side of the old mile square is the state capitol located?
17. Of what building material is the Scottish Rite Cathedral constructed?
18. If you go north on I-65, to which city would you come?
19. What is the name of the large hospital?

Figure 2.12.   Urban trip ticket.

a city plan are all considered. Students notice structures that the teacher has never seen or thought about before, and once the students return to school this provides an interesting research topic for further inquiry.

The rural landscape may be in more danger of disappearing than urban vistas because members of civic planning boards and historic districts often work to protect urban areas. Also, this trip ticket is much more open-ended than the urban trip ticket and is designed to get students to think, question, and interpret. By looking at the context that is obvious on this rural trip (Figure 2.13), students determine things about their world that they may have previously taken for granted. Students look for schools, interurban sheds, interurban bridge abutments, old railroad grades, log cabins, century-old farmhouses, iron or covered bridges, and barns. Depending on the location, they can also look for windmills, fence construction, and round barns. Students look carefully at the rural landscape to find evidence of what they are interpreting.

There may be a need for crowd control devices. These could include a rallying sign to visually indicate where to meet or where the leader is, but an auditory cue of a whistle to get the attention of the group might be important, also. Some teachers like students to wear matching shirts or hats so they can quickly see the members of a group, especially in crowded museum areas that might have multiple groups present. If there is the possibility of multiple groups or crowded areas at night, some groups like luminescent strings that loop around students' necks like glowing necklaces. This is another way of visually keeping track of all of the students and not leaving people behind.

Bring multiple ways of recording the trip through digital or video data retrieval technologies. In small groups, use travel time to teach students how to use these media devices to record the events of the trip. Make the students responsible for carrying them and using them to gather informa-

---

Name:

1. How do you think the small brick structure was used?
2. How is the last brick structure different from this structure?
3. Why is there a stone pillar standing between those two banks of earth?
4. What might have been in this empty space?
5. What do you think the inside of the log cabin looks like?
6. How do you think people made this house modern?
7. How is this bridge different from modern bridges?
8. Why would people have such large barns on their farms?

Figure 2.13.   Rual trip ticket.

tion. The students record memories of the trip and through the data they gather they reinterpret the theme of the trip when they return to school. The data the students bring back to the school reinforces their human memory. Images can be very important for doing public relations work for the school and in celebrating the successful adventures of the group.

The teacher needs to be free to pay fees, guide the driver, meet site officials, and watch the entire group. When the bus gets to the site, the leader needs to be free to meet the museum officials and guides and to direct students to the coat check while the teacher gets a museum pass and map. Before the bus stops at the site review with the students what things can and cannot be touched at the site, and depending on the interpretation of the site, give the students some guiding questions or an assignment to help them examine the site. Also, before the bus stops give the students some preview as to how this site connects with the theme of the trip. Students will ride on the same bus for the entire trip; so when they complete the tour at the site, they should return to the same bus on which they arrived. Make sure to take roll every time the group gets on the bus.

Museums and historic sites close early, usually around 4:00 p.m.; this allows travel time and a 5:00 p.m. meal that avoids the rush of the 6:00 p.m. dinner crowd. When the group eats dinner early, several things happen; it gets the group out of rush-hour traffic and gets the bus off the streets. It also avoids sitting on a bus stuck in rush-hour traffic. By the time the group is finished eating, the roads will be less congested, making it easier to navigate later. The restaurant manager will welcome the group's coming at this earlier time, and the group will find fewer crowds and faster service.

NOSTALGIA DECORATIONS AND AN OPPORTUNITY FOR STUDYING MATERIAL CULTURE

Across North America from the original down-home restaurant or Cheers bar, to multiple small town copies and to the national franchised chains country antique décor can be found in Cracker Barrel, Bob Evans, TGI Friday's, Grindstone Charley's, Ruby Tuesday, O'Charley's, and Applebee's restaurants. Many restaurants have decided to cover their walls with disposable ornaments of a cast-off culture. From the folksy country store to the Cheers bar, nostalgia décor at meal times provides opportunities to study popular consumerist culture. When students enter restaurants with their parents on school study travel experiences or as a result of extra-curricular activities, they are surrounded by a dizzying collection of nostalgic images removed from their proper context and displayed in a seemingly random configuration of artifacts designed to remind people of a comfortable and familiar consumer culture. The students are so accustomed to the popular collection of stuff in these types of spaces that they may not examine it and may just assume that it is a natural feature of the environment.

The first thing to do is to get the students to really see what they are surrounded by; students then determine the use of each artifact. Students start identifying each individual artifact by whether it is two- or three-dimensional. Common two-dimensional items include photos, prints, posters, signs, advertisements, and record jackets. Common three-dimensional items include sports equipment, tools, musical instruments, clothing, toys, and models. By mixing artifacts in large jumbles of displays, students lack a context for identifying and interpreting the items and only get a few cloudy messages: old things are cool, consumerism has a lasting value, and America has always been a land of opportunity for purchasing multiple products and advertisements. Students question the authenticity of the items and question why someone would want to make something look old. Since context has been removed from the artifact, students first try to tie an item to a time and place before determining if they use a similar item today.

The students determine why the items are present. Each piece on the walls was thrown away by someone because they either no longer wanted it or needed it, or because it was old and out of fashion. Students may also wish to consider why this is a popular way to decorate a restaurant—why owners like it, and why patrons like it. Students can discern if there are any political thoughts in any of the artifacts or if there are controversial qualities that would offend any patrons. The items come from the twentieth century and reflect a life that the aging populace will remember as part of their life. Indeed, it could be argued that the artifacts target a wealthy section of society with disposable income and entice them to share some of that income with this present establishment.

Students also question whether an item is timeless or dated; if an item is dated, what makes it stand out as being from a different time period. Students evaluate which purchases stand the test of time and whether they have purchased items that they will quickly tire of or that they suspect will quickly become obsolete (Figure 2.14). What do these items really tell us about society, resources, and the choices that people make with their disposable income? Students need help in looking for social conscience as they attempt to make sense of the experience of the dizzying array of consumer items. Finally, students consider that if this stuff has been saved, how much more of it has been buried in landfills?

One of the hardest parts of planning a group trip is answering the question, "What will the group do after dinner?" If they are in an urban

1. Why was this item discarded?
2. Is the artifact two- or three-dimensional?
3. How was the artifact used?
4. Where was it used?
5. When was it used?
6. Do you use a similar item today?
7. Is it timeless or dated?
8. If it is dated, what makes it stand out?
9. Which purchases stand the test of time?
10. Have you purchased an item that you tired of quickly?
11. Have you purchased an item that quickly became obsolete?

Figure 2.14.   Artifacts in dining spaces.

area, there will be concerts, plays, and some art museums open for late hours. If the days are long, the group can go on a hike to explore natural areas, visit outdoor monuments and memorials or cemeteries; if the days are short, with special arrangements they might get into historic sites. If the group is in a remote location, they can make their own fun with stories, songs, and skits. This after-dinner time may provide an opportunity for the group to experience great active teaching/debriefing or a time for oral reflection, journaling, or working on other assignments.

Another difficult group planning question is, "What can the group do on a Sunday morning?" Most sites are closed until noon, but national and natural properties open earlier. It is a good time for traveling from place to place, and once again special arrangements can be made with local sites. Outdoor monuments, memorials, and cemeteries are open. Early on a Sunday morning is a great time to do urban walking tours because there is little early morning traffic to contend with when either looking for architecture, historic districts, or historic neighborhoods.

On the ride home discuss the field trip with the students; ask them to order the sites by chronology and ask them which sites overlapped in time. Ask the students to evaluate what they liked and disliked about the trip and why, and listen to how the students interpreted the theme of the trip. In addition to reviewing the trip while on the bus, connect a famous person with the site. Also, see if there is a controversial issue connected with the site and determine how the students can explain factions, minorities, and differences of opinion found at the site. On the ride home from the trip, evaluate the experience to determine what portions were valuable enough to keep and which portions should be deleted for future trips; the next day, update the agenda for the following year.

Before getting off the bus thank the volunteers and the bus driver. At the end of a trip students and their parents want to leave immediately after the children get off the bus, often leaving teachers with many of their possessions and all of their trash. To counteract this situation, have students pull all of their items from under their seats; this means that they identify all of their belongings, it slows down their exit, and they leave nothing on the floor. When gear comes out of the back of the bus, all of the common gear comes out first and it is put away, then individual gear comes out. By using this method nothing is forgotten and all items are claimed. Well, alright, there may still be that one lost grayish sock that no one will claim, but it could be much worse.

FINANCING SCHOOL FIELD TRIPS

School boards, superintendents, and legislatures have the fiduciary trust endowed by the citizens of a community to provide money for the education of all students in the nation's public schools. This is their job. If they do not do their job, the people can and should remove them from office. The job of the teacher is to provide instruction. Teachers should not distract themselves from important classroom tasks by engaging in fundraising activities.

I have never seen a school that did not have enough money for a field trip; I will know this school does not have enough money when they stop playing competitive sports games away from school. Until that time comes, all schools that I have seen have enough money for true field trips, but they may not have any political will to take them. To develop political will is once again not the principle job of the teacher. This is the job of the parent organization to make suggestions on how to ensure that school resources are spent for the education of all students. Parents can very effectively lobby the community for increased school spending or reallocation of school funds. Parents can take the message of field-based education directly to administrators, school boards, and legislatures; these people will be influenced and moved by their constituencies.

The other way to develop political will is to ask teachers, administrators, and school board members to live in the school district where they work. This already happens in many small towns, due to proximity. Eventually, most or all of the employees will have children, grandchildren, cousins, nieces, nephews, and neighbors in the schools. No adult connected to his or her school community wants to be the reason that his or her child did not get to go on a field trip. Sooner or later, powerful self interest will incite these decision makers to become advocates for field trips because their children will profit from it.

Foundations

Every school and school district should consider setting up a non-profit foundation to raise money for schools, teacher development, curriculum enhancement, and to provide for students' scholarships. This is another job of the parent organization in conjunction with educators and community leaders. Building an endowment for immediate and long-term educational needs in the community will pay dividends for future years. When using this endowment, the school district might consider piloting field trips with soft money and institutionalizing successful field trips with continuing funding from the school budget. By doing this, teachers experiment with a variety of different programs and locations before determining to make long-term commitments to a specific field trip.

Every town or county should consider creating a community foundation. Part of the mission of a community foundation should be to encourage public education, higher education, and graduate education. By funding public education, community foundations can wisely fund field trips that meet academic standards and celebrate local resources. Helping students to understand and value their communities remain key issues in preventing "brain drain." Community members who benefit from their community can then determine to reinvest in their community.

Grants

Teachers should make applications to school or school district foundations and community foundations. These usually offer resources in small amounts appropriate for field trips. These grants have relatively few application and reporting procedures, thus making them time efficient for teachers. Other larger grants should be left to school development officers or grant writers. While teachers may be tempted to get all of the resources possible for their students, teachers should be cautious of grants because teachers can sink huge amounts of time into writing grants that may or may not be funded. Larger grants may also come with strings attached that take time away from classroom instruction and preparation.

NO-COST FIELD TRIPS

The location of the school may determine where no- or low-cost field trips are possible. Schools located in urban areas or small towns offer the most possibilities for walking out of the school door and into another learning environment. Students enrolled in suburban area schools will need to walk farther, while some suburbs may not be designed for pedestrian traffic. Suburban students are definitely not accustomed to walking great distances, and the resulting gnashing of teeth and wailing from despair may mar the trip. Rural consolidated schools are the most difficult places to provide low-cost field trips, because they are often surrounded by agricultural land that provides limited social studies destinations.

CHAPTER 3

FINDING COMMONWEALTH THROUGH LOCAL COMMUNITY CONNECTIONS

A LOCAL FIELD TRIP

Teachers use a number of instructional strategies to help students develop citizenship skills and learn state and local history content. In many communities teachers include field trips and walking tours to help students learn more about people. The entire third-grade class at Hope Elementary School in Hope, Indiana, learned from older students and from their teacher through a one-day walking tour field trip to the town square, a local history museum, and a cemetery. After exploring these common but overlooked sites and learning about the history of their town, the students found the sites to be both unique and interesting. In the town cemetery, older students performed first-person historical presentations for the third-grade students (Morris, 2009). The older students dressed in their roles and became the characters they represented by speaking in the first person (e.g., saying, "I went to town" rather than saying, "She went to town."). Each older student portrayed a distinguished resident who contributed to the quality of life in the community. Haley (personal communication, May 19, 2000), one of the third-grade students, stated, "I liked when we went to the cemetery; we got to learn about some of the people

The Field Trip Book: Study Travel Experiences in Social Studies
pp. 35–45
Copyright © 2010 by Information Age Publishing

that were back then because there were people acting." Some of the people studied were relatives of the students; other students lived on the same farms or in the homes formerly occupied by the earlier residents.

The third-grade students attended school in a town that their ancestors founded. Many families had long ties to common religious ideas and to multiple generations in the community. Across time the town struggled to keep its school from being absorbed by the county seat. The members of the community worked hard to create a continuing economic base in the town for retail and services. They also worked to develop new housing in the town.

In this example, a veteran teacher, Barbara Johnson, used many of the resources of the community to help her students learn about their town. She used the town itself to teach about history and community, its configuration around the town square, its architecture, its history museum, and its cemetery. She took advantage of the special relationships the location of the town offers that were within walking distance: local businesses for providing a snack, business restrooms for convenience, and the park on the town square for recess activities.

The teacher grounded the experience on the first five of the National Council for the Social Studies (NCSS) Standards: (1) culture; (2) time, continuity, and change; (3) people, places, and environments; (4) individual devolvement and identity; and (5) individuals, groups, and institutions (NCSS, 1994) (see Figure 3.1). Each of these themes helped the students find out more about the place where they live, shop, and attend school (Overton, 2002).

Students appreciated that pride in the local community depended upon an understanding of the history and context of the people (Gentry, 2002), and that people must have one another in order to have a community. The students could not remain inseparable from the community; they are empty without one another (McDermott, 1981). The community members must seek the common good for all members. It remains as imperative as ever to help students find their place in the community and for the community members to want to help all students get the best education possible (Dowden, 2007; Tanner, 1997; Dewey, 1990, 1997). Society holds together because people work together with a common spirit and common aims (Archambault, 1997). For example, students take a field trip to examine a Moravian community that shares both common spirit and aims. This small agricultural town holds together today as it has across the last two centuries.

Having developed prior to Martin Luther's Reformation, the Moravians are sometimes called the first Protestants. Followers of John Huss in the European provinces of Bohemia and Moravia, now part of the modern Czech Republic, rejected the church at Rome. During the late 1700s and early 1800s, the Moravians migrated to North America and established two major communities: Bethlehem, Pennsylvania and Salem, North Carolina. Vigorously evangelical activity occurred when missionaries met with Indians and set out to establish new church communities. The church used its influence to soften the hard edges of capitalism by restraining trade in church towns and protecting its parishioners from the effects of ruthless competition. For example, if there were a baker in town, a young man would be encouraged not to open a new bakery in town for fear that, due to lack of need for two bakeries, both men would become a burden to the community. As admirable as this paternalism was, it did not prove to be pragmatic, and the church moved away from controlling the economy of the towns.

In the twenty-first century, Moravians are alive and well, but in smaller numbers than during colonial times. Some people claim that the Moravians contributed many ideas to popular North American religious practice including the Christmas crèche, the Christmas candlelight service, and the Easter sunrise service with enthusiastic hymns and brass accompaniment. The students knew that they attended school with Moravians, but they may not know that their friends' ancestors played a major role in the history of the town.

This field trip is a great example of how a mixed rural and small town consolidated school went on a no-cost field trip by walking out the door of the classroom and into the world in which they live every day. Their destination was the town square where the students walked from their school and back again. The students used most of the school day exploring sites they went past every day without understanding what they were seeing.

Rationale

Teachers in many communities want their students to learn state and local history content as well as citizenship skills. They may use a number of instructional strategies including field trips and walking tours, which support social studies education to help their students learn more about people and communities. The students in this chapter's example use a combined field trip, walking tour, and first-person presentation to learn state and local history. Students learn social studies content and skills by recreating characters and situations that show members of a community living and working together. Through experiential social studies learning, students learn more about citizenship within a community. Students need opportunities to see how their daily experiences fit into the community (Brophy & Alleman, 2009; Hyland, 2009; Chan, 2007). People fill communities with their lives, stories, and deeds, and these complex pictures of action create a visual historical montage that students learn from others.

Parents, teachers, and community members played a large role in the education of the young members of this town, and this historical trend dated back to the early settlers, who committed to educating all of their children. The community members supported the school and made a commitment to not consolidate their schools with the larger county school system. Evan today the people value the students, wish to maintain the sense of community, and embarce the idea of providing for the children on the community.

The third-grade teacher, Barbara Johnson, said about the field trip,

> I think the main reason we do this is just to develop a sense of pride in their community. So often students in a town this size ... just think they are living in an unimportant area, their town has nothing to offer to the world.... They need to see that real people lived here and did real things that were important to the town while they were here.... Their life has some bearing on what is going to happen to the community in the future. So, as much as anything, I think it's trying to develop a sense of citizenship of doing their part and realizing everyone has worth in the community. (personal communication, May 20, 2000)

The community played a powerful role in determining a curriculum in the local schools (Camicia, 2009; Tali Tal, 2004; Warwick, 2007). Community members wished to inspire pride in the next generation through school, town, church, and family events. There was an underlying sense of inclusiveness in their approach to teaching social studies, and teachers expressed a commitment to developing citizens to improve the future life of the community.

Preparation

The third-grade teacher, Barbara Johnson, prepared for this experience by checking the school calendar for a day without conflicts. She made sure that the public restrooms in town were open to the group. Next, she contacted former students in the fifth through twelfth grades to see when they could help; she also contacted the teachers of those former students to see when they could be released. She sent a letter to the parents describing the project as well as the after-school rehearsal times. The former students researched and wrote scripts from oral history and primary sources; Mrs. Johnson helped them find the limited sources of information and write and review the script to make sure that they helped advance her goals for the field trip. The students worked on the scripts for a month. Since these students were no longer in her class, they worked after school in small groups on multiple nights with Mrs. Johnson to gather material and create their script. Because of the large number of students involved, she could not work with every student on the same night. Then they planned the costumes they needed and practiced their first-person presentations about local people buried in the town cemetery. The scripts needed to be scheduled with the longest ones first graduating to the shortest script last so that groups did not cluster and have to wait for the next presentation. Seventh-grade student Tyler's script is an example of the length of the presentations (see Figure 3.1).

Other former students in the fifth through eighth grades acted as docents, who provided context and helped the third-grade students understand how all the people fit together. Mrs. Johnson worked with the student docents to create a common script and did clerical support to interpret the stops on the tour and the cemetery experience. The student docents gave the students background knowledge about individual stops while under the watchful eye of teachers; their role was subordinate to that of the students doing the first-person presentations. The student docents gained experience and built confidence by speaking in front of groups with limited risk; this also helped prepare them to do future first-person work.

Mrs. Johnson wrote an informational note to the parents telling them about the third-grade students' community exploration. Next, she created a schedule for the adults that included the destination, departure, and arrival times and indicated who was to be at each site at each time to help the office staff, fellow teachers, and aides. The teacher then made plans for transportation to and from the cemetery for everyone.

Mrs. Johnson made slides of the community using both contemporary images and images of the same site as it had appeared in the past, which

---

Reverend Frances Holland

You know how I love botany, which is the study of plants. In fact, I planted all of these trees here. Oh, I'm sorry, let me introduce myself. I am Rev. Frances Holland. I've been principal of the Moravian Female Seminary for Young Ladies for three years. It is a magnificent three-story brick building that houses forty-five young ladies. They study botany, history, literature, Christian evidences, and natural philosophy. They also learn about music, how to sing and draw. I used to live in Pennsylvania, but the Parochial Elders Conference asked me to come over here and start the new girls' seminary. I built a large brick home on South Main Street. Spring Woods is right behind my house. I plant[ed] all kinds of trees here to see if they [would] grow in Hope. I think my closest companion is the dirt under my fingernails. My wife thinks I'm crazy planting all of these trees. I also have two wonderful children, Jane and Prudence. Jane doesn't care for botany, but Prudence helps me every chance she gets. Well, I mustn't keep talking, I need to read more about the Lord.

Figure 3.1.   Tyler's script.

she took from local history collections. She wrote a script to accompany these slides using information from oral history and primary sources. She included historical images and sites beyond walking distance, and she showed this to the students to get them ready for the walk. The students asked multiple questions and offered many stories about the sites in the slides when they made connections between the images on the screen and their lives.

Barbara Johnson shared her thoughts on the value of a handout she created to help introduce students to their town: "Not all children learn well by listening…. Basically, we are trying to meet all forms of learning—reading, hearing, seeing. Hopefully, everybody had a chance to learn … [through] their own style that works" (personal communication, May 20, 2000). The handout included many independent parts and was rich with primary sources. There was a primary source photograph of the town square in 1866—God's Acre Cemetery, a 1910 photo showing the town—a 1920 map of the Yellow Trail, and a photo of mail hacks. As the town was one of the first test areas for rural free delivery, the horse-drawn mail wagons were parked on the square prior to the business of the day. On a copy of the original land plat for 1879, students identified and colored the Main Street, the Moravian Cemetery, the public square, the seminary grounds, the river, Mill Street tributary, and the original town. There was also text describing Rural Mail Delivery, the Yellow Trail, and the history of Hope. Students used this visual and textual information to produce line drawings of their own illustrating the work the children would have done compared to the work that adults would have done at the time Hope was founded. From these illustrations, students could see that all of the members of the community had responsibility to the community and contributed to making the community function effectively. The students made a schedule of all the work they would have done from sun up to sun down and hypothesized the advantages and disadvantages of such a life. Students then read a text on the founding of the town, the Moravian economy, and analyzed it for the advantages and disadvantages of sharing everything. After reading the text on the church formation, students wrote the names of the people who were in each choir. Moravian society used the term *choir* to describe eight gender and social group members in the community that included boys, girls, unmarried men, unmarried women, married men, married women, widowers, and widows.

The Morning of the Walk

On the morning of the walk Mrs. Johnson performed several tasks before school began. Since she was one of the people responsible for the local museum, she made sure it was open and swept before school began.

She stopped by the cemetery to put numbered flags in the ground to show the first-person interpreters where to stand and where to meet their groups. She gathered and left props in the cemetery for the students when they did their presentations, and she also left carbonated drinks on ice in a cooler for the presenters. She loaded the student lunches and drinks in ice-filled coolers, dropped them off at the town square, filled the water cooler with ice and water, and dropped it off at the log cabin with cups and a trash bag.

The Town Walk

Johnson explained that she wanted students to experience events from the past with geographic context: "They will be where it actually happened" (personal communication, May 20, 2000). The obvious limitation to this event was the possibility that the weather could become inclement. On the day of the event students walked to the Female Seminary site where they met a student docent who informed them about the site, continued to the first church in town, and then entered the cemetery. The student docents gave commentaries about the role of the Moravians in establishing the town and attracting settlers to the site in a mass migration. They explained some of the Moravian customs that are still practiced such as the Easter predawn tradition of waking the town with the brass ensembles playing and parading down the Avenue of Spruce to God's Acre, the old part of the town cemetery, in preparation for the Easter Sunrise Service. Here, the flat stones marked the graves where people separated by choirs of gender, age, and marital status were laid in permanent rest. In the cemetery the third-grade students found a dozen first-person historical characters portrayed by former students (Paglin, 2002). After the student docents gave some introductory remarks and the former students made their presentations, the student docents delivered their closing remarks and guided the third-grade students to the location of the next presentation.

At the end of the cemetery experience, the teacher took charge of the tour and led the students through the street into a restored early settler's log cabin to a part of the funeral home with its display of a horse-drawn hearse, to a Moravian tanner's log shop, and finally to the town square. On the square the group divided in half; one half explored the artifacts of the town museum while the other half listened to stories about the town square. In the Yellow Trail Museum the students received a museum handout with pictures of artifacts directing them through each of the three floors and encouraging the students to find artifacts. Students needed to locate approximately ten items listed on each floor; volunteers at the museum answered the questions generated by the students. Children had meaningful social experiences related to the exhibitions; students prefer this type of experience to others (Falk & Dietking, 2000). Students used their background experiences to connect with the new experiences to create new knowledge.

At the town square Mrs. Johnson told stories about people and businesses that impacted the square and helped it change. Some of the stories came from her childhood. Other stories provided context for what is still there such as the pump, the bandstand, and the historical marker at the site of the first church. Still other stories filled in missing gaps about what is gone, such as the spring, as well as some connections to people in the cemetery, like the man who cut his leg while cutting wood for the first church and who is now buried in the cemetery. From hearing some of the stories, the students formed immediate connections with the area where they were standing. For example, while standing on the town square, students learned that after a bear attacked a man in the woods on the town square the women were afraid to walk through the woods of the town square to do their laundry at the spring. Students also explored the bandstand and the storefront postal museum on that same town square.

Debriefing

When students returned to the classroom, they discussed and wrote about their various experiences. During an oral review the students discussed what they liked the most and what they learned. Jonathan, one of the third-grade students, learned about the creation of the town and observed, "I learned what it used to be … when the trees were cut down … and the town was formed in the 1800s" (personal communication, May 19, 2000). Next, students told about what had changed and what had stayed the same. Finally, the students wrote in response to one of the following four prompts: Why is it important to learn about the town? What things stayed the same? What things changed? How do they belong to the community? Third-grade student Isaac wrote this because of his experiences while walking around the community:

> Hope's church changed and the band [stand] changed. The graveyard changed because now people don't get buried in choirs … in God's Acre. Most schoolhouses and log cabins have been moved or destroyed. Rivers and ponds have been covered or buried and the old mills have been burned. They have built new school[s] and buildings. The[y] also built a new town square.

Students shared their responses with the class; the students who had not written on that specific topic promptly added their ideas. Students reviewed factual recall questions with a class team game, and they followed this trip with a bus tour of the county.

When the former students returned to school, Mrs. Johnson accounted for all the period clothing from the older students who were doing the first-person historical presentations. She washed it, sorted it, and then packed it for use in the future. She also made sure she saved copies of all of the scripts for future reference.

Alternatives

Of course, not every elementary school teacher works in a small town, but the format still works well for students in urban and suburban settings. Every neighborhood—indeed, every street—either urban or suburban has a history filled with interesting people and their stories that students can walk to and explore. The suburban teacher might wish to use the courts and cul-de-sacs of the new neighborhood, because nearly every gardener in the addition finds artifacts from Native Peoples. The class could walk down the street and hear parents doing first-person presentations about Indians and their artifacts from the region. The rural-consolidated school, isolated by walls of corn, is the most difficult to interpret though a walking tour, but first-person presentations make it easy for characters from across the county to come to the students rather than having the students travel across the county. Of course, teachers from urban, suburban, or rural areas can always board a school bus and travel to look at a county seat and a town square.

Most elementary school teachers face the unfortunate separation from former students, either physically through separate buildings or institutionally though scheduling and instructional practices. Parents, grandparents, and community volunteers from service clubs, sororities, Daughters of the American Revolution chapters, fraternal societies, and religious auxiliaries can fill the roles of the first-person presentations. The adults have the means to perform short biographical introductions to their characters.

CONCLUSIONS

In this project the students neither marched on city hall nor did they lobby their legislators for consumer protection, but they still conducted work to connect their lives with that of their community. People who care about democracy concern themselves primarily with the common mundane actions and morale of the populace (Elshtain, 1995). Students saw the reciprocity and stability in the area where many of their parents and grandparents have grown up and lived (Arthur, 2000). The story of the community surrounds the students in their daily lives and makes use of that story in their daily experiences. Establishing their links to the community excites these students by helping them to learn information about and develop an appreciation for their community. Students need to confront the social world that surrounds them as they learn about the world. Green (1988) suggests that teachers can point out normal situations in the lives of students to help the students create deeper understanding from the events. At Hope the empowered students worked to interpret their local and visible situations, places, and events; the older students shared information from the past and helped younger students connect it to their lives (NCSS Standard I). Students could no longer just drive by the town square believing that nothing ever happened at the place where they lived (NCSS Standard II). The students saw their homes, playgrounds, religious institutions, and businesses as an important part of their curriculum (Standard III). The students saw daily connections to their community and looked at their common space with more detail, while questioning what it meant to their town (Standard IV). Through this experience students had to determine their relationship to the town (Standard V).

Mrs. Johnson helped to bridge the gap between school and society (Noffke, 2000). Students live in tangled social spaces, and Mrs. Johnson helped them to see that their lives connect to their community. Students learned from older peers in a mentoring experience. Teachers need to find ways to help students make connections to their community and find connections to their lives. Johnson stated, "It's here; we can use it; we can see it . . . . It is the only way kids are going to learn about their community . . . . History is life. You have to go see what it is all about" (personal communication, May 20, 2000). Mrs. Johnson planned an inexpensive field trip that used local resources; by doing this she cut the expense of transportation. Teachers exposed their students to the community in a way that neither required travel nor vast financial resources, thus eliminating barriers that might divide them by class. This kept the focus on the meaningful and the local. Teachers need to encourage children to adopt and to develop sensitivity for the needs of other people, while giving them opportunities to experience how their action can potentially affect the local community (Goodman, 1992). Teachers should include student background knowledge in their lessons on local community topics. Furthermore, teachers need to make use of the immediate, capitalize on the resources at hand, and celebrate the local to help students build meaningful connections into their lessons. Teachers make connections in the community between people by having them work together to examine a common past. Teachers help students to see common, daily connections as well as to connect with the history that includes groups and individuals in a complex story of their town.

CHAPTER 4

INVESTIGATING SMALL TOWNS

COUNTY SEAT FIELD TRIP

Many students now live in large subdivisions in suburban areas. When the fifth-grade class started to talk about county seats, they had no previous experience that would allow them to understand what a county seat was, so the students took a tour of a typical rural county. The students tried to find information about the county, but there was little interpretation to guide them. Almost everything they learned was from reading the built environment. By finding out how a county works, the students could compare their county with this rural county; they could then determine what role they could play in the politics of the county being toured as well as of their own county.

In many communities town government is a relatively small function, but county government is housed in the most formidable of county edifices situated on the town square. To observers the monumental county courthouse in the most prominent area of town speaks to the issue of power residing in county government. Until the middle of the twentieth century, the government most citizens encountered on a daily basis was not the national government; it was the government they could reach within a day's travel time. The county government, which is locally controlled, handled most issues. People still call towns where county business

The Field Trip Book: Study Travel Experiences in Social Studies
pp. 47–61
Copyright © 2010 by Information Age Publishing

is conducted the county seat, and much of county business is conducted in the county courthouse. To understand how people make decisions and how people conduct the business of society, students are encouraged to learn about a typical county seat town. Students learn that the people their parents vote for in county elections handle much of the work of the county through employees who are not elected.

While this is an easy and inexpensive field trip for many students who can literally walk down the street from their schools and into the court-house, for this particular group of students it was more difficult. In the city where they live the functions of city and county had been combined and the county and city buildings merged. This was good for the city, but it was difficult for instructing the students concerning the meaning of a county seat and how it worked. These students needed to take a field trip to the adjacent county to determine how county government worked. Here they could enter the courthouse offices, interview elected officials and their employees, and bring back information about how a county works.

The three C words—*county, country,* and *continent*—are challenging for elementary students to interpret. Not only do they sound similar, but on a map they all look like similar little colored blobs. Certainly, older elementary students can point to those little colored blobs on a map and repeat their definitions, but for working knowledge of how big a county is and how it operates, it is important to go to the site. To help develop the concept and differentiate the three C words, students engaged in a field trip to help differentiate the idea of a county from the other two C words. The focus of the trip was the county seat with guiding questions such as: How does county government work to help organize society? What functions does county government play? Further, they determined how citizens make decisions and work through a political process to administer laws in a democracy.

Students clustered their experiences around three historic communities in the county being visited: the northern area, with its new rapidly growing suburban section; the southern rural farms and factory town; and the central section, which includes the county seat and was home to cultural institutions including a small university and a Masonic Home. Multiple stops occurred in each town, where students compared homes, industries, churches, and cemeteries. Each stop allowed students to define the community in terms of resources and history. They saw the communities not just as a collection of historical artifacts, but also as places where people continued to live and work. In each of these communities, the students took opportunities to compare each community with the one where they lived.

Preparation

Students create maps through direct experience as part of their exploration of the world, and they start by creating maps of their rooms, homes, streets, neighborhoods, and of the entire town. Their purposes for making and using maps may be varied. They make a map of their rooms to help them organize their spaces; they make a map of their homes for emergency plans for fire or tornado; they make a map of their streets to show their parents where they will play after school; they may make a map of their neighborhood to plot where all of their friends live in order to form carpools. For the purpose of their social studies field trip, students created maps of the county and the county seat.

When students learn about the function of a county seat, they get to construct a map of the county; within this map they can map the responsibilities of county government. They show the highways that are maintained. They map the county fairgrounds as well as the soil and water districts. They also compare their map to a voter registration map to show the precincts or wards for conducting elections. They show the jurisdiction of the county sheriffs, the 911 dispatch, the planning and zoning board, the building inspector, and the courts. By the end of the assignment, students easily discuss all of the functions of county government.

Furthermore, they use their maps in solving county problems. They compare their maps to a county land plat to determine how counties keep records on taxes and who owns which land. They make a list of all the places in their neighborhoods that the health department inspects and map them. If there is a wreck at the intersection of two county highways, they determine what would be the closest town the 911 dispatcher could call for help. They can determine a good place to locate a new factory on their maps by taking space, roads, utilities, residences, and the environment into consideration.

In concluding the preparation for the field trip, students meet in small groups to decide public policy issues when the individual or group interests clash or compete.

- What happens if a restaurant does not want to keep its kitchen clean? What can the county health inspector do? Does the county have the right to tell a business what to do? What if it cost the business money? Do the people who eat in the restaurant have a right to know if the restaurant is dirty?
- What happens if a large corporation wants to develop a mega hog farm a mile from the county seat? Residents fear that the smell would blow into the town, and the hog waste would pollute the

ground and drinking water. Who in county government has jurisdiction in this matter?

- A movie theater wants to build a major super-complex with fifteen
screens and theater seating. Everybody wants a new movie theater
in town because of the jobs it will create, but the building inspector
stops construction on the project because the steps are too tall.
According to the county building code, the steps must be no more
than eight inches high, and the movie theater has twelve-inch
steps. The building inspector says that in the dark theater patrons
will be hurt on the steps. Because the steps are made from concrete,
it will take money to remove and replace them, and the local building contractor may go bankrupt and not be able to finish the movie
theater. How can this problem be solved?

South

The students entered the town of Edinburgh. This first site required
some historical detective work; the students could see a large state historical marker describing Thompson's Mill, but there was no mill visible. The
students searched for physical evidence of the once grand but now almost
invisible mill structure. After students combed the site and climbed down
to the river, they found evidence of the mill site in the form of the remains
of a dam, old machinery, and the mill footings. Before leaving the site,
the students took notes from the historical marker by using the flat side of
a crayon and a large piece of paper to capture the image of the cast metal
letters.

Students then walked past some homes, including the Thompson
home, and a church clustered on a hill (Holman & Sucich 2007; Schelling, 2004); the teacher just happened to have pictures and text from a
book that described the unique architecture features of the structures,
which were shared before moving to the site of a demolished school. The
teacher had expected the students to compare the old school to their
school and form questions about why they thought the school had closed
and how they thought it could now be used. When the class got to the site,
however, the school had been completely leveled and the area graded; the
action of the frost and spring rains made this a rich site for surface
archaeology nevertheless. Each student had a meter square to search for
evidence in the area of the now-vanished school, and they discovered what
the elements brought to the surface—small pieces of brick, glass, small
pieces of metal, and wire—the major components of the old school building. The students walked around the site to determine from different col-

ors of soil and vegetation patterns where they thought the outline of the structure had been located.

The students moved by bus to two wood veneer factories with historical markers describing David R. Webb and Amos Hill. Students stopped to take notes from the sign with a crayon rubbing and then saw the veneer factories by bus; the factories were just large enough and the bus was just tall enough to give the students an excellent view from the perimeter of the factories without having to walk through them. Students formed questions such as, "What is veneer?" and "Why are they sprinkling the logs with water?" Students made connections between the current presence of forest resources in the county and the location of the present industry. They also connected the logs to the application of veneer in furniture construction, plywood, paneling, and wood flooring (Karner et al., 2001). Students made the connection between all of the items in their homes and how they were connected to this site as well as how this site connected with the residents of the town.

At the Edinburgh cemetery, students mined data from tombstones as a source of information about the small town (Figure 4.1). The students located several tombstones that belonged to a family and made a time line to record the names and the dates of birth and death. They also listed any additional information available about the members of the family. The students made a list of things that could be inferred about the family, for example: Most of the members died young and many children died at an early age. Students needed to see that families had multiple-year commitments within a community ranging across three to five generations. They used the information gathered from the tombstones to draw a family tree showing multiple generations (Figure 4.2). Students put the oldest parents' names on the trunk and each son or daughter on a branch, along with his or her wife or husband. Then they drew more branches for their children and great-grandchildren. This social science research informed students about the nature of the community; while many people in the early twentieth century stayed in one place, by the twenty-first century few

Ralph Vaughan	Berneice Hanna	Connie Vaughan	Connie V. Halpern	Ralph Vaughan	Berneice H. Vaughan
Born	Born	Born	Died	Died	Died
1913	1917	1937	1973	1991	2002

Figure 4.1. Tombstone data.

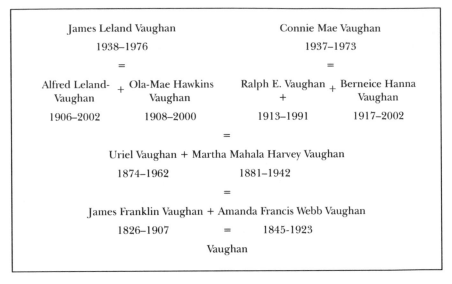

Figure 4.2.   Tombstone generations.

people lived where they grew up, moving multiple times throughout their lives.

The next set of stops was to the former military base at Camp Atterbury. Students took a hike to find the stockade fence from this World War II interment camp and found one of the few remaining original structures on the property—a concrete chapel built by Italian prisoners of war. After the Korean War, the base was deactivated, trees quickly reclaimed the land, and most of the temporary buildings decayed and were torn down. Students searched for footings, coal piles, sign posts, and steps that showed the location of the old camp. Students once again practiced a variation of surface archaeology to determine the vanished landscape that existed in the middle of the twentieth century. As social science researchers, the students investigated this site to determine how it fit into the community, the role it played, and the contributions it made.

The nineteenth century rural cemetery was untouched by the coming of the military base; pioneer family names still rested where family farms and small towns had once stood. Students identified clues from markers representing at least three families that indicated social or economic class, social influence, religion, traits, race, occupations, or cause of death. Students looked for signs of class stratification between lower-, middle-, or upper-class groups of people in this community, compared to the other graveyards. Then students evaluated the similarities and differences

Family #1	Cause of Death	Class	Influence	Occupation	Race	Religion	Traits
Name	Evidence	Evidence	Evidence	Evidence	Evidence	Evidence	Evidence
Name							
Name							
Family #2							
Name	Evidence						
Name							
Name							
Family #3							
Name	Evidence						
Name							
Name							

Figure 4.3. Comparative family traits.

between the families (Figure 4.3). By taking a sociological perspective, students tried to determine what life was like for families in this community. As they continued to develop their perceptions of the community and how the families had fit within it, students looked for evidence from a variety of sources.

The last stop at the site of the camp was a memorial to the veterans who passed through the camp in its function as an induction and training center for World War II. The students took notes from the signs through crayon rubbings and took these back to class with them. Connected to the memorial was a small open-air museum with a variety of army vehicles on display, and students took notes through their drawings. Students sorted them by type and then drew an example from each of the classifications they created (Figure 4.4). For example, they might have chosen to classify the vehicles as airplane, helicopter, fighting vehicle, or truck. They then created a drawing for each of these categories, listed the name of the vehicle, and stated the advantage for using that vehicle.

Central

The group then proceeded to Franklin, the county seat. After making rubbing notes from a historical marker, the group took a tour of the Johnson County Historical Museum (Branting, 2009; Bowdon, 2006; Easley,

Classifications			
Airplane	Helicopter	Fighting Vehicle	Truck
Drawing			
Name of Vehicle			
Advantage			

Figure 4.4.   Drawing as note taking.

2005); this was the only docent-led experience of the entire day, and the museum housed one of the few public restrooms available during the day. The group walked past the old buildings of Franklin College, took rubbing notes from the Indiana Masonic Home sign, and ate their sack lunches in the town park. The historical museum allowed the students to see exhibits of smaller items from Camp Atterbury and photographic enlargements of photos and primary documents from that time. Students also looked at a variety of Victorian antiquities and learned more about the people who occupied the houses, neighborhoods, and commercial buildings they would explore after lunch. Even though this experience was more didactic than their experience of gathering evidence at other sites, the students were still working to gather a picture of life in the community.

In the small town cemetery each student selected a row or an area of the cemetery where they looked for patterns in the use of different shapes and designs of cemetery markers (Mitoraj, 2001; Stevens, 2001, Keegan, 2000). The students drew the shape of the stone, listed the name and the date of death on the marker, and indicated whether there were multiple similar stones in the same style; if so, they just recorded the name and date of death next to the similar drawing. They told the type of material used to construct the marker such as sandstone, limestone, marble, granite, iron, or bronze, and grouped them by flat and upright markers (Figure 4.5). Students documented when different tombstone materials were available for use in the community; they also determined when differing styles for tombstones came into use within the community. Back at school the students compiled all of the data and used time lines to show when a style of marker was first introduced, when it became popular, and when it faded out of style. By using an X for each example to indicate the frequency of the style (Figure 4.6), the students used basic statistical interpretation of their sample to graphically display the data. They analyzed the data to interpret information about the community based on the results. When did the community raise the largest markers? When did the

Flat	Upright	
Flat Rectangle Drawing	Curved Top Slab Drawing	Obelisk Drawing
Pink Granite	Sandstone	Marble
Name	Name	Name
1941	1840	1880
Name		
1957		
Name		
1954		

Figure 4.5.   Marker styles.

Upright Marble Slab With a Half Circle Top											
			X		X	XXX	XX	X	X		X
1810	1820	1830	1840	1850	1860	1870	1880	1890	1900	1910	1920

Figure 4.6.   Marker styles distribution.

community raise the most markers? Based on the time lines, when did the community have the most money? When did flat stones become popular? When did monument materials change? Why did they become popular? When students answered these questions, they were looking into the human history and folk practices of the community.

Using the same row that the students used in Figure 4.5, the students surveyed the cemetery for folk art designs on cemetery markers. By reading and interpreting the information, students determined what was important to the individuals and families. Students could examine changing attitudes toward death and social and religious practices; they could also connect these practices to motifs found regionally and nationally. For each example of design on the tombstone, the students drew a picture of it and recorded the name and date of death; if there were multiple similar carvings, they just recorded the name and date of death next to the similar drawing (Figure 4.7). Students interpreted what they thought the designs meant to the people living in the community and hypothesized about what events might have changed their minds about the decorations

Angel	Book	Chain	Cross	Finger	Gates	Masonic	Rose	Sheep	Sun	Urn	Tree
Name			Name			Name	Name				
Date			Date			Date	Date				
Name						Name					
Date						Date					
						Name					
						Date					

Figure 4.7.   Marker folk art.

Weeping Willow Tree

X	X	XXX	XX	X	X		X				
1810	1820	1830	1840	1850	1860	1870	1880	1890	1900	1910	1920

Figure 4.8.   Folk art distribution.

they used. Back at school they compiled all of the data and used time lines to show when a design was first introduced, when it became popular, and when it faded out of style. By using an X for each example of design, this indicated the frequency of the design used (Figure 4.8). Students analyzed the data to interpret information about the community based on the results; they could see the role played by social groups and military organizations. Furthermore, they could see the rising individualization over traditional folk art preferences with the introduction of technological advances into the monument industry. What designs became popular earliest? Why did other designs become popular? What military signs were present and when were they popular? What social clubs were present and when were they popular? Did more religious symbols show up at any particular time and were the symbols specific to a particular religious sect? Students examined community attitudes toward mortality and grieving through gathering examples of aesthetic representations and symbols.

From the cemetery the group went to more lively areas of neighborhoods found in the heart of the old town. Students looked at the basic plan for the town, the county courthouse, or the county seat located on the town square (Bell & Henning, 2007; Maher, 2004). Students took rubbed notes from the historical marker before finding a memorial to Civil War soldiers in the form of a fountain, a plaque for memorializing Spanish-American War soldiers, and a panel celebrating those who served in wars from World War I through the conflict in Vietnam. Off the town square was the town hall that sparked a debate about what the town did and what the county did before going inside to see what the signs said about the different functions of local government. Both of these buildings provided necessary restroom facilities for this type of trip.

Students then took a walk down the main street while looking at the commercial architecture (Groce, Grace, & Colby, 2005; Argiro, 2004; Alibrandi, Beal, Thompson, & Wilson, 2000). Many of the store fronts on the lower level had been changed and modernized, but if the students looked up to the second, third, and fourth floors they could see what the town looked like over one hundred years ago. Locked in time the original Italianate, Queen Anne, and Romanesque commercial buildings stood as sentinels over the busy streets. The students used a flyer produced by Historic Landmarks Foundation of Indiana, "On the Street Where You Live: Be a Building Watcher!" (2002), to find five examples of the types of architecture listed in the flyer. Through this analysis they could examine when much of the original growth and development of the town occurred. They could also see how the growth of the town and the architectural styles selected connected to the architectural fashion of the rest of the nation.

They turned off Main Street and moved into a residential neighborhood just north of the courthouse at the juncture of Yandes Street and East King Street to read the exterior of the houses (Figure 4.9). In this old neighborhood students used questions to get them to think about the architectural elements and materials of individual residences. Students needed to consider what a family would want to add to make an old house comfortable in the twenty-first century. Students examined why members of the community continued to use historic structures for homes when many other types of residential structures now existed in the community. They also determined how people lived at one time in the town, including the normal size of a house in this area. The last stop in town was a protected historic district at the corner of North Main Street and Martin Place to look at the residential architecture in Victorian context (Figure 4.10). At this site not only were the houses restored to their original prime, but the community context had been preserved—complete with brick streets, limestone curbs and sidewalks, iron fences, gas street lights, and Victorian flower urns. Students got a taste of what it would have been like to live on this street one hundred plus years ago. In this area students probed what it would be like to live with all of these neighbors in a Victo-

Materials
- From the foundation to roof, what materials were used to build the house?
- Compare the origin of the native versus imported materials.
- Clay, sand, and water were combined to make brick; in what ways have raw materials been modified?

Construction
- How was the house constructed?
- What level of technology is reflected in the construction?

Design
- Sketch the basic structure of the house including the number of stories and the basic shape.
- Explain why and /or how this house represents an architectural style or styles.
- Describe the ornamentation.
- How does this design compare in quality to similar houses?

Function
- What was the building's original purpose?
- What other objectives (such as aesthetic, ceremonial, indicator of status, or symbolic) did the building serve?

History
- Has the function of the building changed over time?
- What structural changes have been made in the building?
- In what way has the original style been altered?

Meaning
- What does this building tell you about the culture that produced it?
- What does it tell about the people who used it?
- Why has this building been preserved or allowed to fall into disrepair?
- In what ways does this building relate to its environment or deviate from its surroundings?

Figure 4.9.   House reading.

rian community and why people went to all of the effort to restore the neighborhood rather than trying to make it modern.

North

The last stop was a small town overgrown by strip malls, suburban sprawl, and commercial chain stores and restaurants. Surely there could not be any history in an area that was completely covered in asphalt. At the entrance to the largest mall was a lone historical marker. The students were familiar with this part of the county, since it was the closest to their school; even though they had gone past this sign many times, they saw

Art
- Is public art present?
  Flowerpots, urns, or statues

City Services
- What city services are provided to this neighborhood?
  Sidewalks, curbs, streets then and now, water, gas, electricity, cable TV, phones

Environmental Concerns
- What is missing today that would have been present when the neighborhood was established?
  Flies, animal waste, odors, garbage, mud

Trends
- Is there evidence that the neighborhood is moving up or down?

Landscape
- How are the spaces between homes defined?
  Fences

Unity
- What connection or similarities exist between the homes?
  Architects, lots, placement of the house on the lot

Figure 4.10.   Neighborhood.

and read it for the first time. Dodging cars, the students made some notes from the sign and returned to their cars for a quick trip to the oldest part of the town to explore yet another historical marker and cemetery.

Students looked for trends by seeking information to document family relations, civil and military service, fashion trends in funeral markers, naming customs, and causes of mortality (Figures 4.11 and 4.12). Military traditions figured prominently in the represented markers of the cemetery. Despite being surrounded by shopping malls, this cemetery had many interesting stones, and students searched to find information about the individuals buried here.

Throughout the entire trip students had acted as investigators tracking down evidence, reading the built environment, and learning about a typical county. Students could see the residents of this county and compared them to the city where they lived. Students could see the institutions and structures in the community and could determine how residents interacted within the community. When the students returned to their classroom, they had multiple sets of notes the size of outdoor markers. The easiest way to work with them was to put them on the floor, order them, and then attach them to the hall walls with masking tape. Students took information from these notes to write about their experiences and the his-

1. What are the names of three brothers?
2. How far apart were they in age?
3. Find the names of three persons that held important government jobs.
4. Find and copy the names and the dates of death from three markers that contain metal as part of the memorial.
5. Find a wealthy and influential family plot and record the name of the father. Why is he remembered?
6. List three first or family names no longer in use.
7. List three soldiers' names, ranks, and birth and death dates. Veterans of which war(s)?
8. Find names for two people born in a foreign country.
9. List the name of one person who died of an unusual cause.

Figure 4.11.   Social cemetery search.

List the name on the stone showing:

- American Legion
- Bench
- Bird
- Broken Column
- Bronze Woman
- Cannon
- Chain Links
- Civil War Confederate Soldier
- Civil War Union Soldier
- Cross
- Crown
- Finger Pointed Up
- Flag
- Grand Army of the Republic
- Granite
- Holding Hands
- Log
- Marble
- Mason
- Mausoleum
- Open Book
- Order of Rail Road Conductors
- Rock
- Rose
- Sandstone
- Stone Tree
- Sword
- Vine
- War of 1812 Veteran
- Weeping Willow Tree
- Woodmen of the World
- World War II

Figure 4.12.   Cemetery search.

Teachers help students learn about:

II.   Time, continuity, and change
III.   People, places, and environments
IV.   Power, authority, and governance
VII.   Production, distribution, and consumption

Figure 4.13.   NCSS (1994) national standards.

tory they constructed from reading the built environment. They visited three small but not uninteresting towns as they conducted their investigation. They expressed how people influence, take action, and relate to one another in their community; they understood more about life in a county seat (Figure 4.13).

CHAPTER 5

INVESTIGATING
URBAN SPACES AND PLACES

THE THEME-BASED URBAN FIELD TRIP

Urban spaces and places not only need to be explored at many levels, but they can be visited multiple times with different lenses to focus the experience on various themes. Students and teachers find many places to explore in urban areas, but sticking to a specific theme is more difficult because so many venues abound. When students examine an urban space, they will use a theme to organize their day; they will form questions based on this theme, which they will use to direct their learning about the sites. Students, therefore, make multiple field trips to the same place, and by focusing on different themes and raising different questions, they acquire different ideas each time they return to the site. When fourth-grade students reach a specific destination, they look at the site as a connection to their local studies (Figure 5.1). They seek to understand how that particular site reflects their theme of local studies, and they take information and skills from that experience that will allow them to learn from other sites in the future.

Students go on field trips to bring information they learned on-site back to the classroom; using this information, they then create new products that focus on their role as a citizen. Consideration of the students' age determines the type and form of notes appropriate for the students to

The Field Trip Book: Study Travel Experiences in Social Studies
pp. 63–73
Copyright © 2010 by Information Age Publishing

7:30 a.m.	Depart
7:45 a.m.	Mary Bryan's grave
8:00 a.m.	Depart
8:15 a.m.	Hanna House
9:00 a.m.	Depart
9:15 a.m.	Indiana State Museum (Amish Clothes, Early Children's Clothes, Earth Science, Freetown Village, Golden Age of Radio, Main Street, Natural History, Regional Artists)
10:45 a.m.	Depart
11:00 a.m.	Riley Home
12:00 p.m.	Depart
12:15 p.m.	Fast food lunch
12:45 p.m.	Depart
1:00 p.m.	City Center (*Indianapolis Indeed!* and *Indianapolis Today*)
1:30 p.m.	Depart
1:45 p.m.	Indiana Medical History Museum
2:45 p.m.	Depart
3:00 p.m.	Eiteljorg Museum (Eastern Woodland Program)
3:45 p.m.	Depart
4:00 p.m.	Indiana Museum of Art (Indiana Artist Program)
5:00 p.m.	Depart
5:30 p.m.	Return to school

Figure 5.1.   Indianapolis: The city and county.

bring back to the classroom. Few students are born knowing how to sort through the massive amounts of information found in an urban area. They do not know how to make sense of it or to determine what information is most important. While field trips are great ways for students to learn serendipitously, teachers cannot count on that knowledge and therefore need to have a plan for how students will learn and gather information. Giving students an armature for note taking will help them to be successful in knowing what they are expected to gather from the experience.

Cities are fascinating places due to the concentration of museums and institutions that students see. Teachers often take students on field trips that become a long list of places to visit without any meaningful connections. Rather than trying to see everything in one day, consider targeting specific places and galleries. The theme might be "Nashville's National Contributions," "Savannah's Economic Ties to the World," or "Work and Leisure in Charleston." Each site the students visit then ties into that theme, and they then gather information around that theme. By using a theme-based field trip, students return to a site multiple times or to a site that they frequent with their parents, and they find new aspects to explore.

Preparation

To prepare the students to go to a series of urban places, the students need the following equipment: pencils and erasers, clipboards, and their data retrieval chart. Before taking students to see different sites, they need to construct a data retrieval chart based on questions the students raised in class prior to the trip. The teacher might ask, "What do we want to learn when we are at these sites?" After listing the questions, the students cluster these questions into groups. The teachers further refine those clusters into a single idea or concept. The students make a chart by listing the names of the sites to be visited that day on the left-hand side (e.g., Indianapolis Museum of Art, Indianapolis Motor Speedway, Indiana World War Memorial). Across the top of the sheet, list the concepts: Change, Economics, Human/Environmental Interactions, Leisure, Government, and Technology. Arrange in rows and columns and leave space for students to write their notes in each cell created; students then take these focused notes which they have written in the cells about the sites back to school.

Students utilize their time best by starting their investigation early in the day; thus, they gather information all day before returning to their school. It is helpful to arrange to be an early group at the most popular destinations, therefore beating the crowds. Because the school day usually starts before the museum day, students may need to plan to visit other places prior to going to big museums. Cemeteries and private, prominent, local homes are good early morning destinations because they have no set open hours. The teacher needs to watch the time carefully throughout the day, lest any one activity consume more time than its objective merits. The teacher needs to especially be aware of how rapidly the period after lunch can pass, especially because the school day usually ends long before the museum closes.

Large museums such as children's museums, state museums, or art museums offer specific programs, and groups must conform to the programs of these large institutions. Larger institutions usually allow little flexibility for the creative teacher because these institutions are dependent upon large numbers of visitors to justify their funding requests. Thus, it is important for the members of the class and the teacher to be very selective in what they focus on in the museum. They must identify and focus on the galleries and exhibits that specifically support the main ideas of the trip; in this case the connections will be made with local history. Next, check the educational programming catalogue to see if there are any specialized tours or programs that connect to the theme of the tour. For example, galleries on the land, natural resources, and bio-zones in the state help establish a foundation of knowledge for students who will learn even more about these areas on other trips. The recreated main street in the museum provides a contrast between the streets of the past and those that the students will walk later in the afternoon and thus provides a point of comparison between the past and the present. Other exhibits provide new experiences for learning about ethnic and religious groups, artists, and radio entertainment.

When students visit a city, they need to first learn what opportunities the city offers; therefore, one of the first places to visit is the city's welcome center that features a short video as well as models of the city, thus providing an overview of the wealth of educational and entertainment opportunities or possibilities available in the city. This place provides a preview or review of all of the stops encountered during the day. At other sites the students also explore the home of a regional poet, where they compare the restoration and the preservation of both the building and the furnishings. Students also explore changes in medical technology, noting how those changes improved the quality of life for people as well as the way doctors prepared to work with patients. It is important for the students to get an overview of the community as well as the specific details that support the connections between art and science that enrich life in the city (Mislove & Strange, 2008; Brouillette, 2006; Fattal, 2004; McCloskey, 2004).

Urban Art Museums

When the students visit a city art museum, they do not go there to experience the entire span of time nor to see the entire collection, but rather to discover specifically how the people in their state have seen life through art and how this view of art changes over time (Whitmer, Luke, & Adams, 2000). At another art museum, which focuses on the work of indigenous people, students again look not at all the work of all people, but at the creative work of people who had connections with just their area. At first glance this approach seems provincial, but the emphasis on different people from different places is compounded the next year, as students return to the urban space to make connections between their city, nation, and world. Students get experiences with western and non-western arts and crafts, and they value the production of these art materials across time. The students begin to understand how the artist sees and understands the world, how an artist chooses to depict that world, and how that view is connected to time, place, events, and personal philosophy.

In the fifth grade, students look at sites in the same urban space to find connections to national and international events (Figure 5.2). The students may repeat some of the sites, but this time they are examining sites in light of national connections. One of the first events of the day is to find people in a cemetery who had nationally significant reputations. At a cemetery the teachers assign the students a variety of tombstones, and the students then classify the people represented into one of five groups: artists, entertainers, industrialists, politicians, and outlaws (Figure 5.3). From this sorting exercise students find out more about the work of famous people and the contributions they made. Students connect this knowledge with economic and political events, which they have heard about in their other explorations.

Students get an overview of military history by looking at public monuments that honor contributions to military efforts (Nespor, 2000). There is probably a War Memorial Commission that cares for all of the monuments as part of the state or city government. When observing monuments, students first need to look at the setting, then they need to examine the exterior of the monument, and finally they need to look at the inside space and the interpretation of the space. From each of these areas the students get ideas about local implications of international events. Students not only look at the landscape but at the structure, the interior, and the exhibits to determine the messages of power and authority that are built into the monument (Figure 5.4). Students can make a

7:30 a.m.	Depart from school
8:00 a.m.	Crown Hill Cemetery (John Dillinger, Benjamin Harrison, Eli Lilly, James W. Riley)
8:45 a.m.	Depart
9:00 a.m.	Indianapolis Speedway Museum and Track Lap
10:00 a.m.	Depart
10:30 a.m.	Monument Circle
11:00 a.m.	Depart
11:15 a.m.	World War Memorial
11:45 a.m.	Depart
12:00 p.m.	Fast food lunch
1:00 p.m.	Depart
1:15 p.m.	Morris - Butler Home
2:15 p.m.	Depart
2:30 p.m.	Benjamin Harrison Home
4:15 p.m.	Depart
4:30 p.m.	Return to school

Figure 5.2.   Indianapolis in the nation and world.

Name	Artist	Entertainer	Industrialist	Outlaw	Politician
John Dillinger				X	
Paul Hadley	X				
Benjamin Harrison					X
Eli Lilly			X		
James W. Riley		X			

Figure 5.3.   Cemetery data retrieval sheet.

Landscape
• How has space been used?
• How has the land been arranged?
• What place does water have in this arrangement?

Structure
• What is the design of the structure?
• What materials have been used?
• How have statues been used?
• Did the period of time when the building was created influence the design of the structure?

Interior
• What emotional response do you get from the space?
• What materials have been used?
• What symbols have been used?
• How much of the building elements are decorative and how much are functional?

Exhibits
• What evidence do you see of propaganda?
• How does this exhibit reflect celebration?

Message
• How does the landscape reflect power?
• How does the monument's exterior reflect nationalism?
• How does the monument's interior reflect militarism?
• How do the exhibits reflect authority?
• How does the monument reflect patriotism?

Figure 5.4.   War memorial reading form.

case for propaganda from the war posters found in the exhibits, and they can look for evidence of militarism, nationalism, and patriotism within the symbolism of the structure.

The homes of politicians help students understand the contributions the citizens of the city have made toward national and international events; this can be very misleading, however. A poor tour can easily turn into an explanation of the Victorian way of life or a decorative arts tour when what is really wanted is how the house reflects the life and times of the person. Students need to see evidence from both artifacts and the context of the house in order to determine how this person was effective and how the person's life intersected with both other influential persons and the common citizens. Students see how life in a particular time period occurred in an urban setting by looking at the backstairs section of the house; they also see the social implications of Victorian entertaining practices from the very formal front spaces of the house. If the purpose of the visit is political then the focus needs to remain on the rise and successes of the politician through national and international achievements.

Exposure to the typical Victorian house museum presents students with the experience of life styles that contrast with their present modes of living. The importance of the students' visit hinges on the connections they make with Victorian living across the nation as well as their reflections upon interpretive society through consumer goods, design, esthetics, and fashion. For a contrasting house museum, the students return to the art museum, which they visited the year before, to visit a house museum that represents a family's country home of the early twentieth century. In their return visit of the century-old home, Oldfields, they reflect on the esthetic vision blending art, architecture, and landscape design as artifacts of money and power. Students need to look at both of these houses as artifacts from a particular period of time; by considering the art, the architecture, and the landscape design, they then determine what the site tells them about the nation during this period.

In order to explore image and culture, students go to a local racetrack, where they take a lap around the track and explore the accompanying museum; as a result, they construct ideas of international reputation, image, media exposure, economics, and entertainment. The concept of image in the twentieth-first century shapes concepts of place and esteem in a consumer culture driven by media and advertising. The image of fast cars and high stakes winners is invaluable for the city because of the international attention it brings to the location. The roots of this modern phenomenon are connected to the historical development of the city as a testing ground for the pioneer industry of automobiles and automobile parts. Students need to gather information and evaluate the site to determine what the site contributes to society.

Media outlets are also important places for students to explore; here they see the local TV or radio stations and newspaper office. In a trip to the TV station students see the offices, the computers for video editing, sets, camera equipment, and anchor desks. They meet the weather correspondent and see the blue screen and the monitors. One group even learned that one day when the weather correspondent wore the wrong color blue necktie, a storm moved across his abdomen on the news because the computer picked up the color of his blue tie as the blue screen. The students are allowed to watch very quietly from behind the cameras as the news is broadcast, and during the commercials they may ask the anchors questions about their jobs, how they prepare, and the disadvantages of media. Media outlets are places where the image of the urban area is defined, distorted, expanded, and refined by various events. When students examine the source of their news, they become more sophisticated as consumers of both the news and advertising.

All of the sites in this chapter are sources of data when using urban spaces as resources, but urban cemeteries are another source of data that students take from the travel experience back to the classroom. Sometimes the markers, statuary, chapels, signs, and mausoleums are so distinctive that they merit recording via photos and bringing back to the classroom in order to discuss them as features found in the cemetery. Students use this data to develop additional ideas in the classroom. Students turn the photos or the rubbings produced from markers into extensive time lines. At each site in the city, students learn more about a sense of place connected with a theme, and they gather information as they interpret the site into their own construction of knowledge (Koetsch, D'Acquisto, Kurin, Juffer, & Goldberg, 2002).

Local History

It has been said that local history is not lucrative for authors or historians, but it is certainly more affordable for teachers and students. When comparing the costs associated with state and local sites to those sites that interpret national or international views or events, there is a decided increase in the cost of the latter (Figures 5.5 and 5.6). In fact, the state and local admission fees are less than one-half the price of the national and international costs. The implications are clear: Knowledge about local history is not valued nor as highly esteemed as knowledge of national or international events. Good teachers use these local and state information sources, however, to help their students gather, analyze, and evaluate material that they can use later in the classroom(Dallmer, 2007; Michels & Maxwell, 2006; McCall & Ristow, 2003). By using these sources, teachers help students to bridge the gap between local, state, national, and international events (Figure 5.7).

Eiteljorg Museum	$1.50 child, $3.00 adult
Indiana Medical History Museum	$1.00 student, $2.00 adult
James Whitcomb Riley Home	$0.25 child, $1.00 adult
Total per Child	$2.75

Figure 5.5.   Fees for state and local urban trip.

Indianapolis Speedway Museum	$2.00 adult
Indianapolis Speedway Track Lap	$2.00 per person
Morris - Butler Home	$1.00 per person
Benjamin Harrison Home	$1.00 child, $2.00 adult
Total per Child	$6.00

Figure 5.6.   Fees for national and international urban trip.

Debriefing

Students bring their notes back to class on their data retrieval sheets (NCSS, 1994) (Figure 5.8). When they talk about their experience, they pool their information on big charts of paper with the concept and the location listed at the top, such as "Indianapolis Museum of Art/Leisure." Students move from place to place copying their information on each piece of chart paper until they have shared all of their information. Then in groups clustered by concept (such as "Leisure"), they write stories about their trip comparing the sites they visited. While this will give several students comparable analysis sections of their paper, they would need to end by discussing how this idea impacts citizenship for themselves or for others (Figure 5.9). They need to determine if there are issues that might be controversial for individuals or groups in society, such as "Are the bronze statues of naked Greeks pornographic?" What happens in society when some people say they are and some people say they are not?

- *Archeological Sites*: Students visit prehistoric, historic, or industrial archeology sites, where they learn about the first people, early settlement, or early industry from signage or docents.
- *Art Museums*: By looking at artifacts, students examine the contributions of ethnic groups and women, and they learn about the context of the art and how the art reflects the context of the time.
- *Cemeteries*: Students learn about many different traditions including religious, artistic, ethnic, regional, and industrial. Cemeteries illustrate the lives of individuals and provide clues about interpreting culture.
- *Ethnic Museums*: Students explore specialized collections to hear the stories celebrating the contributions of Blacks, Fins, first peoples, Jews, Poles, women, and many other ethnic groups.
- *Factories*: Visitors examine products, ideas, laborers, management, economics, and trade in these sites.
- *Government Buildings*: Students tour fire stations, police stations, state capitols, and government buildings to learn about life as a citizen.
- *Historic Districts*: Visitors discern residential patterns, business and commercial sections, ethnic communities, leisure activities, planned communities, military paths, and manufacturing.
- *History Museums*: Students tour general collections of artifacts and primary sources that interpret themes, or one specific collection that interprets one particular theme.
- *House Museums*: Students meet both famous and common people as they tour houses that illustrate the lives of typical people from the time, architectural styles, artists, musicians, politicians, leaders of commerce, religious leaders, literary luminaries, political figures, or make connections to military commanders.
- *Military Bases*: Visitors to these sites explain stories of conflict between Indians and settlers, response to world war or cold war, or growth of the military across time.
- *Parks*: Students usually go to parks to play, but as examples of urban planning or sets for Great Depression relief projects, parks have a history in explaining how people live in urban spaces.
- *Private Residences*: Examples of adaptive reuse help students see how people continue to use homes across time.
- *Science and Engineering Museums*: These institutions help students understand changes in technology and medicine, as well as how the choices they make continue to impact their lives.
- *Sports Complexes*: When students use the history of sport, they look at how people use their leisure time and how that idea has changed over time.
- *Utilities*: Students rarely think about how environmental and energy choices are made in their community; when they visit utilities, they learn how basic services are provided by government or businesses including water treatment, electric generation, steam plants, sewer treatment, natural gas, phone, landfill, cable, and recycling.
- *War Memorials*: When students visit memorials, they honor sacrifice and accomplishments from many or specific conflicts with groups of people who most likely are now our allies.

Figure 5.7.   Urban field trip sites.

II.   Time, continuity, and change
III. People, places, and environments
V.   Individuals, groups, and institutions
VI.   Power, authority, and governance
VIII. Science, technology, and society

Figure 5.8.   NCSS (1994) national standards.

For assessment, the teacher could use a rubric on a 4-point scale:

Identified the Concept
  4   Identified, defined, and gave an example of the concept
  3   Identified and defined the concept
  2   Identified the concept
  1   Did not identify the concept

Compared the Concept
  4   Listed three institutions and gave more than one similarity and more than one difference
  3   Listed three institutions and gave one similarity and one difference
  2   Listed two institutions and gave one similarity
  1   Did not compare the concept

Connection to Citizenship
  4   Made a connection to citizenship and gave more than one example
  3   Made a connection to citizenship and gave one example
  2   Made a connection to citizenship
  1   Did not make a connection to citizenship

Controversial Issue
  4   Identified a controversial issue and provided more than one example
  3   Identified a controversial issue and provided an example
  2   Identified a controversial issue
  1   Did not identify a controversial issue

Figure 5.9.   Assessment rubic.

CHAPTER 6

FINDING STATE ADVENTURES AS INVESTIGATORS

INTRODUCTION

Students need to be investigators of social studies sites, and they can investigate in many ways. Their investigation can be a very physical exploration of the geography of an area, or they might investigate static exhibits. They might use drama in their investigations or they may have a specific assignment. If their only investigation is limited to listening to a content expert at the site, then the regular classroom drill of listening to a teacher has merely changed voices. The active student enjoys investigations out of the classroom, because there are so many things to explore in the world.

As teachers plan field experiences, it is important for them to think about what students learned, what they thought, and how they reacted to the experience. The latter a perspective that is often left unconsidered. Of course, this is a week-long field trip, but most people do not have to contend with the vast geography of west Texas. Many teachers will be able to use the information provided here including enactive field trip experiences and what the experience meant to the students who participated to create their own one-day or half-day field trips.

The Field Trip Book: Study Travel Experiences in Social Studies
pp. 75–98
Copyright © 2010 by Information Age Publishing
All rights of reproduction in any form reserved.

"I WONDER WHAT WILL HAPPEN NEXT"

The seventh-grade students from Lubbock, Texas, took a weeklong class trip to study central Texas as part of their seventh-grade social studies curriculum. They traveled by bus to spend time at sites of state and local interest in central Texas. The students wanted to see where Texas history occurred and the sites that were described in their textbook. Students prepared for the trip, kept journals during the trip, and created a newspaper to use for debriefing after the trip. Although the students participated in a teacher-directed experience, they interpreted the experience to direct their own learning. The research question was: How do students extend their definition of community through field trip experiences in their state?

Teachers think about planning the trip in three phases: before, during, and after. They design specific experiences to help students learn at each of these points in the process of taking a field trip. They also think of four specific parts while on the trip: travel time, docents, independent student activities, and student interaction with static exhibits. All of these parts can be used to help students find out more about a site; they may all be used at one site or four different field trips could each use a part. They also consider how each part of the process and each part of the trip reinforce and interact with other aspects of the trip.

Before the Trip

Prior to the trip, the teacher should tour all the sites before selecting the most interactive sites for the students. Teachers look for sites that help to raise controversial issues for student discussion and exploration. Oftentimes the site will not provide this without interpretive help from a teacher to probe different perspectives. Experiences that help students learn about ideas that shaped the state and its people take priority over miscellaneous collections of old stuff. The teacher sets up tours to help the students focus on important ideas and actively experience the exhibits.

Many students get an opportunity to study their state and local region in social studies class; the students should not just hop on the bus and start riding however. They must have a good preparation so that they know what they will see while they are on-site and realize how this experience is significant to their education. Students spent two and one-half weeks focusing on a trip to central Texas. They began their study travel preparation by working in groups and by dividing the state into regions, defining the attractions and notable features in that area, and finding or creating illustrations on a three-fold backboard to illustrate the region.

Each group shared their research about their assigned region. An extension of this project included providing a potential itinerary for a day trip. The students selected sites and attractions that related to social studies, researched them to make sure they were pragmatic, and then presented their plans to the other groups. The class evaluated each plan and selected a plan by voting and compromising to determine their route—in this case, central Texas.

When the seventh-grade teacher, Mrs. McNeely, announced the trip, she asked the students to write what they knew about the trip or the sites on the paper-covered walls with markers (Figure 6.1). The students brought a large amount of prior knowledge and information with them into the classroom; the teacher wanted to capitalize on these experiences. From there, Mrs. McNeely worked to correct any misconceptions, folklore, or myths before proceeding to other background material. She gave a brief preview of the trip by using a wall map, an overhead projector, and transparencies.

Students also had classroom journals in which they recorded some of their ideas before the trip. Seventh-grade student Jonathan stated, "I also expect to learn about the history of San Antonio and the history of Austin. I also want to learn about the history of how Austin became the capitol." Next, Mrs. McNeely passed out state highway maps of Texas and had the students use highlighters to trace their journey for each day of their trip

---

- **Alamo:** Mission used in the Texas War for Independence
- **Ft. Concho:** American military outpost for operations against the Indians on the Texas frontier
- **Ft. McKavitt:** American military outpost for operations against the Indians on the Texas frontier
- **Fredricksburg Museum:** Interprets German settlement in the hill country of Texas
- **Goliad:** Site were Texans surrendered to General Cos during the Texas War for Independence only to be massacred
- **La Bahia Spanish Mission:** A well preserved Spanish religious outpost
- **LBJ Ranch National Historical Park:** Ranch and home of Lyndon Baines Johnson
- **National Museum of the Pacific War:** World War II military history
- **Paint Rock:** Prehistoric petroglyphs created by indigenous people
- **Presidio:** Spanish Colonial military post
- **San Jose Mission (San Antonio Mission National Historical Park):** One of three missions preserved in the area by the National Park Service
- **Texas State Capitol:** Seat of state government

Figure 6.1. Central Texas sites.

on the map as well as to color the sites they would see while on the trip. Students compared their predictions of where they were going with the geographic facts when they saw the relationships between sites and the travel routes. Next, they created a time line of all the events and places they planned to visit on the trip and used both the journals and the time lines to record their trip experiences. Furthermore, students reordered the sites and events in chronological order; this was particularly difficult for students if a site experienced continuous occupation or if a site had more than one historical event associated with it.

The teacher planned the trip early enough so that she was able to take advantage of pre-packaged materials provided by the Texas state capitol in Austin; the students used these materials to interpret what they would see at each site. During these activities students worked with photos, artwork, documents, and letters to discover information about the sites. The teacher modified the instructions and the students worked in groups; this worked well since many of these materials contained primary sources. She also obtained copies of the Texas Constitution and had students use the index to find issues that interested them. Students identified issues that they found important, but by working in groups they were also exposed to the ideas researched and presented by the other students.

To help the students learn how to use primary sources prior to visiting a site interpreting the life of Lyndon B. Johnson, Mrs. McNeely found six political cartoons depicting Johnson, and students discussed the issues in the cartoons (Schwartz, 1995; Forman & Calvert, 1993; Yarrington, 1987). One cartoon depicted Senator Johnson between two kicking donkeys; one was marked "liberal democrats" and the other marked "conservative democrats." Students determined that Johnson pacified both factions to get them to work together. The other cartoon showed Johnson showing America his scar in the shape of Vietnam, and students contributed information about Vietnam from their literature class. Students interpreted this cartoon to mean that Johnson's presidency had a dark shadow hanging over it and that Vietnam forever marked him.

During the Trip

The seventh-grade class spent one week in the fall traveling to sites of local, state, and national significance to gather information to use when they returned to school. The students traveled to central Texas to see sites connected with early people including sites related to their settlement, independence, and governance. They took this trip as a part of their social studies curriculum so they could see where history actually occurred. Together the students traveled on one chartered coach, and they made multiple stops to get tours from local experts. The trip included spending five days and four nights at a base camp in the hill country of Texas and taking side trips from that central location. One seventh-grade student, Modiv, said in her journal,

> I think that I will learn many things on this trip. I would like to learn about how Texas became a state in the United States. I would also like to learn how … [Native Americans] took care of Texas, and how the Texas government works. I hope to learn many things about early Texans also.

It took time for students to have enough experience with the events to absorb them into their lives. Students needed time on the site to take everything in and to digest the information. At each site Mrs. McNeely reflected upon what the students could do, explore, and experience to help them meet the objectives of the trip. Mrs. McNeely actively looked for situations associated with conflict or accord between cultures and tried to focus on the contributions of others or of forgotten ethnic groups. At Paint Rock, a prehistoric site on private land, a huge rock slab aligned with one of the pictographs as if to form a viewing or ceremonial platform. At this site each person made a map of Paint Rock and plotted where he or she would dig, if he or she were an archeologist, in order to see if other rock slabs might be found. At this site during periods of solstice and equinox, the rocks cast shadows across pictographs and petroglyphs. Students also speculated about shadows cast onto other rock paintings at different times of the year. Students made and tested their predictions in these activities. One student, Lauren, wrote in her journal, "At Paint Rock we saw so many different kinds of signs that the Comanches wrote with all sorts of signs with mysterious meanings. We saw many bear claws and drooping corn crops with [a] heavy sun."

Travel Time

Teacher-directed travel assignments including historic, geographic, and journaling opportunities helped students interpret their travel experiences. Teachers, who planned instructional activities during travel time, made every minute count toward learning. During the trip the students had assignments held in three-ring binders so that nothing fell out on the bus or at the different sites. Each three-ring binder provided a writing surface for students and displayed their names on the exterior for easy identification. These assignments provided documentation to justify the expenditure of released time from classes at the school building.

The binder contained a variety of activities for the students while the bus was in motion; the teacher provided information through background essays on the sites, battle flags, and the six governments that represented

Texans. The Texas Department of Transportation provided the students with information about Texas wildflowers and a booklet segmented by region illustrating Texas attractions. The highway map fit neatly inside the pocket of the three-ring binder; the binder also contained a geography exercise in which students labeled a map of Texas including the adjacent country, states bordering Texas, and Texas cities, rivers, and bodies of water. Mrs. McNeely included a map of the Alamo in San Antonio at the time of its defense; another map of the Alamo showed its original configuration superimposed on the modern city streets. This was easy to make by photocopying a simple line drawing onto a transparency and then photocopying the transparency over a map. The teacher also included the time line that the students made so that they could add to it; the students received comprehension and divergent questions that corresponded to each site where they stopped. The students found journal pages at the back of their binders where they made an entry for every day of the trip. They also had time to work on the binder materials including their journals; these materials helped the students to preview and debrief while traveling between sites.

Educators blended narratives and activities to help students learn while they traveled. On the trip students had many different stops, but between sites the students could listen to ten-minute stories about what they had seen or would see. These mini lectures helped preview and review data between sites. Because the students liked ghost stories, sharing these before or after visiting a site provided a different source of information; the teacher asked the students to compare these stories with historical accounts. Students had to hypothesize about what scared the people who told these stories; they then had to evaluate and give reasons why the stories still scare people today.

Before touring a site the students found the multimedia orientation programs and models at the visitor centers useful. These presentations allowed students exposure through media and reinforced content through multiple experiences at the site. For example, students saw and heard multimedia exhibits, experienced audiovisual overviews, and listened to docents talk about the events at the Alamo. The students saw models of the town and the Alamo along with static exhibits before seeing the video presentation. Each of these experiences helped students to scaffold content into a story line that they could remember.

Docents

Museum education personnel conducted formal interpretation with programming designed to interpret the site. The students got multiple perspectives when they traveled. It was particularly easy for students to get one view from an expert and to think there was only one side to the story. The National Park Service provided a good example of multiple perspectives when they interpreted the Lyndon B. Johnson Ranch National Historical Park near Johnson City, Texas. Johnson himself narrated the tour on tape. The park service included his quotations as well as the quotations from his contemporary supporters and detractors.

On study travel trips students met experts in the field who interacted with the students in a variety of ways. When students visited government buildings, the elected officials and clerical staff took time to speak with school groups. Docent-led tours usually focused on a particular theme and then helped students see corresponding parts of the galleries in order to interpret the theme. Furthermore, docents played an important role in providing demonstrations for students at the historic sites. At these times students got to see skills demonstrated that are not readily available in the classroom. For example, at Fort Concho in San Angelo, Texas, students got to see what a site looked like in the past and how docents conduct daily life activities at restored sites. The interpretation consisted of a lesson from the school day in the restored school as well as observing the soldiers firing their rifles for the students. Students joined in this experience; they followed behind the soldiers, marched across the parade ground, selected a bunk, and dressed in military uniforms, hats, and shoes. In the hospital the students randomly drew a slip of paper with a disease written on it. Each student lay on a bed in the ward. One of the students arrived as the doctor to give a cure, which was printed on a three-by-five card, or he ordered the attendants to haul the dead body to the morgue.

Students also tailored the experience to satisfy their needs by asking questions in front of the group while walking with the docent to the next site or after the tour. On the rare occasions when students had down time after a tour with a docent, the student questions could be particularly interesting with students asking multiple questions to clarify their understanding. Student questions and interest in topics reinforced the role of the docent and motivated the guide to provide even more information. Since students shaped the interview, they got information that interested them. The result was more like an inquiry project for the students who were exploring their own interests.

At some sites the teacher essentially acted as a docent to provide assistance in interpreting static exhibits. Teachers pointed out the highlights, brought interesting stories into the tour which were not told by the exhibit, helped students spend more time with the collection, and answered impromptu questions. Mrs. McNeely carried artifacts, photos, artwork, quotations, and maps to interpret sites. The visual aides helped the students see vanished details, focus on a major point of the site, or see what was currently on the site in a different context. Mrs. McNeely knew that this type of assistance was valuable in helping the students to deepen their understanding when they visited a site.

Independent Student Activities

Students worked on-site with many different types of activities independent of close supervision. Students do not usually profit from self-guided tours unless the students have an assignment on which they can focus. Students commonly preview the entire site before going back to a particular segment of the site that interests them. This may be very disconcerting to a linear teacher. Many military sites have limited signage or interpretation. Students used crayons and paper to make rubbings of all the available historical markers to gather information from the trip. Students collected a variety of free flyers available at tourist attractions to reinforce historical content from the sites. In the Plaza of Presidents at Fredricksburg, Texas, students used graphic organizers to make four columns labeled *Administration, Air Force, Army,* or *Navy* in order to chart twentieth-century presidential World War II service. The students saw that military service propelled military leaders into political leadership. Students needed interaction with each site, but it was particularly difficult to interpret ruin sites. Students drew blueprints for their ideas for reconstructing the ruins of the Spanish colonial fort or Presidio at Menard based on the evidence of the footings.

At Fort McKavett near Menard, Texas, the students searched for the original footings, and they drew how they thought the fort once looked based on the foundations. The students used a treasure map of instructions and a compass to start at the arsenal, move to the officers' quarters, barracks, latrine, and finally to find the quartermaster's warehouse, a building that was no longer standing. Students also did surface archeology at Ft. McKavett; within a one-meter string square each student had two minutes to find artifacts that would indicate prior habitation on the ground without digging. What did the debris they found tell us about life here? Students had to leave any artifacts they found. Students used artistic imagination to restore the ruins of Commander Ranald McKinzie's house in an illustration. With partners they also used graph paper to make a map of the fort footings. At the Fort McKavett Visitor's Center, students conducted a scavenger hunt with questions that had been provided (Figure 6.2).

Other military structures, this time from the Spanish Colonial Period, also impressed the students favorably. Sam wrote in his journal, "Goliad is really neat. I love the architecture. The buildings were beautiful ... [with a] great design. The Presidio was equally interesting. The way [the] Presidio was built really appeals to me." Students used the fortification with thick stone walls and walkways covered with rolling arches to act out their

- What four ethnic groups met in this area?
- What was the defensive plan of Texas?
- Who was McKavett?
- What are dragoons if they do not eat knights?
- What happened after the fort was abandoned?
- What was McKenzie's role?
- What connections does the fort have to baseball?
- What was the role of the Buffalo Soldier?
- How did people get in trouble at the fort?
- How was the fort restored?
- How does archeology help people find out about the fort?
- How is Lubbock connected to this site?

Figure 6.2. Fort McKavett scavenger hunt questions.

next assignment. The Mission Impossible simulation activity helped students focus on questions for La Bahia, a Spanish Mission at Goliad, Texas (Figure 6.3). To teach the concept of interior lines of defense, the students used gross motor skills and pre-printed task cards. Although this strategy had not actually been used at Goliad, military leaders did use it in other situations (Figure 6.4).

The students also used role-playing at Goliad to recreate some of the feelings of the site; the students became the prisoners from the captured garrison. The prisoners marched down the road with their hands tied loosely with rubber bands behind their backs and under the guard of

- What structures were at the mission?
- How did the Spanish defend themselves?
- What was the fewest number of bastions needed for defense?
- Select a diorama.
  - o Where are you in it?
  - o What are you saying?
  - o To whom are you talking?
- What jobs did the Native Americans do?
- Is there evidence that the mission was not successful?

Figure 6.3. Mission impossible.

The strategy for defending this fort is to have a fast mobile reserve force that can go anywhere there is danger. Open your fate cards and do what they tell you to do. After you have discovered what it tells you, select the next card.

- Fire your rifle from the rifle port on the north wall.
- Reinforce the southeast ramp and defend against the attackers scaling the wall using ladders. Push all of them away from the wall.
- Get water from the well and pour it on the main gate, which the attackers have set on fire.
- Set up cannon to fire through the Mission Gate.
- Fire through the west rifle ports.
- Pour boiling water from the southeast ramp onto the attackers to scald them.
- Fire down the wall from the southwest ramp with the cannon.

Figure 6.4.   Simulation.

other students. The guards stopped to form a single rank along one side of the road. The student prisoners turned their backs to their guards, and the words rang out, "Ready. Aim. Fire!" At this point the teacher lit a string of firecrackers, and the students dropped in the road near the monument as if they were victims of the massacre at Goliad.

Students also role-played the myth of crossing the line when they saw the plaque and bronze line set in the ground in the front of the Alamo. William Travis drew in the dirt with his sword and asked his men to cross over to defend the Alamo with him. The students recreated the event by crossing over the plaque in front of the Alamo. Students also role-played cleaning up the Alamo after the battle and made an inventory of all the things that had been left behind. They found the items left that had once belonged to Davy Crockett, William Travis, and Santa Anna. Jonathan said, "I really liked seeing the original artifacts at the Alamo.... I like to see original things so ... [they really] caught my attention" (interview).

Student Interaction With Static Exhibits

Students also engaged in role-play at the National Museum of the Pacific War in Fredricksburg, Texas. The group members started together with a video introduction before moving on to the deck of the submarine. The students found themselves off the shore of Pearl Harbor role-playing Japanese sailors about to climb into a mini-sub. They saluted and got their instructions from their commander, and then they raised their arms and yelled, "Banzai!" The group moved to the electric map showing illuminated invasion routes across the Pacific Ocean before walking onto an aircraft carrier hangar deck. A signal man directed a plane into position. The students saluted and then cheered the planes as they took off in an animation with sound and light effects. In the next exhibit some manne-quins talked about their experiences in the war, but just then, following the teacher's instructions, the students had to dive for cover during an air raid. Once they hit the dirt, they crawled to the steel drums near a Quon-set hut in the exhibit for shelter. At a large picture of island fighting, the students created a tableau by standing next to the big picture and assum-ing positions as if they were an extension of the picture. The students told what they thought and how they felt. Finally, students came down the gangplank, where they decided through role-playing how they would react now that they were at home and the war was over. The teacher sent the group back through the exhibit on their own to listen to radios/audi-tory programs and watch video programs. They also looked for cartoons, weapons, clothing, models, prisoner of war artifacts, and letters from home. They read captions and looked at pictures. Inside, they all got a chance to explore the 20mm gun; outside, they explored the three pieces of navy equipment, and they found the midget sub.

Enactive Experiences

Preservationists have sometimes maintained a whole community site for visitors, but these can sometimes be overwhelming because of the large scale of interpretation. To help overcome the possibility of informa-tion overload each student got a job in the San Jose Mission in San Anto-nio National Memorial as a soldier, baker, priest, or farmer. Students explored the mission in small groups. They found a place to interpret from the perspective of their character; for example, a baker might choose to interpret a bake oven. The students found out as much as they could about their job; then at a set time they returned to the whole group. Later, each person acted as a tour guide for the whole group in their part of the San Jose Mission while sharing the information they had discov-ered. Through exploration, students gained an understanding of how many people lived together in a democratic society and how they fit into that society. The students from one successful trip looked at how they learned about their community and how they related to it by using local and state historical sites, an idea important to young adolescents.

After the Trip

The students spent a week in social studies class debriefing as well as completing a follow-up project. When students returned to the classroom, they recorded their experiences in their journals and traded photos to

There is a chain of missions along the San Antonio River. There are five missions including Mission San Antonio de Valero (commonly known as the Alamo), Mission San Jose, Mission Conception, Mission San Juan, and Mission Espada. There are two reasons for the missions: to convert the Native Americans to Christianity and to make the Native American accept Spanish ... culture. Some of the Spanish Missions are still being used as Catholic churches. San Jose is still being used as a church. The seventh-grade class was fortunate to go and see two of the five missions including the Alamo and Mission San Jose. San Jose was very big ... [with] a window called the Rose Window. The reason it is called the Rose Window is because of the rose design around the window.... It was very interesting to see what happened in the heart of the city of San Antonio. The Alamo is called the "Cradle of Texas Liberty." (Michelle and Miranda)

Figure 6.5.   Student newspaper article about the San Antonio missions.

David Crockett, William Travis, and Jim Bowie were some of the people who fought for Texas. The Alamo was a mission before it became a fort. The Alamo is a mission that was called at first The San Antonio De Valero Mission. This mission was made by the Viceroy of Mexico, in the year of 1716.

The Alamo was constructed in 1722. The Alamo has been preserved into a state monument. Santa Anna, was a general, who fought against Texas for Mexico. Santa Anna came to the Alamo with a force of two thousand men on February 23, 1836. Only one hundred fifty-five men under the command of William Travis guarded the Alamo. This is one of the most famous battles of Texas' independence. All of the men that were defending the Alamo were killed, but Texans had fought hard killing six hundred Mexican soldiers. At the Battle of San Jacinto Santa Anna was defeated. (by Chase and Jonathan)

Figure 6.6.   Seventh-grade students study the history of the Alamo.

recount the events of the trip. They drew upon their journals and their photography to produce a newspaper that summarized their experiences (Figures 6.5 and 6.6). This issue of the paper focused on student analysis and evaluation of the trip. Students did additional research to fill in any other necessary details and to check facts; in rounding out their story, they became involved with historical research and writing. The newspaper served as a preview for prospective students and parents. The teacher assessed the newspaper, which the students created, for historic under-standing, connections to the present, primary sources used, multicultural voices, and implications for the future (NCSS,1994).

FORMING CONNECTIONS TO COMMUNITY
THROUGH STATE TRAVEL

On this trip students gathered information during a five-day field trip to find out more about state history. The students spent two weeks preparing for the trip through the social studies class activity using maps, timeline, primary sources, and rock art. Students listened to docents, experienced audio-visuals, explored on their own, and read static labels. When they debriefed, they created stories about their experiences and wrote historical sketches about the sites which they had visited. On the trip they kept a notebook that included their journal, specific questions for each site, readings, a time line, and a map. Twenty-four seventh-grade students went on this trip; three of them were Asian and the rest were Anglo. I took a constructivist and interpretivist perspective in conducting this research, and I used phenomenology in examining the characteristics of the students' reactions to the trip. My role as participant observer was as a guest observer traveling with the students to take field notes, but I was neither in charge of the trip nor was I a teacher. The following is an example of my field notes: "Students saw the ring in the Imax film when they go to the Alamo itself, they were interest[ed] in looking at the cases and they saw the actual ring and were very, very pleased to see that. I really saw them making connections there." At the beginning and at the end of the project, all of the students participated in individual interviews. Students kept audio journals via a hand-held cassette tape recorder on which they documented their thoughts, questions, and what they determined as the most important points about various events. I collected artifacts in the form of student work from their notebooks, and I triangulated them with the field notes and interviews.

FUGUES: A REOCCURING IDEA

Students spoke about how educators can teach them through field trips and how they best learn in the field. They revealed that they need to feel trusted, that they can take part in the decision-making process, and that they value the importance of social interaction and content knowledge in their learning. Knowledge was not accepted without challenge and students engaged in questioning. Students on field trips made empathic connections with people from the past, valued the experience, esteemed a sense of place, and also valued some time alone while on a field trip. Many different things were happening under the surface of field trip events in the thinking of the students.

Trust

One fugue to emerge from the students was the idea of trust; students felt that the teacher trusted the students in unstructured and structured situations. When the students had free time to eat and walk around a mall, the teacher gave the instructions that they had to remain together in groups, when to return, and that they needed to remain in the mall—but that gave them a long leash. "You get to choose groups, instead of the teacher choosing the groups, you would get to choose" (Sam, post-trip individual interview). Sam pointed out that elements of this situation hinged on an implicit contractual understanding by all parties. At a local natural feature steeped in local legend, the students continued to practice their covenant; the students remained safe and yet also practiced autonomy within prescribed boundaries. They assumed responsibility to handle their freedom, and the students valued the amount of freedom that they had. "We had so much fun climbing up and down the boulder. I went down the other side and climbed up a very steep part of the rock ... we were adventuring up and down everywhere" (Saskia, journal entry). Students trusted one another in the difficult terrain, and the teacher trusted them in this area. Students helped one another navigate across the obstacles and helped the teacher and the group by safely getting back on time.

Voting

The students and teacher made some decisions through majority rule votes, and the student recognized opportunities for decision-making through voting with multiple viable possibilities. They realized the results of their votes would impact the direction of the field trip. "We got to vote on what we wanted to do; it wasn't just one choice" (Robb, individual interview). Students recognized the voting as an important part of the trip and realized that it was neither a sham nor a facade. Students knew the difference and appreciated the opportunities that the trip presented. "With our spare time we would vote on ... what to do" (Jonathan, post-trip individual interview). Students had experienced teacher choices before that had few options or no real choice but were presented to manipulate the students and allow the teacher to say it was the students' choice. While not all decisions were open for debate, the students realized that some meaningful topics were open for discussion. "They just let us make our own choices on where we wanted to go and what we wanted to do" (Patrick, post-trip individual interview). Patrick liked selecting how to spend his free time, and he took part in making decisions. While students did not engage in completely open-ended decision making, students did get to participate when they selected sites and locations.

Social

A third fugue was the social nature of the trip. Students got to be with all of the people in their class, not just the ones in their section of the class. Students commented on how they bonded together as a class and how much this meant to them to get to do this. Students had transportation time to converse. An important aspect of the trip was to help the students build a sense of community by establishing personal relationships with their peers. "[We] used it [to] try to socialize with people that were not in my class" (Vanessa, individual interview). "The best part of the whole trip was going around with my friends" (Michelle, written journal). The experience of spending large amounts of time together allowed students to spend prolonged periods of time in interpersonal communication. The intense communication and prolonged time together allowed students to have a taste of living as a community.

Knowledge

Students realized that knowledge was an integral part of the experience and that the entire trip served as a vehicle for instruction. The information was both new and relevant to the students. "I was learning twenty-four, five" (Vanessa, post-trip individual interview). "I thought it was important because it would teach us things that we didn't know, and it would just tell us things that we needed to know" (Chase, post-trip individual interview). The information was both valuable immediately and for future use. Furthermore, the trip was not a terminal point for knowledge; it was an incitement to learn more. Students left the trip motivated to learn about topics that interested them, and students used complex thought processes to critique this knowledge. Evaluation of the information that came to the students allowed them to discriminate between what sounded plausible and implausible before accepting or rejecting the knowledge. When students did not get enough information, they were disappointed. "I like the Pioneer Museum because it was chock-full of information! I also like the L. B. J. ranch because I got to learn a little bit about L. B. J. However, I wish I could learn more. He sounds very interesting" (Modiv, journal entry). Students commented positively about the time for learning and for deep, meaningful exposure to content. Students, however, did not accept all knowledge without dissent.

Student Evaluation, Discrimination, and Rejection of Knowledge

Students actively evaluated the knowledge they received; they sorted the knowledge they accepted, and they disallowed some knowledge. The students rejected some knowledge as unimportant or incorrect when they were in the field.

> A big rock.... I'm not exactly sure what it is, but it doesn't seem like it would be a burial site. It may have been some kind of ... a spiritual temple or something. It is probably not a burial site because traditional Indian burial sites have never been exactly like that.... The Indians that live on this plane had been studied for a long time and historians know what type of burial they had.... It may just have been inhumanly impossible to lift that rock over to put it over a body to bury it. I thought they would probably have had more studies on it instead of making that man guess about what it was. I wonder if they have done any dating on this to find out if all the signs were done the same time or in diverse times. I saw a date on the graffiti that said 9/16/14. That couldn't have been 1814—the fence was put up in 1907. Hmmmm. I wonder what he means by, he said that virtually all of the graffiti was stopped. (Sam, audio journal)

This site did not conform to the previous learning Sam had experienced. He also questioned the knowledge of the guide, questioned the lack of understanding of the site, and the lack of contextual information that might be available from ethnographers.

> Dr. Morris, I don't understand why this place is a nation park. Maybe a state park, or maybe even a city park, but why a state park? All it is is a big ranch ... and then it's a state park.... It's both. This is just weird ... It shouldn't be ... [this] is not [a] tourist place.... I know that the President wanted it to be [a] park and all, but it's just, there's nothing here that's exciting. So what if there are a bunch of flowers and cows.... I mean, it's cool coming here to a national park, but I don't see why it is a national park, that is all. (Jonathan, audio journal)

Here, Jonathan realizes that the historic site did not quite measure up to other federal historic sites and questions the standards set for property admission without understanding the tax advantages of estate planning. He does not see why President Johnson would have placed his ranch in federal and state hands, or why those two governmental bodies would have accepted them from the President.

"Everything moves slower with a guide. They tend to stop every five feet and say, 'This rock is a rock,' or something very uninformative" (Sam, pre-trip individual interview). Sam was more critical of the inane statements docents sometimes used with groups of school students that neither provided depth of understanding nor helped to focus the students on themes, generalization, controversy, or problem solving. Other students criticized docents for what they failed to provide about groups of minorities. "I didn't think it was fair that all they talked about was the Comanche. They did not say anything about the Apaches. Nothing" (Miranda, pre-trip individual interview). Students questioned history that left out groups of people, places, or important events. Students also discarded information if it intuitively did not make sense, "When it's something that doesn't sound true" (Nicholas, pre-trip individual interview). Though vague, students engaged in a process where they sorted and rejected information that sounded bogus. Students evaluated, sorted, accepted, or rejected the knowledge gathered from field experiences. This process of students winnowing knowledge demonstrates the critical thought that occurs during study travel experiences.

Questioning

When students traveled on field trips, they engaged in a process of asking questions that they initiated. This process can be disrupted by inhibitions or peer pressure, but the questions emerged nonetheless. "I had a few questions. I didn't really want to ask because I was scared to ask them. I was kind of wondering what a few of the hospital towels were used for because I didn't understand the words that they wrote on [the exhibit signs]" (Elizabeth, audio journal).

Interpretive signage can be a problem, but a more significant problem was self-censorship. Students sometimes refused to ask questions, but the counterbalance was when students confounded their prior understandings by a direct experience on a field trip.

> I had heard about … the Alamo having the fort, but I didn't know the whole fort was once a mission. I just thought that one little building was, and I knew that that was the mission for the fort and I did not know that it was first a mission. (Jonathan, post-trip interview)

By going to the actual site, the misconception was corrected by seeing the site in a context richer than a video or the picture in the textbook. Once on the site the students could rapidly develop questions. "I was actually wanting to learn more about the Germans and I remember I knew that I asked … a lot of questions, and I knew that I was going to find out more" (Vanessa, post-trip individual interview). When students asked their own questions, they had ownership over their learning. Through student interaction with people and places, student questions build con-

cepts and bulldoze misconceptions. "I wonder what kind of building tech-
niques they used, they had to use to make it look that old" (Sam, audio
journal). Here, Sam moved into complex questions about historical preservation, engineering, and aesthetics. Some students entered a place and
the questions poured out of their minds in a seeming rapid-fire succes-
sion.

Is it an active church? ...

So none of this is real? ...

Oh, is this pretty close to what it looked like back then, or did he look back
at papers? ...

Was there anything left? ...

What are those over there? ...

And did you ever find any tombstones, or were they just buried in the front
yard? (Michelle, audio journal)

Just one experience can touch off a string of questions, and just one
question can explode a misconception. Just one question can lead to a
new thought or a whole new area for exploration, and new exploration is
learning that the student initiates and owns.

Empathy

With questions and new explorations, students find empathic experiences on field trips that allow them to explore the circumstances of people in different times or places. They may stimulate their empathy with
artifacts of a time or place. "I just imagine what stuff they had, what they
didn't have, and how I would be in that position" (Patrick, pre-trip individual interview). After a field trip Patrick could easily connect with other
people. Students found historical images that were either disturbing or
celebratory in museums and cultural centers. "Well, sometimes they felt
really sad because, I mean, a lot of people fought and they died and their
children died very young. And then other times, it's like wow, we got
through it, and so that makes me happy" (Lauren, pre-trip interview). It is
important that students understand and experience the good and the bad
stories from the past and present and empathize with others. This experience showed how easy it is for students to encounter feel-good interpretations in museums. Even though it is possible for students to have
emotional experiences, these experiences need to be connected to intellectual content so that they don't flow into romanticism.

Experiential

Students responded to the empirical nature of the study travel experience; they enjoyed going, doing, and being a part of the experience. By learning from all of their senses, they directly learned from the site. "I liked [not just] hearing about the history, but seeing it actually" (Natalia, post-trip individual interview). Students get multiple opportunities for mono-sensual experiences in school, but multiple sensory events come naturally during study travel experiences. Students learn kinesthetically on study travel experiences by encountering textures in context with other sensory stimuli. "I liked to touch the rabbit fur.... Hands-on experience and seeing actual artifacts is more fun and educational than just reading out of a book and only seeing pictures" (Nicholas, audio journal). Students saw their school learning as two-dimensional compared to the real-world learning of the field trip. Students combined learning through the senses of sight, touch, and hearing on the field trip. "You said these was built by the Franciscans. Were they Spanish monks that worked it?" (Nick, audio journal). Students also addressed questions while using their multiple senses. Students got to directly experience their learning when they were on site recreating daily events in the legislative process. At the capitol students used a committee hearing room to act out how a bill becomes a law through the legislative process.

> We kind of made a play. We all played a different part of it. I thought that was a very interesting way to learn. There's a few questions running through my head that I think I am a little confused about which part you are supposed to play in it and how it worked at the beginning, because it is kind of confusing because you don't know if you have to speak for yourself or for everybody else. (Elizabeth, audio journal)

Students used auditory, kinesthetic, and visual senses to learn from their study travel experiences as they engaged in actively constructing knowledge from their experiences.

Artifacts/Built Environment

Students used their empirical experiences with artifacts in the context of the built environment to learn during the study travel experience. Artifacts connected students with both familiar and foreign experiences that allowed them to assimilate new knowledge after experiencing the site. "I really like artifacts because ... you find something new every time" (Evan, pre-trip individual interview). The open-ended nature of artifacts allowed students to develop increasingly more complex interpretations as they encountered more sophisticated ideas about human relations. Students had expectations about what they would learn when they traveled. "I saw all the original artifacts I had heard about" (Jonathan, post-trip individual interview). They used their pre-trip preparation to identify what they would encounter on the trip. The students identified with the historic nature of the site and made a connection with the stories from that site.

> I think the real things can tell their own stories and replicas really don't have much to say.... It's kind of like when we went to Paint Rock. The things were real and it feels like you were there with the Indians while they were sitting there telling you about [them].... You feel like you know them personally when you are in a real thing. (Saskia, audio journal)

They developed a sense of place, connecting with both the place and the people that once inhabited the place. Students connected the authenticity of the experience with their understanding of the learning events they experienced on the field trip. Students used artifacts and the built environment as an important component of learning during the field trips.

Independence

Students showed their independence by learning on their own and at their own pace. "I liked learning about it on my own. They do it to their own thinking, and I like to do it to my own looking" (Patrick, post-trip individual interview). Patrick liked to move on his own through the galleries. Some students wanted to learn even more in-depth than their peers.

> I would give more time at places and let people look at stuff because sometimes there's a lot of stuff to read about the people and we didn't have a lot of time. And I was always in a rush, and I didn't have enough time 'cause we needed to like spend a whole lot of time at the capitol 'cause we really wanted to see that, so then we would only have like two minutes to see a church.... Give us more time. (Carolyn, post-trip individual interview)

Carolyn really wanted to do more in-depth exploration at the sites and was frustrated when it did not happen. She enjoyed learning at her own pace. Students enjoyed the independence they had at the different sites.

SUB-PATTERNS

Choices

Students exercised limited decision-making skills in determining how they could make choices in this environment. Students did exercise decision-making in how they would conduct themselves on the trip. "We got to make choices ... [about] who we want[ed] to ... go with, where we wanted to eat, where to meet.... It was more social choices" (Vanessa, post-trip individual interview). Students especially identified the choices they had on social arrangements with their peers. Students also identified other choices they made on more substantive issues.

> I like had choice about what to do on the bus and where to go when we went places. I had a choice if I didn't want to climb the rock.... I could have done things different with my time. I could have maybe read more on the bus instead of listening to music or I could have ... spent more time at other places.... I could have made different decisions or different choices.... I could have spent time with different people. (Jonathan, post-trip individual interview)

Jonathan identified personal choices he made with his time. These choices allowed students to exercise good decision-making skills within a relatively controlled environment, making choices that had real consequences.

Social Learning

Students enjoyed learning within a social context. The students worked with their peers prior to leaving school to prepare to visit historical sites on the trip. "When you talk with your friends, ... that's what really prepared me" (Sam, pre-trip individual interview). When the students traveled to the site, they talked about what they were going to see. When the students explored the site, they talked about it. "Usually in groups of three or two and we just kind of talk about, 'Wow, you know, this is really interesting'" (Emily, pre-trip individual interview). The students communicated their enthusiasm for learning in the field with their peers. They also saw the communication as a liberating power in learning. "Let the people talk, and they will learn a lot" (Vanessa, post-trip individual interview). The students talked about the site as they departed; they even talked about the trip during their free time. "The free time was great because we all got to talk about our day and the trip!" (Elizabeth, written journal). Students reinforced their understandings, reflections, and experiences through their conversations. This reinforcement also helped the students to socially construct a value of the trip within their peer community. "Talking about it with all my friends—they helped me remember" (Lauren, post-trip individual interview). Through learning with a peer group, the content and the experience was more memorable for the students. The students reinforced their learning in formal and informal times through verbal communication. The students verbally interacted to prepare, experience, and debrief from the field trip experience.

PATTERNS

Community/Self Understanding

Students developed greater insights into how they interacted with the members of their community. Their understandings of themselves also deepened. "I found out something that's happened or how it could've affected me, or some of the inventions, things we use every day. Just how things have changed over the years and what's new, and old civilizations, about how they lived" (Evan, pre-trip individual interview). In this example, Evan saw connections between groups of people and his life. This connection between an individual and others in the group was an important bond. "I really got to know this person.... We finally all got together and ... we all got a lot closer" (Vanessa, post-trip interview). Vanessa saw the merits of helping peers understand one another in order to become a closer group. Students understood the connections between themselves and their peers as they traveled on the experience together. Students connected with one another to form a closer community by understanding more about themselves and their relations with other members of their group.

Communal Living

The students practiced a form of communal living in which they took their meals in common and spent all of their days together. From this common experience, they became closer to one another. "I think we're closer, now that we've had to live with each other, twenty-four, five" (Michelle, post-trip interview). The students lived together as a group sharing their space and their trip with each other. They interacted for the entire duration of the trip without much time by themselves.

> Well, we usually don't get to talk that much at school because, you know, classes or break is only twenty minutes, lunch is only thirty or something like that.... But, for instance, we got to talk more, we got to learn a lot more about each other, we got to see more of their personality more and how they act toward other people. (Vanessa, post-trip interview)

Vanessa enjoyed seeing how her peers related with one another. Students lived in closer proximity than they lived even in their family groups when they shared space, food, learning, and diversions with one another. The interactive experience of being in close proximity for prolonged periods of time without distractions that would splinter the group was an important factor in the success of the group.

CONCLUSIONS

There are some limitations in this example. This study travel experience was taken by a private school and each family paid a significant amount of money to participate on this week-long trip. Other schools may not have the commitment to participating in a week-long trip or the families may not have the resources to fund it.

The next step in researching this topic would need to explore whether extra-curricular programs, such as history clubs, museum-sponsored travel, or summer enrichment, could be just as successful with adolescents. The other consideration would need to examine whether family or individual travel promotes the same sense of community in adolescents.

Students needed exposure to the multiple groups of people depicted in the many stops made on this trip. Natallia said, "The sites helped you actually feel like you were back then in all the hardships and everything. So you actually were put in the person's place." When students met these people, the students learned more about the diverse nation where they live; students needed opportunities to explore the near, the close at hand, and the accessible. Students needed exposure to state and local studies; they needed to know what happened in their state, county, township, and town. When students studied the local area, they could see how democratic processes and practices impacted them as well as the people they encountered. Students moved from thinking of democracy as a remote and abstract concept to talking about it as an immediate and pressing concern.

Teachers planned educational trips to show students conflicts within a democracy. Teachers also needed to continue to look for opportunities to show diversity when students traveled to state and local sites. Natallia observed, "Mrs. McNeely won't take us anywhere without us either experiencing … or learning something." Teachers communicated to students their expectations of important social understandings and helped students to see these understandings as important for a democratic society. Finally, teachers helped students to accomplish understanding at the sites through preparation and debriefings that helped them connect to their state community.

The students on this trip documented what they learned in a well-planned study travel experience. Further student growth was documented in areas not traditionally thought of as academic. The example also provided a means of listening to what students say about their learning as they participate in study travel experiences.

To the students the importance of the study travel experience was academic accomplishment with important social and personal implications in which the students found meaning in working as a group of semi-autonomous learners. Students found that it was enjoyable to learn social studies while they traveled to geographically, politically, and historically significant sites.

The importance of the study travel experience to the teachers was that they were able to plan a method that generated powerful results in the learning of social studies. Teachers often forget about state sites as possible ways to interpret events of national significance, but this example serves as a reminder that they can use these sites in designing successful study travel experiences that assist students in forming their own opinions and gathering information for use in the classroom.

I.	Culture
II.	Time, continuity, and change
III.	People, places, and environments
IV.	Individuals, groups, and institutions
V.	Power, authority, and governance
VI.	Civic ideals and practices

Figure 6.7.   NCSS (1994) national standards.

CHAPTER 7

NATIONAL CONNECTIONS TO THE PAST AND PRESENT DEMOCRACY

INTRODUCTION

People made history in our own backyards. The history of the nation is not a set of far off and remote events; it is actually the experience of the people we meet every day. It is the experience we create through our daily existence. We need to help our students capture those experiences in order to understand that we are part of the wash of history. We participate in it, we live through it, and sometimes we even help shape it; we are all a part of it. We can help students experience history by using multiple methods of exploration when students encounter historical content through creative interpretation methods.

Students can experience multiple ways to explore nationally important events and sites. The students need to engage through drama, investigation, first-person presentations, role playing, taking on the role of the tour guide themselves, and being observant of what is going on around them. They gather evidence from primary sources and first-hand experiences to discern what life was like in the past. At each point they are constructing their knowledge about history by using sources of evidence. They use these experiences to understand some of the major events of

The Field Trip Book: Study Travel Experiences in Social Studies
pp. 99–116
Copyright © 2010 by Information Age Publishing
99

I.	Culture
II.	Time, continuity, and change
III.	People, places, and environments
IV.	Individual development and identity
V.	Individuals, groups, and institutions
VI.	Power, authority, and governance
VII.	Production, distribution, and consumption
VIII.	Science, technology, and society
IX.	Civic ideals and practice

Figure 7.1.   NCSS (1994) national standards.

history, and they use these tools to consider what it means to be an American citizen.

Many elements were combined into one extended field trip to teach about democracy (Figure 7.1). This model field trip unit shows how one teacher, Mrs. McNeely, and a class of fifth-grade students learned about life in Virginia by preparing, traveling to the site, and then debriefing.

VIRGINIA FIELD TRIP

It is important to market all field trips by creating excitement for them. The group leader should create flyers that tell when and where the group is going, how it ties to the curriculum, and the major instructional purpose of the trip (Figure 7.2). Then the teacher must determine and list the major activities and adventures that the students will have, starting each one with an action verb. If the leader cannot think of anything stimulating to say, the students view this as a bad sign for what has and has not been planned for and with the students. The flyer serves as an important tool for planning and for evaluating the trip; it is used to measure if this really was an exciting and interesting event. The parents and students who received the flyer understood the communicated academic advantages of taking the trip and the adventurous qualities of exploration.

To begin the preparation (Figure 7.3), the teacher wanted the students to learn about traveling across the Atlantic Ocean to Jamestown (Morris, 2000A). After the students mapped out a space on the floor with masking tape to demonstrate the dimensions of one of the ships bound for Virginia, the students performed some of the work they would have done as sailors on that ship. The tape helped illustrate the confining space that

Virginia 2000!
The focus of this study travel experience is to compliment the exploration
of U. S. studies in the 5th-grade year.

Students will focus on two ideas:
1) Exploring the English Colonial Period
2) Examining the Revolutionary War

Enter an army camp
Listen to ghost stories
Enter a 300-year-old fort
Follow a pirate to his death
Dine in a 300-year-old tavern
Hear the cries of an accused witch
Be amazed by the governor's garden
Find evidence of a 300-year-old murder
Enter a two-hundred-year-old mental asylum
Find your way down streets filled with crafts shops
Explore a three-hundred-year-old town by candlelight
Step into the oldest college building in the United States
Climb the trenches and fortifications of a Revolutionary War battlefield
Find out what George Washington would have done when he was your age
Make yourself at home in George Washington's house
Stand on the deck of a Revolutionary War gun boat
Walk in the footsteps of the Lees of Virginia
Help a craftsman in the building trades area
Find out about your jobs if you were at sea
Listen to the music of 200 years ago
Enter a Native American village
Join the enslaved community
Visit a 200-year-old farm
Join the colonial militia
Find a vanished town

Plus adventures and surprises!

On your 5th Grade Trip!

Figure 7.2. Trip flyer

limited the colonists and sailors. Upon arriving in Virginia, attention moved from the boats to the establishment of the colony; students then used role-play to act out the story of John Smith and Pocahontas (Morris & Welch, 2000). When the students used the role-play, they determined reasons why the colonists and the native population got along as well as reasons for their long-term disagreements. Both of these experiences

---

Jamestown
- Ship dimensions mapped on the floor
- Students act out performing jobs of sailors

Williamsburg
- Archeology dig of Colonial and Revolutionary War artifacts
- First-person presentation of George Mason using the Virginia kit and slide presentation
- Colonial learning centers
- A taste of Virginia

Stratford Hall
- Colonial schoolroom simulation

Revolution
- Slides of Jefferson
- Capt. John Doyle first-person presentation and George Rogers Clark slide presentation
- Students select a Virginia patriot to research

Figure 7.3.   Preparation activities.

helped the students think about how the colonists came to a new and very alien world. The teacher needed to help the students understand the span of time between Jamestown and the flowering of colonial culture in Williamsburg. In a later activity students acted out the surrender events on the actual field at Yorktown.

The students explored learning centers about colonial and revolutionary Virginia (Obenchain & Morris, 2010). These centers helped the students to recognize issues, places, events, and attitudes that they might encounter in Williamsburg and explained how this site related to other colonies. To prepare students for the stops in Williamsburg, the teacher conducted an archeology dig simulation with the students using plastic sheet squares to represent the dig site and artifacts for deductive thinking and hypothesis generation (Obenchain & Morris, 2010). This helped the students become familiar with the artifacts and primary sources while making inferences about colonial Virginia. Each student applied this information to a specific person whom they were researching in an attempt to provide a connection with that individual. After selecting a person from the *Official Guide to Colonial Williamsburg* (2002) and using the aforementioned information, each student created a first-person presentation about their character (Obenchain & Morris, 2010) (Figure 7.4). These presentations helped students to show a more human face that the empty buildings do not show by themselves. Each individual represented a group of people who lived in Williamsburg; students polished their pre-

- Anne Blair
- Betsey Braxton
- Bristol
- William Byrd II
- Caesar
- Christiana Campbell
- Adam Craig
- Martha Cripps
- Eve
- Governor Francis Fauquier
- John Greenhow
- Anthony Hay
- James
- William Marshman
- Walker Maury
- William Moody, Jr.
- Randolph Family
- Peter Pelham
- Clementina Rind
- Sarah
- St. George Tucker
- Benjamin Waller
- Adam Waterford

Figure 7.4. Williamsburg first-person characters.

sentations before they left on the trip. During the trip the students acted as content experts to explain the person whom each student had studied.

The teacher gave a first-person presentation of George Mason, using a kit of artifacts gathered from Virginia and slides taken at Mason's home, Gunston Hall. The students saw how the teacher did the first-person presentation and how the teacher incorporated artifacts and visual images. To teach about the American Revolution, the teacher presented another first-person presentation with slides about one of the men who marched with George Rogers Clark. These two different portraits of men of that time introduced some of the qualities and leadership characteristics possessed by people of that generation. In addition to their historical figure discussed above students also selected a Virginia patriot to research (Figure 7.5). The number and caliber of talented individuals at that time and place provided many interesting people from which the students chose.

- Carter Braxton
- Benjamin Harrison
- Henry
- Jefferson
- Francis Lightfoot Lee
- Richard Henry Lee
- Marshall
- Mason
- Thomas Nelson
- Washington
- Wythe

Figure 7.5.   Virginia patriot research.

Each of them made significant contributions that carried the country toward independence. All of these experiences helped the students to learn more about lives that led the nation to independence and gave them more information that they could use later in the trip.

The students participated in a "Taste of Virginia" in which they created samples of the types of food the colonists would have eaten and recreated the open hearth cooking experiences to prepare the food (Figure 7.6). For students to experience preparing and sampling a colonial meal, the teacher printed the recipes and taped one copy of each recipe to each of the five tables. The students had easy-to-follow instructions that included ingredients and told what equipment to use when cooking. All of their utensils and ingredients as well as a trash bag were in a box on each table, and a dirty clothes bag was under each table. One table per group was placed outside in a ring ahead of time, and one fire per group was set up inside the ring. Students worked outside of the ring except when it was time to cook.

Students got to experience life on a plantation where the owners hired a tutor for the privileged students old enough to attend school. Relatives, neighbors, and children of overseers all attended this school, or students had their lessons in the house before going away to boarding school. To prepare for the visit to Stratford Hall, the home of the Lee Family, the students reenacted lessons in a colonial schoolroom by working sums on slates for arithmetic, working with a map of Virginia in geography, learning the Kings and Queens of England in history, copying a Proverb using quill and ink for penmanship, reading some quotations of Adam Smith, and reading a Psalm (Figure 7.7). Students of that time period also

Group I: Biscuits
- Get water: *water jug*
- Start fire/get coals on *Dutch Oven: Aluminum foil pan liner, hot pad, coal tongs*
- Find recipe and do as it says (get butter and buttermilk from the butter group): *mixing bowl, wooden spoon, measuring spoon, measuring cup, sharp knife, cutting board*
- Wash and dry dishes inside: *soap, towel*
- Offer biscuits, butter, and honey samples to other groups: *plastic knives, paper plates, spoon for honey*
- Put trash in the *trash bag*
- Wipe off the table with your towel
- Put the cloths in your bag under the table

Group II:
Butter
- Get water: *water jug*
- Put cream in the *churn*
- Beat until you see yellow lumps
- Scrape butter out of churn: *wooden spoon, butter washing bowl*
- Pour off and save the buttermilk: *buttermilk bowl*
- Pour cold water over the butter and wash out the rest of the buttermilk
- Save the butter: *butter bowl*
- Offer butter to the biscuit group and the mashed potatoes group
- Wash and dry dishes inside: *soap, towel*
- Put trash in the *trash bag*
- Wipe off the table with your towel
- Put the cloths in your bag under the table
Green beans
- Get water: *water jug*
- Fill *pot* half-full with water
- Snap beans (break the end and the strings off the beans): *3 knives*
- Put the beans in the pot
- Put pot on the *tripod, hot pad*
- Watch that the pot does not boil over and put out the fire: *wooden spoon*
- Wash and dry dishes inside: *soap, towel*
- Offer green beans and apple cider to other groups: *plates, forks, paper cups*
- Put trash in the *trash bag*
- Wipe off the table with your towel
- Put the cloths in your bag under the table

Group III:
Mashed Potatoes
- Get water: *water jug*
- Fill *pot* half-full with water
- Fill *pot* half-full with potatoes
- Put the pot on the *tripod*
- Watch that the pot does not boil over and put out the fire:
- Test the potatoes to see if they are done by sticking them with a *fork* (the fork should go in easily)
- When they are done, drain water, get butter from the butter group

(Figure continues on next page)

Figure 7.6.   Colonial meal.

- Melt butter in a *skillet*: *wooden spoon, hot pad* (if you see smoke take the skillet off the fire immediately or it will burn)
- Put your *towel* on the table and put the skillet on top of it
- Put the potatoes in the skillet and mash them: *masher*
- Add salt and pepper: *wooden spoon*
- Wash and dry dishes inside: *soap*
- Offer mashed potatoes and milk to the other groups: *paper plates, plastic forks, paper cups*
- Put trash in the *trash bag*
- Wipe off the table with your towel
- Put the cloths in your bag under the table

Ham
- Cut ham into cubes: *knives*
- Put ham in *skillet*
- Put skillet on *grill*
- Move ham around to keep it from burning: *wooden spoon*
- When ham browns take off the fire (if you see smoke, remove from the fire; it will burn)
- Place towel on table and put skillet on that: *wooden spoon*
- Wash and dry dishes inside: *soap, towel*
- Offer other groups ham and milk: *paper plates, plastic forks, paper cups*
- Put trash in the *trash bag*
- Wipe off the table with your towel
- Put the cloths in your bag under the table

Group IV:
Gingerbread
- Get water: *water jug*
- Put coals on the *Dutch Oven:coal tongs, lifter, hot pad*
- Follow the recipe for gingerbread: *mixing bowl, wooden spoon, measuring spoon, measuring cup, pan liner*
- Wash and dry dishes inside: *soap, towel*
- Offer other groups gingerbread and whipped cream: p*aper plates, plastic forks, paper cups*
- Put trash in the *trash bag*
- Wipe off the table with your towel
- Put the cloths in your bag under the table
- Whipped Cream
- Get water: *water jug*
- Pour one cup cream in a *mixing bowl*
- Add one half *cup* of sugar
- Add one tea*spoon* of vanilla
- Stir until foamy: *fork*
- Wash and dry dishes inside: *soap, towel*
- Offer other groups gingerbread and whipped cream: *paper plates, plastic forks, paper cups*
- Put trash in the *trash bag*
- Wipe off the table with your towel
- Put the cloths in your bag under the table

Figure 7.6.   (Continued).

- Arithmetic: Sums on slates
- Geography: VA map
- History: Kings and Queens of England
- Penmanship: Quill and ink—Proverbs
- Reading: Adam Smith
- Religion: Psalm

Figure 7.7.   Colonial school.

received lessons in dance, etiquette, music, and fencing. The students on the field experience compared their school to the education that children received in colonial Virginia. Students evaluated why the curriculum had changed over time and whether they thought one type of curriculum was better than another.

When students visited Williamsburg, they saw aspects of both colonial life and the lives of the people who led the revolution. Students needed to have experiences in Williamsburg that blended the ticketed admission and the educational experiences planned by the class. The Colonial Williamsburg Foundation staff offered many musical or dramatic ticketed events presented in the evening that the group enjoyed. Students used the town as a learning environment while coupling their own investigations with the site programs.

On the site of the field trip, the students were responsible to be co-docents with the teacher and the site host (Figures 7.8 and 7.9). The students acted as instructors rather than being shepherded from place to place. This meant that prior to the trip the students needed to prepare and research what they would see at the site. They needed to determine how they would present information to their peers and how they would keep the attention of their peers. They also needed to ask open-ended questions from their peers. At each site in Williamsburg the students presented their previously prepared first-person historical presentations for their peers (Figure 7.10).

From the chronologically earliest experiences on the field trip, the students needed to have interactive experiences at the site. At Jamestown a student was selected to be signed up as a ship's boy. At first it sounded glamorous but when the students started to see all of the work that the ship's boy did, they started to reconsider this dubious opportunity. When the students saw the danger of being at sea, they thought again about whether or not it would be a good idea to go to sea. In a similar experience later at Yorktown, a student had the opportunity to sign up to be in the army in the encampment of the Continental Soldiers.

Sunday
Depart by air from airport
3:00 p.m.   Bus departs from Reagan National Airport
3:30 p.m.   Mt. Vernon *703-780-3383*
4:00 p.m.   Depart
7:00 p.m.   Dinner at lodging
8:00 p.m.   Depart
             VA Capitol
             War Memorial
10:00 p.m.   Lights out

Monday
6:00 a.m.   Rise and shine
6:30 a.m.   Depart
7:00 a.m.   Breakfast *(fast food)*
7:30 a.m.   Depart
9:45 a.m.   Stratford Hall Plantation *804-493-8038*
12:00 p.m.   Lunch *(in the Stratford Hall Dining Room)*
1:30 p.m.   George Washington Birthplace National Monument *804-224-1732*
4:30 p.m.   Depart
6:00 p.m.   Dinner at lodging
7:00 p.m.   Depart
8:00 p.m.   Play
10:00 p.m.   Lights out

Tuesday
6:00 a.m.   Rise and shine
8:00 a.m.   Breakfast at lodging
8:30 a.m.   Depart
9:30 a.m.   Jamestown Settlement *604-229-1607*
                 Visitors Center
                 Indian Village
                 Discovery, Godspeed, and Susan Constant
                 James Fort
12:00 a.m.   Lunch at Jamestown Settlement Cafe
1:00 a.m.   Jamestown Island
                 Jamestown Visitor Center *804-229-1733*
                 Fort Site
                 New Towne
2:00 p.m.   Ranger program
3:00 p.m.   Depart
3:30 p.m.   William and Mary - Courthouse - Wren Building *804-221-4000*
5:00 p.m.   Dinner in Williamsburg
8:00 p.m.   Lantern tour of Williamsburg
9:00 p.m.   Depart
10:00 p.m.   Lights out

Wednesday
8:00 a.m.   Breakfast at lodging
8:30 a.m.   Depart for Williamsburg
9:30 a.m.   Colonial Williamsburg *1-800-447-8679*
                 Public Hospital of 1773

(Figure continues on next page)

Figure 7.8.   Sample itinerary for colonial and revolutionary Virginia.

	Building Trades Area
12:00 p.m.	Lunch at Shield's Tavern
1:00 p.m.	Self Guided Tour
2:00 p.m.	Tour of Historic Trade Shops
3:00 p.m.	Governor's Palace
4:00 p.m.	Capitol
5:30 p.m.	Dinner in Williamsburg
7:00 p.m.	Cry Witch dramatic trial
8:30 p.m.	Musical program
9:00 p.m.	Depart
10:00 p.m.	Lights out

Thursday

8:00 a.m.	Breakfast at lodging
8:30 a.m.	Depart for Yorktown
9:30 a.m.	Yorktown Victory Center *804-898-3076*
	Film: *The Road to Yorktown*
	Military encampment
	Middle class colonial Virginia farm
12:00 p.m.	Lunch
1:00 p.m.	Tour Yorktown Battlefield
2:00 a.m.	Battlefield Visitors Center *804-887-1776*
2:30 p.m.	Depart
3:00 p.m.	Carter's Grove *804-229-1000*
	Slave cabins
	Wolstenholme Towne
5:00 p.m.	Depart
5:30 p.m.	Dinner in Williamsburg
7:00 p.m.	Trial of Blackbeard
8:00 p.m.	Ghost Tales
9:00 p.m.	Depart
10:00 p.m.	Lights out

Friday

8:00 a.m.	Breakfast at lodging
8:30 a.m.	Depart
10:30 a.m.	Thomas Jefferson Visitors Center *804-293-4188*
11:30 a.m.	Lunch fast food
12:30 p.m.	Monticello *804-984-9822*
5:00 p.m.	Depart
5:30 p.m.	Dinner *(Charlottesville, VA)*
7:00 p.m.	The Lawn of the University of Virginia
7:30 p.m.	Depart
10:00 p.m.	Lights out

Saturday

6:00 a.m.	Pack and load the bus
6:30 a.m.	Depart
7:30 a.m.	Breakfast in route fast food
9:30 a.m.	Gunston Hall *703-550-9220*
11:30 a.m.	Depart
12:00 p.m.	Lunch *(in airport)*
1:00 p.m.	Reagan Airport check in and check baggage

Figure 7.8.   (Continued).

These figures are based on 25 students and 5 adults.

We could handle up to a total of 44 people on the trip.

With smaller numbers we would, of course, use a van instead of a bus.

I like to use university dorms to cut costs rather than staying in a private conference center.

Day #1		
Day #2		
Breakfast	$ 5.00 × 30	$ 150
Day #3		
Dinner	$ 10.00 × 30	$ 300
Day #4		
Dinner	$10.00 × 30	$ 300
Day #5		
Lunch	$ 5.00 × 30	$ 150
Dinner	$ 5.00 × 30	$ 150
Day #6		
Lunch	$ 5.00 × 30	$ 150
Dinner	$ 10.00 × 30	$ 300
Day #7		
Breakfast	$ 5.00 × 30	$ 150
Lunch	$ 10.00 × 30	$ 300
Sub Total		*$ 1,950*

Lodging

	$30.00 × 30 per person × 6 nights	$ 5,400
Meals at Roslyn		
	Evening 2 × $ 10.00 × 30	$ 600
	Breakfast 4 × $ 8.00 × 30	$ 960
Sub Total		*$ 6,960*

Bus

	7 days × $ 700.00 per day	$ 4,900
Gratuity	30 people × $ 1.00 × 7 days	$ 210
Sub Total		*$ 5,110*

Mt. Vernon

	$ 4.50 × 25	$ 112.50
	$ 8.50 × 5	$ 42.50
Sub Total		*$ 155.00*

Stratford Hall

	$ 4.50 × 25	$ 106.25
Lunch	$ 13.00 × 30	$ 390.00
Sub Total		*$ 496.25*

(Figure continues on next page)

Figure 7.9.   Virginia trip expenses.

Williamsburg		
	$ 10.00 × 25	$ 250.00
Governor's Palace	$ 5.50 × 30	$ 165.00
Carter's Grove	$ 5.50 × 30	$ 165.00
Lantern Tour	$ 8.00 × 25	$ 200.00
	$ 10.00 × 5	$ 50.00
Evening Program	$ 40.00 × 2	$ 80.00
	$ 50.00 × 2	$ 100.00
Tavern Lunch	$ 10 × 30	$ 300.00
Sub Total		*$ 1,310.00*
Jamestown Settlement & Yorktown Victory Center		
	$ 6.00 × 30	$ 180.00
	2 Ranger Programs	$ 60.00
Sub Total		*$ 240.00*
Monticello		
	$ 6.00 × 25	$ 150.00
	$ 5.00 × 11	$ 55.00
Study tour	$ 7.00 × 30	$ 210.00
Sub Total		*$ 415.00*
Gunston Hall		
	$ 10.00 × 30	*$ 300.00*
Staff		
Teacher	1 × $ 1,250.00	$1,250.00
Counselors	4 × $ 200.00	$ 800.00
Sub Total		*$ 2,050.00*
Total		**$ 18,986.25**
Cost per child		**$ 759.45**

Figure 7.9. (Continued).

All of the students got into the action at Crime Scene Investigation Wolstenholme Towne. Students participated in an investigation when they followed clues to help them find out who died on the site and under what circumstances. They discovered that a woman died in an Indian raid in 1622. Next, students needed to learn more about the context of the death and how it related to early Virginia history. Finally, students learned about the history of the particular site and how it has changed over time (Trofanenko, 2008; Barton, 2001).

Each day students had an agenda to follow that was keyed to the sites scheduled for the day and connected to primary sources. Students received a role-playing prompt that took them on a mission from place to place either looking for something, trying to deliver something, or trying

• Anne Blair and Betsey Braxton:	John Blair House
• Bristol:	Brush-Everand House
• William Byrd II:	Capitol
• Christiana Campbell:	Christiana Campbell's Tavern
• Peter Pelham:	Gaol
• Governor Francis Fauquier, William Marshman, and James:	Governor's Palace
• John Greenhow:	Greenhow Store and Lumberyard
• Anthony Hay:	Hay's Cabinetmaking Shop
• Clementina Rind:	Ludwell-Paridise House
• Martha Cripps and William Moody, Jr.:	Market Square
• Adam Craig:	Public Record's Office
• Peyton Randolph, John Randolph, and Eve:	Randolph House
• St. George Tucker:	St. George Tucker House
• Benjamin Waller:	Benjamin Waller House
• Caesar and Sarah:	Wetherburn's Tavern
• Adam Waterford:	Windmill
• Walker Maury:	Wren Building

Figure 7.10.   First-person presentations and Williamsburg sites.

to solve a problem. On the first day at Williamsburg, the students looked for Mr. Jefferson by following primary source clues through the town in search of his National Treasure, his preparation for leadership. The next day the students had primary source dispatches to deliver to Mr. Wythe that guided them through Williamsburg. Later in the trip students on the grounds of Mt. Vernon each received numbered clues telling them where George Washington might be. By following the clues and reading excerpts from a primary source, students saw the outbuildings on the plantation while they learned about the plantation in Washington's own words. Each of these missions allowed the students to pretend, learn through using primary sources, and provided a theme for the day.

While at Williamsburg a couple of nods toward commercialism might be made in relatively good taste. Students should enjoy at least one lunch in a historic tavern to get a feel for how the structures might have been used in the past. Authentic meals, good food service, and quality entertainment are found under these roofs. If the students must shop, try to take them to the most authentic Greenhow, Prentis, or Tarpley stores in Williamsburg. They stock inventories that include quality reproduction items in displays that are compatible with the 1700s. While both experiences separate the visitors from their money, they are less garish than postcard shops and stores selling the "Virginia is for Lovers" bumper stickers.

Before students leave they should evaluate the Williamsburg site with two questions. First, "What can we not see here that should be here?" Second, "What is here that should not be here?" Students do not question the interpretation of the past unless they are challenged to do so. This very carefully cultivated visitor destination is limited by the very things that it attempts to interpret. For example, the streets of Williamsburg would have been dirt, hence, there would have been dust in the summer and mud whenever it rained. Think of hundreds of visitors tracking mud into the historic structures, and it becomes a curator's nightmare. There would have been significant amounts of garbage, animal wastes, and animals roaming the streets. The spiffy docents in their very clean clothes would have smelled putrid, they would have had bad teeth, and some of them would have had smallpox scars on their faces. None of these things would be acceptable to modern visitors, and students need to be able to thoughtfully discern these issues.

In the evening the teacher passed out copies of a commercial play about the revolution and had students act it out as an evening amusement. Scholastic (Appelbaum & Catanese, 2003) commercially produced these plays (Fink, 2009). Students liked to perform the plays, and the teachers needed to plan something with the students in the evenings. It made sense for the teachers to use the time for instruction, but it was helpful to have a type of instruction that the students enjoyed. Because the events were scripted and the plays were active, the students did not need a lot of advanced preparation. Students were engaged all of the time with the plays, so the chaperones could play along with the students by also assuming roles.

On the steps of the Virginia State Capitol, the teacher used primary source material from Jefferson to describe the state house. She also used pictures to describe the architecture, shared photos from the Civil War to show what the area once looked like, and pointed out the additions to the structure. Students stepped over to the Washington Statue to give their patriot reports before the other students. Since they completed these reports before leaving school, they now served as content experts. When they shared their information about Virginia patriots, many of them stood at the base of the equestrian Washingotn statue and in front of a life-sized statue of the patriot about whom they were speaking.

Students immediately debriefed with several questions to review where they had been and what they had done (Figure 7.11). Using these questions, students talked about why sites are important, why institutions maintain sites, and what people gave up to see these sites. Students described their observations at each site and then tried to sequence the events that occurred at each site. Students saw connections between their lives and events from another time and place (Briley,

- Who opened this site to the public? Why does the institution maintain the site?
- Why is the site important?
- What do people give up to see the site? What else could you have done today?
- Place the sites in chronological order.

Figure 7.11.   Debriefing questions.

2000). These questions helped students to remember what they had done and to order their thoughts about the many aspects of the trip. They saw an area that provided many national connections, and through their field trip they saw applications from history to democracy both in the past and the present.

ASSESSMENT

Students started their assessment prior to traveling on the trip (Figure 7.12). They learned how to put together a scrapbook with six sections documenting the six themes studied on the trip (Figure 7.13). Those six themes included: African-Americans, Economics, Family Life, Making a Nation, Religion, and Women. For each section students wrote what they knew and what they wanted to know. On the trip they gathered handouts and photos or took their own photos. When students returned to their school, they wrote what they had learned about each theme. They looked at not only what content they had learned but what misconceptions they

I.   Scrap Book: Six sections documenting each theme. For each site write what you:
   1.   Know (write about each of the six themes)
   2.   Want to Know (individual questions before the students leave)
   3.   Learned (information on return)
   4.   Find photos or take photos about the section
   5.   Save handouts from the trip
II.   Slide Program: Select a site. Tell the story of the site:
   1.   What happened there?
   2.   Who was involved?
   3.   Why is it important?
Include information about how it relates to our six interpretation themes on this trip
III.   Group Project: Virtual Field Trip

Figure 7.12.   Assessment assignments.

- African Americans
- Economics
- Family Life
- Making a Nation
- Religion
- Women

Figure 7.13.   Field trip themes.

1. Mount Vernon
2. Stratford Hall
3. Pope's Creek
4. Jamestown Fort
5. Indian Village
6. Jamestown Ships
7. Jamestown Site
8. Yorktown Battlefield
9. Yeoman's Farm
10. Colonial Troop Encampment
11. Carter's Grove
12. Slave Quarters
13. Wolstenholme Towne
14. Monticello
15. Williamsburg
    - Governor's Palace
    - Capitol
    - Raleigh Tavern
    - Hospital of 1773
    - Bruton Parish Church
    - Courthouse
    - Magazine
    - Wren Building of William and Mary
    - Blacksmith Shop
    - Carpenter Shop

Figure 7.14.   PowerPoint presentation topics.

had had and how their ideas of colonial life had changed as a result of visiting the sites.

Students also selected a location and created a PowerPoint presentation about it (Figure 7.14); they told the story of the site: who was there, what happened, and why it was important. They worked with a digital camera and PowerPoint to include each of the six themes in the slide show; after the trip they put all of the slide shows together and created a virtual field trip. The students evaluated their knowledge as they selected the photos they wished to include; they determined what to include in order to tell the story and what was irrelevant. In determining who was there, what happened, and why it was important, they selected the most important events to describe. They put together a compelling story that helped them communicate to their audience of peers and parents the importance of what they were saying about the site.

CHAPTER 8

THE EIGHTH-GRADE STUDY TRAVEL TRIP TO WASHINGTON, DC

INTRODUCTION

Every year the spring budding of the cherry trees signals another onslaught of the yellow school buses and the charter coaches rolling thousands of students into the federal district for the pilgrimage to the nation's capitol (Coy, 2009; Potter, 2007). The eighth-grade students in Lubbock, Texas, and their teachers took a trip to Washington, DC to study in the national capitol. They spent two weeks preparing for the trip, one week on the trip, and three weeks debriefing after they returned to school. The students spent their time seeing the United States' government in operation, exploring the sites, and digesting the large city. They not only saw national treasures, but they also participated in the performing arts and the cultural exhibits pertaining to history and government as an important part of their social studies curriculum. Washingtonians design their interpretations to handle large groups of people with static displays, audio-visual programs, or docents. The bulk of responsibility, therefore, falls by default to the resourcefulness of teachers to help their students construct meaning from this larger-than-life urban symbol of national power and heritage.

The Field Trip Book: Study Travel Experiences in Social Studies
pp. 117–127
Copyright © 2010 by Information Age Publishing

The trip to Washington, DC is almost a right of passage for eighth graders, but the dreaded trip can be anti-intellectual. At the National Archives students push to the front of the line to see the Constitution, but often they do not realize that they are walking past the Emancipation Proclamation. Students too often enter the Smithsonian and attempt to see it all in two hours, which is an amazing feat considering the size and complexity of the exhibitions. Without processing their experiences, some adolescents experience a mind-numbing charter coach chase from superficial destination, to fast food restaurant, to pool time. This model of a Washington, DC field trip offers examples of positive experiences for a class trip that helped eighth-grade students learn about government and history in the nation's capitol.

THE TRIP TO WASHINGTON, DC

The first thing to notice about this example is that the trip did not occur in isolation. Even though the students spent one week on the field trip, they spent two weeks preparing to go on the field trip and three weeks debriefing after the trip. The second important thing to note in this chapter is that the students spent their time preparing to be the guide for their peers. These students gave their peers a tour of the national capitol. The third thing to observe is that the students used the information they brought back from this trip to create projects whereby they could share this information with others in their school and home.

Most students study American history in eighth grade as part of their social studies scope and sequence (Langhorst, 2007; Rabb, 2007; Chu, 2004; Levstik & Barton, 2005; Findley, 2002). Students investigate topics that are often related to and supported by stops found in the nation's capitol. Students need opportunities to create their own questions while they examine sites, events, and people. Students ask questions such as, "How does the national government work?" The teacher's role shifts from evaluator to collaborator, and students are encouraged to find their own solutions by developing sustained arguments (Mitchell & Parker, 2008; LeCompte, 2006; Roser & Keehn, 2002; Logan, 2000). A rigorous social studies curriculum supports content of broad scope and methods that allow students to form, select, and investigate their questions. Classroom educational practices need to combat the charges of a vacuous social studies curriculum lacking cohesion between content, scope, and methods and neutered by political considerations (Rodgers, Hawthorne, & Wheeler, 2008; Duplass, 2007; Michels & Maxwell, 2006; Misco, 2005). In selecting their questions students cultivate deep and sophisticated explanations. Students who travel get the double advantage of a broad curriculum and progressive questioning opportunities.

Preparation Before the Trip

The entire eighth-grade class was able to attend this study travel experience. To prepare for their trip to Washington, DC, the students each selected a site from their itinerary (Figure 8.1) by lottery. Each student was given the opportunity to become the class tour guide for his or her selected site. The students obtained information by reading at least three published sources about the site before preparing a 10-minute presentation that would be given to the class (Figure 8.2). Within their presentation, students examined why the site is important and what happens there. The students selected a controversy that related to the site, which was an interesting assignment because they tried to remain as unbiased as possible. Students attempted to be fair by presenting both sides of the controversial issue. Mrs. McNeely, the social studies teacher, encouraged students to practice their talks before they gave the presentations so that they would not read directly from their papers, thus making it more of an interactive and real-life tour guide experience.

Because the group of students would be visiting Washington, DC, it was important for them to learn about their local representative who works at the capitol. Legislators often enjoy hearing from and talking with students who are visiting from their home districts. Prior to the trip the teacher made an appointment with the representative's staff member for a photo shoot on the steps of the United States Capitol. Prior to the trip, students developed specific questions to ask their congressional representative. They checked newspapers, news magazines, National Public Radio, and national TV news to find what issues faced the nation. Many of the questions focused on elections, domestic issues, and international issues. Students conducted research to determine on which congressional committees their representative served and what issues the committee faced, and they asked the representative about his position on these various issues. The students also asked questions about how the representative campaigns, raises funds, serves constituencies, forms legislation, defines budget issues, and works with party leaders. They did background research to find out what experiences the representative had during his or her term in office so that they could ask additional appropriate questions. Students peer reviewed their questions to help each person think about the clarity and appropriateness of his or her questions (Figure 8.3).

The students designed open-ended questions that enabled the representative to answer beyond mere yes or no responses. A member of the

Monday
8:00 a.m.   Depart Lubbock International Airport Lubbock, Texas
3:00 p.m.   Arrive Regan National Airport Washington, DC
3:30 p.m.   Meet bus
4:00 p.m.   Check into hotel
5:00 p.m.   Dinner at hotel
6:00 p.m.   Lincoln Monument
7:00 p.m.   Vietnam Memorial
            Vietnam Women's Memorial
            Einstein Statue
8:00 p.m.   Korean Memorial
9:00 p.m.   Return to hotel

Tuesday
7:00 a.m.   Breakfast in hotel
8:00 a.m.   White House Tour
9:30 a.m.   White House Visitor's Center
10:30 a.m. Library of Congress tour
12:00 p.m. Lunch Union Station
1:00 p.m.   Meet U.S. Representative
1:30 p.m.   U.S. Capitol tour
3:00 p.m.   U.S. Supreme Court tour
5:00 p.m.   Dinner in hotel
6:00 p.m.   Jefferson Memorial
7:00 p.m.   FDR Memorial
8:00 p.m.   George Mason Memorial
8:30 p.m.   Kennedy Center
9:00 p.m.   Return to Hotel

Wednesday
7:00 a.m.   Breakfast in hotel
8:00 a.m.   Kennedy Grave
9:00 a.m.   Lay a wreath at the Tomb of the Unknowns at Arlington National Cemetery
10:00 a.m. Custis-Lee Mansion
11:00 a.m. National Archives
1:00 p.m.   Lunch at Old Post Office
2:00 p.m.   Ford's Theater
2:30 p.m.   Ford's Theater Museum
3:30 p.m.   House where Lincoln died
5:00 p.m.   Dinner in hotel
6:00 p.m.   Walking Tour of Arlington, Virginia

Thursday
7:00 a.m.   Breakfast in hotel
8:00 a.m.   International Spy Museum
12:00 p.m. Lunch

(Figure continues on next page)

Figure 8.1.   Itinerary for Washington, DC.

1:00 p.m.	Fredrick Douglas House
3:30 p.m.	Smithsonian Air and Space Museum
5:00 p.m.	Dinner in hotel
6:00 p.m.	World War II Memorial
7:00 p.m.	Washington Monument
8:00 p.m.	Marines Memorial
9:00 p.m.	Return to hotel

Friday

7:00 a.m.	Breakfast in hotel
8:00 a.m.	Smithsonian Museum of American History
12:30 p.m.	Depart Regan National Airport Washington, DC
8:00 p.m.	Arrive Lubbock International Airport Lubbock, Texas

Figure 8.1. (Continued).

_____ (3) Three explanations of why the site is important
_____ (3) Three explanations of what happens at this location
_____ (10) One point for every minute up to 10
_____ (5) Free from notes: one point for every two minutes without looking at notes
_____ (4) Poised: standing straight, smiling, looking at the audience, audible
_____ (3) Pick a controversy that relates to the site
_____ (3) Give both sides equal time
_____ (3) Fair to both sides; strong arguments for both
_____ (34) Total

Figure 8.2. Tour guide oral presentation self-evaluation.

representative's staff met the group prior to their tour of the capitol, and then the students met with their congressman for a photo and an informal question-and-answer time. Students spoke about the issues that they found interesting and wanted to investigate further.

To accompany their presentations about their sites, the students prepared three-fold brochures with the aid of the computer program Publisher. The students gathered colored pictures as visual aids using either a scanner or a color copier. They included color pictures, captions, text to describe the purpose for the building, and arguments stating both sides of any controversy involving the building (Figure 8.4). They summarized their findings including why the site is important and what happened there. This way students have a souvenir of their stop and their peers'

Students critique the following questions raised by their peers on a scale of 1 to 5, with 5 being the highest.

_____ Informs the class as to the representative's political philosophy
_____ Explores a controversial issue
_____ Demonstrates open-endedness: More than one word required
_____ Starts with how or why
_____ Draws upon the representative's experiences in Washington, DC

Figure 8.3.   Question evaluation rubic.

_____ (3)   Gives three explanations of why the site is important
_____ (3)   Gives three explanations of what happens at this location
_____ (3)   Chose a controversy that relates to the site
_____ (3)   Presents both sides with equal time
_____ (3)   Is fair to both sides: strong arguments for both with no loaded language
_____ (3)   Uses at least three colored pictures
_____ (3)   Has strong layout and design: pleasing to the eye
_____ (3)   Uses captions for photographs
_____ (3)   Includes bibliography: 3 published sites, accurate citations
_____ (27) Total

Figure 8.4.   Site brochure student evaluation.

presentations. Along with constructing their brochures, they practiced including the items required from the self-evaluation rubric in the oral presentations.

Students flew from the Lubbock, Texas, airport to the Regan National Airport in Washington, DC, where a charter bus was waiting for them to use for the week. Funding was provided by parents who paid for their children to go on this school trip.

On-Site Data Collection

When students got to the site that they had selected in the classroom prior to the trip, they shared their information with the class and passed out the travel brochure that they had prepared about the site. Students either had a visual aid to which they referred during and after the presentation or they saved the brochure to use for notes when they returned home. By becoming the class expert for one particular site and presenting part of the tour, each student in this class controlled part of the trip, which made it more meaningful because they had a stake in the learning process.

On field trips students tend to expect some sort of interaction or they evaluate the site as being boring and unworthy of their time; it is imperative, therefore, that the students have some rather meaningful experience at each site (Ohn & Wade, 2009; Rubin & Giarelli, 2007; Berman, 2004; Wennik, 2004; Wolk, 2003; Allen, 2000). The teachers planned many activities for the students to do at each site. For example, at the Korean War Memorial this group of eighth-grade students brought paper and crayons to perform a rubbing from the faces on the wall to bring these images back to the classroom as a form of note taking for a future project. At the Vietnam Memorial students looked for their family names in the directory near the wall. Not every student actually found his or her name on the wall, but they were all able to experience touching the cold, smooth stone wall. Students captured larger blocks of text when they photographed quotations from John F. Kennedy's grave as a form of note taking for a future project. Students were able to learn more about what this former president stood for based on some of his quotations. The photographs helped students capture an image of the quotes, which allowed them to discuss and interpret them at a later date.

At the Franklin Delano Roosevelt Memorial, students used their bodies to finish, add to, or reinterpret a sculpture, and thus freeze the action. Students interacted with the life-size bronze statues by joining the action in tableau; they explained how their actions contributed to the understanding of the memorial. For example, one set of bronze statues depicted men standing in line and slumped under the weight of the Great Depression. Eighth grader Jonathan, who also slumped over, joined the line showing his connection with the artist and the feelings of all people oppressed by economic disaster. Other students followed his lead and joined in interpreting the statue. At another bronze statue where a man was listening to a radio broadcast, Evan jumped behind the radio to provide the voice coming from the radio and other students gathered around to listen. The actions by these students emphasized the artist's vision of Roosevelt being the power behind the broadcast—a man communicating with the people of his country. At the big, sloppy statue of Einstein students were able to climb on the statue sharing the artist's understanding that Einstein was not someone aloof and unknowable but was an intimate and personable acquaintance to many. The freedom from barricades and the large inviting lap beckoned students to climb up and explore. The pop icon of Einstein and the students' fascination with genius provided a stage for student interaction at this site. The students involved themselves with each site, and the teacher invited the students to interact with the sites to keep boredom at bay.

Other sites did not require the deep interaction suggested above, but the students did need some focus provided by the teacher. The questions teachers asked focused on large ideas and helped students construct meaning to interpret each particular site. At the Frederick Douglas House students used a guiding question: How do the furniture and artifacts in this house reflect his political beliefs? Students then used this question to view the material culture to determine Frederick Douglas' political philosophies, which they had previously studied in the classroom.

The teacher also included a bit of mystery to keep students involved in the study travel experience (Figure 8.5). The students became detectives at Ford's Theater by looking for clues about President Lincoln's assassination. They received instructions to find two pieces of physical evidence from the assassination and to provide their evidence with the facts after they had investigated a crime scene. In the Ford's Theater Museum students divided into groups to find the name of one conspirator and tell what happened to him. Basing their reports on the evidence that they found, students reported on how they thought the murder occurred. The eighth graders also acted out part of the play Lincoln watched that night, which gave students a hands-on learning experience at that particular site. Whether using guiding questions or a nod toward the dramatic, the students mentally engaged with the site.

A field trip to Washington, DC is not complete without a trip to the White House on Pennsylvania Avenue. On the tour of the White House students explored the following critical guiding questions:

- Should the president live like a European monarch when people are starving?
- What evidence is available that this is an American house versus a modern European palace?

Man's voice: You sockdologizng old mantrap!

Audience: *laughter*

Man's voice: Sic semper tyrannis!

Woman's scream

Man's voice: Stop that man!

Figure 8.5.   Bus microphone play.

Both questions required that students look at evidence found on the tour of the White House and then confirm their beliefs to determine an answer.

Some sites required a combination of knowledge-level questions to help students see specific items along with broader open-ended and higher-level thinking questions. At the National Archives the teacher asked the class to think about and answer the following questions:

- What document displays peaceful transfer of power?
- What did Franklin Delano Roosevelt do to solve the problems of the Great Depression?
- What steps could the conservators at the National Archives take to preserve documents?
- In your opinion, should documents be on display for people to see or be kept someplace where ink does not fade? Support your answer.

The students used the same combination of gathering data and reflective introspection to learn while visiting the Supreme Court. The function of the Supreme Court is sometimes difficult for students to envision and understand. Students used a combination of sources to investigate democratic ideals at this site, as well as looking at how the court building, interiors, and displays communicate abstract ideas such as liberty.

The trip allowed students to gather information about the nation's capitol using multiple sources of data. Furthermore, students served as a source of information for their peers while on the trip. Students interacted in many ways to harvest information from the sites and brought that information back to school.

After the Trip

On the first day back in the classroom, the students worked to create individual scrapbooks on Washington, DC that included all of the sites that they visited on the trip. They wrote an introduction for the scrapbook and included the purpose for going on the trip; they also included the opportunity cost (what they gave up to go on the trip). Since the trip was required, each student gave up something. It might be free time to visit with friends at the mall, time playing video games, or interacting with a computer. Furthermore, they discussed what responsibilities they assumed on the trip and how they engaged in decision making. After the introductory section they allocated one page for each site on the trip. For every site, they included a picture, a caption, told why they thought the site was important, and explained how they felt when they visited the site. On the last pages of their scrapbooks the students wrote a conclusion in which they evaluated the entire Washington, DC trip. In this conclusion they listed the experiences from the trip that they would repeat given the chance, detailed the events they would change, described what they learned, and reflected on how they changed as a person because of the trip.

The rubric for the scrapbook helped the students know how to determine points in the grading process. Each product showed a different aspect of what the students learned, demonstrated how they learned it, and provided an illustration of the application of that knowledge. By looking at knowledge, process, and application students, parents, and teachers determined the success of the students' learning from the sites. Students had products that they could explain to their peers, teachers, and parents.

Students had a rubric provided by the teacher to guide them in the creation of the project. Before he or she left for the trip each student made sure he or she included everything of value required by the teacher and yet had room for individual creativity in the preparation of materials. Students demonstrated their characteristics of individuality while also expressing their competencies with projects.

After returning to their social studies classroom and using the rubric, the students included controversial issues, reporting both sides of each issue (NCSS, 1994) (Figure 8.6). Students each took an opinion and explained his or her line of reasoning while documenting why he or she thought this position was correct. Each student also listed multiple reasons that supported his or her position. In another place in their scrapbooks they needed to demonstrate balanced treatment of a controversial issue, because the scrapbook required the students to evaluate their work through a process of reviewing, revising, and reflecting upon their work in comparison to the rubric.

II.   Time, continuity, and change
III.   People, places, and environments
V.   Individuals, groups, and institutions
VI.   Power, authority, and governance
X.   Civic ideals and practice

Figure 8.6.   NCSS (1994) national standards.

Students received bonus points for artistic endeavors; however, the lack of artistic endeavors did not diminish the score. These individual accomplishments with media materials personalized projects that could easily have become multiple repetitive checklists. The individualization this provided also differentiated the products into unique products. The student earned points for achieving the criteria, and students had multiple opportunities to demonstrate their accomplishments. Students not only prepared before the trip, but they constructed knowledge during the trip, and demonstrated what they learned with products that their peers and parents could see following the trip.

CHAPTER 9

ENACTIVE INVESTIGATIONS IN A (BATTLE)FIELD

INTRODUCTION

The citizen only exists within the context of a community. In a democracy it is important for students to learn to be good citizens and to be strong contributors to the community. Brosio (2000) states that democratic education is necessary in perpetuating a healthy democracy. Students must connect to their communities through the people they encounter in those communities. Because the abstraction of a community is difficult for many young learners to comprehend, educators must work to connect community to faces. The bonds must be made person to person; Burch (2000) states that the glue that holds a community and hence a democracy together is eros. Both love for self and love for others are important ingredients in creating a sense of community and an ethic of participation. Educators help students heighten this sense of love and trust in situations requiring students to work together on common tasks. Educators help students when they use high adventure activities for the purpose of community formation and peace education (Arweck & Nesbitt, 2008; Quezada & Christopherson, 2005). Students engage in these activities by developing trust in the members of the group. Students work on their common tasks in a field situation that possesses natural qualities of adventure. When the students engage with the community, they are able to feel

The Field Trip Book: Study Travel Experiences in Social Studies
pp. 129–157
Copyright © 2010 by Information Age Publishing

a sense of belonging that helps them see the challenge of forming connections to others.

The K–12 educational experiences of many students include individual social science courses, but rarely do these courses promote a fusion of disciplines (McCall, 2006, 2002; http://www.cr.nps.gov/nr/twhp/; http://www.cubekc.org/). To be a group requires that people spend time together to understand one another and especially to listen to one another. With the aid of shared understandings, students can see multiple connections to disciplines. If students engage in inquiry projects, they can then use the study travel experience to form an integrated curriculum. Furthermore, students who travel together have the necessary common experience to think of themselves as a group. A study travel experience is a natural event with which to focus integrated instruction around social studies themes.

Due to the magnificent will and memory of the members of the Grand Army of the Republic and the United Confederate Veterans, as well as the determination of modern members of groups such as the Civil War Preservation Trust, vast stretches of land that were former sites of Civil War battles have been saved through the United States Department of the Interior. At these sites there may be a visitor's center, a few historic structures, or the land may have preserved features such as a sunken road, a pond, or a rock fence. The flora and topography may have remained the same: a stand of timber, a wheat field, a peach orchard, or a stream. While there may be some bronze or stone markers and occasionally even a cannon for interpretation, until the teacher builds context the site simply looks like a field. It takes significant effort to set the stage for a field trip to these sites because before the site has meaning to young visitors the imagination can only go so far without structured stimulation.

CONTEXT

Visiting battlefields demonstrates the ultimate controversial example of when diplomacy failed between two groups of people. The natural state of mankind, peace, is disrupted and people turn to violence, and then return to a state of peace. Whether it is strife between the North and South, Tory or Whig, American or British, Indian and Anglo, or Mexican and Texan, the sites of these contentious events dot the landscape. Most of the time it is up to the teacher to give historical meaning to the site by interpreting military and political events. In order to set the stage some stories of women, children, and minorities that might be hidden by traditional interpretation of the site can be taught to students. This could call into question the historiography of the site in order to determine how people have explained the site in the past, how it is explained today, and speculation as to how it might be interpreted in the future. It might require taking an in-depth economic, geographic, and sociological perspective to overcome hagiographic interpretations of events.

INTERACTIVE INTERPRETATION OF CIVIL WAR SITES

A group of students from Texas prepared, experienced, and debriefed from a trip to American Civil War battlefields in the east as part of their social studies curriculum. All three phases of the student trip engaged the students with powerful learning in social studies. The students learned about the Civil War on the grounds where the actual events occurred in order to learn more about the people involved in the conflict. Their teacher asked the students to participate with the content at the site and included ideas for assessment.

A group of students traveled to Antietam as part of their studies, and they spent one day at the site as part of a class research trip. They saw the national historical park grounds and then interpreted the site on their own. Students used parts of the battlefield to understand what happened at the site; they used a variety of interactive experiences on the site to interpret the events that had occurred there. Students need a combination of content knowledge, action, and adventure to help them to learn and to retain their experiences. Through both their experiences and their interaction they became curious about events and people whose lives changed on the battlefield over a hundred years ago.

When students travel with their teacher they relate to their peers in the experience. In the field students do not need to conform to a school model that champions capitalism's individual, material, and competitive society (Beach & Dovemark, 2009; McLellan & Martin, 2005). With their teacher they determine their purpose for taking the trip and what they will see on-site. They then work with their peers to explore the sites in groups. The students use the interaction between their group and their teacher to explore the site's Web page to determine where to spend the most time on the site (e.g., Antietam National Battlefield, http:// www.nps.gov/anti/index.htm). The Web page can provide much information for students, while encouraging students to talk with their peers to determine what would be the most interesting things to see and do. Furthermore, the Web provides students with a way to explore the site before traveling to it; students work in groups to explore the significance of the sites. For students to travel successfully they must by necessity practice cooperation, establish community, and work for the common good.

Preparation Before the Trip

Students need information about the issues that concerned people in the past and still concern people today. Students see how their lives connect to the people who lived at the time of the Civl War and fought over those issues. To that end the teacher provided the students with a book of essays (Horwitz, 1999) to provide background about the war and to establish the importance of the war in the present. Catton was writing in the shadow of the World War II, and he discussed the yet unfulfilled promise of equal rights after the Civil War, a war for the purpose of liberation. Students examined his text to see what had been accomplished since he wrote it, and who was left out by it. They examined issues that they thought had not yet responded to the Civil War's extension of liberty to all people who lived in the country. They compared this civil war to civil wars in other places and examined the results of those wars. Students determined what connections their lives had to the Civil War in the twenty-first century.

Students also had choices when they went to the DVD computer learning stations. Students watched Ken Burns' (1990) *Civil War #1: "The Beginning of the War,"* and got to see a clip from *Glory* (1989) showing Robert Gould Shaw writing home to his mother about the approaching battle of Antietam and of daily life in the army. Students were able see the scale of the action and the large number of troops it took to fight the war. Before playing the students were asked to look for evidence of Robert's education, social standing, and why he was fighting the war. When the DVD stopped, students were asked to predict what would happen next; they were required to give reasons why they thought the way they did. Students got to see another video clip of the railroad yard at Atlanta from the film *Gone with the Wind* (1939). After the clip the students were prompted to talk about which wounded soldier the ambulance drivers transported first, what wounds would be priority, and who had the most chance of surviving a Civil War wound. Students also saw clips from Ken Burns' Civil War film about the battle of Antietam to help them establish a chronology of events and gain a working knowledge of the major characters. Students also saw another brief clip from *Glory* in which Robert Gould Shaw's father introduces him to Massachusetts Governor Andrews and Frederick Douglas. The video clip was prefaced with two questions: "Why does Robert jump at the sound, and what was startling about the party?" At the end the students were asked, "How does Robert feel about getting to lead African American troops?" After seeing films about the Civil War, students could select to take a virtual tour of the present day battlefield at Antietam. Students could preview the sites they would be traveling to see; they were able to find out some of the events that occurred on the site. Student choice of activities allows students to spend time learning about what most interests them.

In addition to the DVD and computer centers students visited learning centers set up in the room to learn about the Civil War from documents and artifacts. At one center replicas of United States and Confederate currency ("Barry'd Treasure: Civil War Relics," http://www.iglou.com/btreasure/currency.htm) were on display. Students examined the symbols to determine what each government valued and why the government selected to put it on their currency. Students discussed who printed the currency, which currency was worth more, and why it was more valuable. Another learning station contained posters of Civil War photographs and maps. Students determined how photography changed the way people saw the war, what fascinated people about Lincoln's image, and whether most photographers worked inside or outside and under what circumstances. Another station allowed students to create a Civil War time line incorporating all the information they had discovered. Students went to other learning stations in the room to learn from artifacts. At a display of Civil War flags students examined the flags and read text describing the flags; they determined why the flags all looked different and why there were so many variations.

On-Site Data Collection Trip to Antietam and Gettysburg

On the first day students met a first-person character, a sergeant from the Stonewall Brigade, which got its nickname from their commander's conduct at the Battle of Bull Run. The soldiers called this group foot cavalry because they walked as far as the cavalry rides, and in battle they were shock troops. They hit the enemy on the flank. He talked about why he was fighting, which included the right to take slave property anywhere in the United States, the right of a state to nullify federal law, and the right of a state to secede.

Students stopped in the East Woods of Antietam to recreate Civil War photography. Students wearing jeans and a shirt put on a Civil War jacket and hat, crossed their arms, and wore a serious look on their faces. The group also had the option to add period eyeglasses, brogans, cap box belts, cartridge boxes, haversacks, or canteens. Students used a digital camera to take pictures of their peers. Photoshop was later used to change the colors to sepia.

At the Dunker Church a member of the Iron Brigade met students for a first-person presentation about the battle. Students learned about the back-and-forth fight that occurred across the corn field and around the Dunker Church from a person who had been there to see the action. The character spoke about his feelings, the troop movements, and the reactions of the men. The character also connected with the students by telling them about the contributions of young soldiers who had fought there. In addition to showing the students historic photos, the first-person presentation helped students make a personal connection to the events that actually happened on the battlefield.

At Bloody Lane students walked down the path and counted every step from the time they get off the bus until they got back on the bus. After the battle it was impossible to go down the lane without stepping on or over a body with every pace. Students got some idea of the number of casualties they would have seen just in their brief walk. Students were better able to form a picture in their minds of the carnage as they lay on the ground and moaned or called out for water. They compared the lane as it is today with pictures taken shortly after the battle.

At Burnside's Bridge the group divided into half; one half went up to the heights and the other went goes to the approach of the Bridge. The group on the heights pretended to be sharp shooters with Whitworth rifles and scopes; to do this each sharp shooter made the OK sign with the thumbs and first fingers of both hands. One of these they put close to their eye, and the other they put at arm's length to get the idea of the scope. They could pretend to shoot each enemy in sight, but they had to leave twenty seconds between shots as timed on their watches. The other half of the group charged Burnside's Bridge and ran up the hill; after each side had done their jobs, the groups changed places.

At Antietam students had the opportunity to work in a field hospital as surgeons, patients, or orderlies. Students selected these roles at random. Attendants drew fate cards to see how each student had gotten there; the options included a nurse from the community, U. S. Sanitary Commission ("The Sanitary Commission and Other Relief Agencies," 2002), a soldier detailed to care for the wounded, an ambulance driver, or a private citizen traveling to meet the army and provide relief. Attendants put the wounded soldiers on Civil War blankets and sheets. All patients had limb wounds, and students who were patients drew fate cards for upper arm, lower arm, hand, upper leg, lower leg, or foot wounds. The doctor drew a fate card to see what drugs were available; the possibilities were chloroform, ether, morphine, opium, or alcohol. If the card read *morphine* or *opium*, the attendant gave the soldier a shot with a drinking straw, and if the card read *alcohol*, the attendant pretended to get the student drunk from the canteen. If the card read *ether* or *chloroform*, they had to cover the patient's nose and mouth lightly with a funnel ("Anesthetics in The Civil War," 2006). Next, the surgeon was ready to use the belt as a tourniquet above the area to be removed, remove the skin and muscle (newspaper) with the knife, cut the tendons (cardboard) with the scissors, saw the bone (dowel rod), file the bone, and sew the wound closed (needle, thread, and two pieces of fabric). The patient had a squirt bottle of blood (red food coloring, corn syrup, and duck sauce) that they could use on the surgeon's and attendants' hands, faces, and tools if they hurt the patient or if the patient thought they were working slowly. After the surgery the patient drew another fate card to see whether or how they recovered. The options included going into shock and dying, waking up during the operations and needing more anesthesia, death by loss of blood, death by overdose of anesthesia, death by blood poisoning, death by gangrene, or waking up and throwing up from the anesthesia but surviving with limited infection. In a field hospital students learn many of the grim realities of the world of Civil War medicine.

Students were required to take another perspective, inhabit it, and act on it. They each had an opportunity to look at a primary source and reading it to him/herself while looking over the battlefield. Students read sections of the Emancipation Proclamation and role played four characters: Jefferson Davis, Queen Victoria of England, the foreign affairs minister of France, and Abraham Lincoln. Students had to evaluate whether the military or the political significance of the battle was more important to each person and what both meant to the group of people the person represented. Students personalized the recitation, the importance of this document, and its impact on these characters and nations after the battle.

Students needed to know about people like themselves who were at this site. By playing an identity game, they found out about many of the people at the site and what they had done. Students were assigned a Civil War character, which was taped to their back. They did not know who they were and could not be told their names except through yes and no questions. Each student attempted to find the other person who had an identity that corresponded to the one taped to his or her own back. Students played this as two separate games, with the topics of young soldiers of the Civil War or women (Wiley, 1995, 1997). (The game can also be played as one large group depending on the number of people in the group). Through this game students found not only who their own characters were but also who the other characters were as each student searched for his or her assigned identity.

In groups of three, students created a Civil War archeology dig (Easley, 2005; Boothe, 2000); first the students included a drawing of what the site looked like in 1865 and marked the coordinates. Then the students added a drawing of each dig site including at least three pits with the coordinates marked. The students included a list of artifacts and features found in each pit; students also listed at least one primary source to document each artifact in the pit. To conclude, the students wrote an archeologist's narrative including their interpretation of what each pit

____ (5) Drawing of the site
    ____ (1) Coordinates
    ____ (1) Authenticity
    ____ (3) Three features

____ (15) Drawing of the three pits
    ____ (3) Coordinates marked on each pit
    ____ (3) A drawing of each of the three pits
    ____ (9) Includes three features in each of the three pits

____ (36) Create a separate list of three artifacts found in each of the three pits
    ____ (9) List of each artifact that could be found after 150 years in the ground
    ____ (9) Describe each artifact
    ____ (9) Picture of each artifact
    ____ (9) Each artifact is authentic to the time

____ (12) What did the first pit represent?
    ____ (1) A point for determining what the pit represents.
    ____ (9) A point for each sentence in the paragraph that supports the outline.
    ____ (1) A point for the proper citation.
    ____ (1) A point for a quotation that supports the ideas in the body of the paper.
    ____ (1 Bonus Point) For using a primary source including diaries, letters, or
    public records

____ (5) Drawing of the site
    ____ (1) Coordinates
    ____ (1) Authenticity
    ____ (3) Three features

____ (15) Drawing of the three pits
    ____ (3) Coordinates marked on each pit
    ____ (3) A drawing of each on the three pits
    ____ (9) Includes three features in each of the three pits

____ (36) Create a separate list of three artifacts found in each of the three pits
    ____ (9) List of each artifact that could be found after 150 years in the ground
    ____ (9) Describe each artifact
    ____ (9) Picture of each artifact
    ____ (9) Each artifact is authentic to the time

____ (12) What did the first pit represent?
    ____ (1) A point for determining what the pit represents.
    ____ (9) A point for each sentence in the paragraph that supports the outline.
    ____ (1) A point for the proper citation.
    ____ (1) A point for a quotation that supports the ideas in the body of the paper.

____ (1 Bonus Point) For using a primary source including diaries, letters, or public
records

Figure 9.1.   Archeological pit rubric.

- Topic: What was the pit?
- Statement: How do these artifacts help us know what happened here?
- Example of artifacts: Describe the artifacts found in the pit.
- Why? Why do these artifacts tell archeologist about the people who were here?
- Statement: Make a connection between the artifact found and a document from that time.
- Quotation: Quote and cite a publication that describes a person from the Civil War referring to one of these artifacts.
- Why? Why does this quotation tell us about the people who live here?
- Why? Why is this information important in the interpretation of the site?
- Conclusion: So what? Why is this important? Why is the topic sentence important? How and why does this knowledge bring us to the next paragraph?

Figure 9.2.   Teacher archeological pit model.

___ (12) Using the paragraph guide found above, what did the second pit represent?
    ___ (1) A point for determining what the pit represents.
    ___ (9) A point for each sentence in the paragraph that supports the outline.
    ___ (1) A point for the proper citation
    ___ (1) A point for a quotation that supports the idea in the body of the paper.
    ___ (1 Bonus point) For using a primary source including diaries, letters, or public records
___ (12) Using the paragraph guide found above, what did the third pit represent?
    ___ (1) A point for determining what the pit represented.
    ___ (9) A point for each sentence in the paragraph that supports the outline.
    ___ (1) A point for the proper citation.
    ___ (1) A point for a quotation that supports the idea in the body of the paper.
    ___ (1 Bonus Point) For using a primary source, including diaries, letters, or public records
___ (6) Conclusion paragraph
    ___ (3) In two or three sentences summarize what it tells us about life in the 1860s when interpreted together.
    ___ (3) In two or three sentences summarize why this information is important to understanding that time.

Figure 9.3.   Archeological report rubric.

represented, what the pits communicated about life in 1865 when interpreted together, and why this was important information (Figure 9.1). Students were required to both demonstrate their understandings of archeology and the Civil War to successfully complete this task. Students created an archeologist's narrative to practice the formulation of historical hypotheses, and students completed an archeology dig evaluation (Figures 9.2 and 9.3).

Students created three different snapshots of the Civil War for interpretation. They had to create a story, gather the tools necessary to interpret it, and arrange the tools in such a fashion as to communicate the story to the observer. In this evaluation students documented their thinking and the gathering of evidence. The students provided a model for communication displaying thinking and evidence that supported a hypothesis.

Students had the option of using primary sources to help them interpret the pits (Hopkinson & Farmer, 2001; Martin, 2001; McElmeel, 2001). The students summed up all of their findings in a concluding paragraph in which, like real archeologists, they put forward their best guesses. Students took their three snapshots of Civil War life and wove them together. The students told their stories in three tubleaus expressing interactions and interrelations between the three pits. This assessment helped students creatively reflect upon and interpret their Civil War knowledge.

INTERACTIVE INTERPRETATION AT GETTYSBURG

A group of students traveled to Gettysburg as part of their studies; they spent one day at the site as part of a class research trip. After they saw the national historical park grounds and visitors' center, they then interpreted the site on their own. Students used parts of the battlefield away from the crowds to understand what happened at the site. Students used a variety of interactive experiences on the site to interpret the events; during these experiences, students moved from observers to participating learners. Students constructed meaning about events through games, drama, and activities that looked like play to the students but this involvement allowed them to become interested in finding out more about the site.

In traveling to the site of Civil War battles and conducting research, the students brought their cognitive, social-emotional, and moral qualities to these interactions while integrating their experiences in and out of school (Bobek, Zaff, Li, & Lerner, 2009; Gallavan & Fabbi, 2004). All of these qualities have an impact upon students' success when learning on the site of a Civil War battle. There are wide varieties of resources available to help prepare students for such a trip. Educators planning to explore Gettysburg on- or off-site should examine the Web site http://www.nps.gov/gett/index.htm for an abundance of teaching ideas and resources. From virtual trips to quotations, this is an excellent source for new ideas about teaching the Civil War. Teaching with Historic Places also offers a lesson on Gettysburg (http://www.cr.nps.gov/nr/twhp/wwwlps/lessons/44gettys/44gettys.htm). By tapping into these resources, teachers can find out about the site without traveling to it. Students used a combination of primary sources to explore the Gettysburg battlefield and employed their emerging social, emotional, and ethical qualities. Finally, students used content from Internet sources combined with their growing experiences to interpret the events of the Civil War.

Trip Preparation

In preparation for studying on site, students learned about the larger context of the war and its causes including the role of slavery before engaging in the unit. The students got to read and compare how various authors have interpreted Gettysburg from a reading packet (Boritt, 1999; Catton, 1962, 1963a, 1963b; 1965; Foote, 1986a, 1986b; Freeman, 1971; 1995; Hess, 2001; Sandburg, 1974; Rhodes, 1999; McPherson, 1988; Nevins, 1992; Nolan, 1983). Students did not read all of the essays; rather, they picked two readings about Gettysburg by lottery and compared them. Students then were placed into small groups to discuss their readings. Here the students examined where the authors agreed or disagreed, what the authors were attempting to emphasize, and the authors' respective points of view or themes. The groups then reported their findings by sharing their information with the entire class. Finally, the students compared what Wiley (1995, 1997) says about the men who fought on each side; his work detailing the common soldier provides a social history about the people who fought in the war. After reading the two chapters the students created a data retrieval chart, determined the categories to be included, compared the two Wiley readings, and cited evidence from the readings. The students divided the top fields of the retrieval chart into two parts: North and South. Next, they separated the side fields into the following categories: African Americans, education, ethnic groups, social status, student choice, and young soldiers.

Students selected sections that they wanted to compare from the reading; this allowed them a voice in identifying the most important ideas. Students compared contentions from the 1860s with the issues of today, considered how historians report different events in what they write, and discovered how social history is also part of the whole story. All writers have a bias, and the students attempted to determine the bias of each author. Each author selects different sources that help tell the story, and the selection of sources determines the outcome of the narrative. The selection and documentation of primary sources becomes very important in the creation of the narrative.

Students also had choices when they went to the DVD and computer learning stations. They saw Ken Burns' (1990) *Civil War #9: "The End of the War,"* and clips from the "Gettysburg" section of Burns' *Civil War #5.* After seeing films about the Civil War, students could select to take a virtual tour of the present day battlefield at Gettysburg. Students could preview the sites they would travel to see, or they could find out about some of the events that occurred on the site. Student choice of activity allows students to spend time learning about what interests them most. Students must make wise decisions about how they will use their time, what to do with extra time, what they can do in class, and what they can do at home.

Along with the DVD and computer centers listed above, students visit learning centers that are set up in the room to learn about the Civil War from documents and artifacts. In one station students looked at reprints from *Harper's Weekly Illustrated Newspaper* (http://www.civilwarliterature.com). Students looked for a part of the paper that is similar and a part that is different from the newspaper today. Students scanned the headlines and determined whether the people at that time thought the event was very important or not. Students also examined the ads to see what products did and did not continue to sell. Students noticed political cartoons and tried to determine what perspectives the artists held.

The next learning center featured a brick wall covered with Civil War recruiting posters (http://www.irishbrigadegiftshop.com/souvenir.html# posters). Students had to determine who recruited military personnel and the reasons soldiers gave for joining the army. They compared the reasons why people enlisted and the reasons people enlist today. The brick wall also had bricks with names of inventions that influenced the war; by raising the flaps on those bricks, students could see and read how the inventions had changed the war. Students found out how technology changed the way the war proceeded and determined what differences the technology would have made in their lives if they had been soldiers. Students evaluated whether the technology changes would have encouraged them or discouraged them from signing up for the military.

Students discovered that multiple events happened at the same time on different fronts during the Civil War. For example, John Hunt Morgan raided Indiana and Ohio at the same time that fighting occurred at Gettysburg and Vicksburg. Students created a map of Morgan's Raid at one station by using primary and secondary sources to plot the route (Mitchell, 2001; Ramage, 1995). Students needed to determine whether cavalry raids allowed military leaders to widen the scope later in the war for the type of war Sherman and Sheridan fought. They also determined who constituted enemy combatants in the civilian population and under what circumstances a property could become a target for military operations.

Students compared street fighting to cavalry raids and determined which would be more justified in a combat situation.

While some events such as political or military campaigns were large, other events were more personal in nature, such as individual tastes in the use of leisure time. In another station students listened to music from the Civil War (http://www.civilwarmusicstore.com/) to determine what types of music the men listened to in the field, at home, on parade, and in camp. Students predicted how the soldiers interpreted the music they heard in their daily lives. Students reacted to both melody and lyrics and found them to be uplifting marching songs or melancholy emotional songs. The students considered what they learned about the people who sang these songs and hypothesized about why these songs had been popular. The students considered what songs soldiers sing today, what the songs say about the soldiers, and why these songs are popular.

Students learned about both political and social history and got additional experience similar to a soldier at the time from artifacts. A first-person presentation of a soldier from the 19th Indiana (Morris, 2009) shared with the class about life in the Civil War and the Iron Brigade's role in the battle. The students met this character later on the field of battle at Gettysburg, where he talked about how he was fighting and why he thought others were or were not fighting. He let students try on his uniform and explore the equipment he carried. These items were almost a part of him, because he had carried them and fought with them across multiple states and for many years. When the students opened his haversack and backpack in addition to his cartridge box, cap box, and canteen, they found a diary, a pencil, an identification coin, a straight razor and carrying case, coin money (and/or postal stamps) and carrying case, a tintype picture in a leather case, a Bible and carrying case, rifle tools (wiper, tompion, nipple wrench/screw drivers, worm, and punches), a candle, a clay pipe, a pen and carrying case, an ink well, paper, playing cards, button polishing brush, a round mirror with cover, a comb, a *housewife* (scissors, needles, buttons, thread, pins, thimble), a hatchet, a cooking pot, hardtack, a combination fork/spoon/knife, boxed and canned foods, and a plate (Rolph & Clark, 1961; Morris, 2000B).

Next, the first-person presentation of a Civil War soldier explained the three branches of Civil War service (artillery, cavalry, and infantry) by using a variety of hats with different colors of hat cord and different insignias for each division and distinction between troops. These differences in attire allowed the soldier to quickly see where his group was and where other positions in the army were. Finally, the students got to march in formation, performing simple commands such as *attention, at ease, right* and *left face, about face, dress the line,* and *forward march*. In a battle it was easy for the men to be quickly separated so they had to move quickly as a group to respond to the movements of the enemy and to coordinate their attacks. The students attempted to do this in the same manner.

Assessments

Students researched a person who was at Gettysburg during the Civil War. The possibilities included a person from the Army of Northern Virginia, Pickett's Division, Army of the Potomac, Hood's Texas Brigade, Iron Brigade, the U. S. Sanitary Commission, a conscientious objector, a farmer, a nurse, a photographer, a politician, a relative, a spy, or a Gettysburg resident. Each student found a connection to themselves either in age, a family relative, or someone from their home area, and each student found out what his or her person did at the site and where they were on the site. Students then made a map of their person's route from the time of leaving home to returning home. Students also found out what their characters did before or after the war. Students looked for other stories they could tell about their characters such as personal details, primary sources, public records, and their connections to the big issues of the day (Dean, 1999; Hess, 1997; Jimerson, 1994; Linderman, 1989; McPherson, 1998; Mitchell, 1997). Students used a rubric (Figure 9.4) to evaluate the Civil War person from the past project.

Each student received instruction on how to write a model paragraph starting with a topic sentence and ending with a concluding sentence (Figure 9.5). Students were required to make statements, provide evidence, and interpret the evidence presented. Students received bonus points for using primary sources, and students were encouraged to provide documentation for their ideas in formal writing (Figures 9.6 and 9.8). Through researching a person associated with the site where they are going to travel, it is to be hoped that students will make a physical connection to

```
Check if Present              Example Notes
_____ Personal connection
_____ Prior to war
_____ War travel map
_____ Personal details
_____ Big issues
_____ Where in battle
_____ Did in battle
_____ After war
```

Figure 9.4.   Person from the past rubric.

I. Topic sentence: lays out an idea, thought, or opinion that is important
    A. Statement of observation, fact, or opinion
        1. Example, evidence, or quotation supporting the statement
        2. Why the example, evidence, or quotation supports the statement
    B. Statement of observation, fact, or opinion
        1. Example, evidence, or quotation supporting the statement
        2. Why the example, evidence, or quotation supports the statement
    C. Statement of observation, fact, or opinion
        1. Example, evidence, or quotation supporting the statement
        2. Why the example, evidence, or quotation supports the statement
    D. How do these three statements support the topic sentence?
    E. What conclusion has been reached from these facts?

Figure 9.5.   Outline paragraph.

- Topic Sentence: What is the main idea of this paragraph?
- Statement: State an idea you have.
- Quotation: Provide evidence with a quotation (words from reading surrounded by quotation marks) and citation (author's last name, year, page number of a primary [a document created by a person who was there] or a secondary [a narrative created after the fact] source that support the statements made.
- Why: Why is this evidence appropriate to support the statement?
- Why: Why is this important idea related to the topic sentence?
- Conclusion: So what? Why is this important? Why is the topic sentence important?
- How and why does this knowledge bring us to the next paragraph?

Figure 9.6.   Model paragraph.

that person on the site. The person's name or unit may be marked on a monument at the site or the primary sources the student uses may refer to a specific recognizable place. Students also need to know that people may have had one particular time in the limelight, but in many cases their lives overlap the event on either end.

The life of the person connects to the big issues of the war and the time. The person may have had leadership roles in the army or back home because of conduct or ideological positions connected to the issues of the age (Mitchell, 1995). Those issues may have defined or been defined by where the soldier went; the map traces the events of a soldier's life and shows how they got to travel because of the war. Students who excel in researching their characters can show their accomplishments on their maps. In graphic form the students can show both early and later

- Create a map tracing where the soldier started and where the war took him.
- Leadership position at home
- Where troops mustered.
- Personal connection to a big issue of the war or the time.
- Battle locations.
- Leadership position in the army.
- Discharge location.
- Burial.
- One point for each field filled with a justifiable answer (an oral argument made to defend this).
- One additional point for presence of evidence; evidence consists of a quotation from the reading that supports the argument.

____ (14) Total

Figure 9.7.   Preparation rubric.

____ (1) Select a person and list this person as the title of the paper.
____ (9) In the first paragraph repeat the name of the person and determine what relationship or connections he has to you.
    ____ (1) Making a connection between the reader and a soldier.
    ____ (6) Each sentence in the paragraph supports the above outline.
    ____ (1) Proper citation.
    ____ (1) A quotation that supports the idea in the body of the paper.
    ____ (1 Bonus point) For using a primary source, including diaries, letters, or public records
    ____ (3 Bonus Points) For including personal anecdotes, details, or stories in the format of three sentences: statement, quotation, and why

Figure 9.8.   Civil War person from the past rubric.

periods in the lives of their soldiers including troop musterings, battles, discharges, and burials (Figure 9.7). Students sum up the individuals' experiences in a form that allows them to summarize and communicate their findings.

On the Fields of Gettysburg

Students used structured role-play to investigate the events at the site. They found a site where the participants from their hometown were located, and they followed those soldiers across all three days of the battle. Students role-played out history (Morris & Welch, 2000) at the site of the fighting on the first day of Gettysburg. They divided into two groups and picked up a hat to indicate whether they were on the side of the North or the South as they role-played the experience of the Iron Brigade. Students received parts, roles, and quotations then they role-played the fighting on Seminary Ridge and around the Railroad Cut, and role-played the death of Reynolds, the capture of Archer, the events at the rail and dirt barricade near the seminary, and the resulting obliteration of the Iron Brigade.

Students performed a historic reenactment using the many cannons and limbers located on the battlefield. At the Peach Orchard, students pretended to load and fire artillery in the face of cavalry and infantry charges. Students saw copies of ordinance (http://www.aaamunitions.com), artillery supplies (http://milkcreek.com/shop/index.php), and diagrams of tools before getting the names, numbers, and job descriptions of their positions around the gun (National Civil War Association, 2005). Each student had a role that the student first practiced aloud and then silently. Once the students knew how to load and operate the cannon, the other students, who acted as cavalry and infantry, charged the battery. If the infantry or cavalry touched the cannon before the artillery crew said "Boom," the infantry and cavalry won. If the artillery crew said "Boom," indicating that they had completed the loading process before the infantry and cavalry reached them, the artillery won.

Students next got to enact a play adapted from Freeman (1995). The section about the Peach Orchard lends itself to becoming a play based on the actual words and documents written by the original players with little effort (Morris & Welch, 2000). Students find plays exciting and teachers can adapt plays for students from primary or secondary sources. Primary sources are particularly good ways to get material for plays because the soldiers can then speak for themselves. The teacher looks for sections of dialogue or fast-paced action with many characters and limits the role of the narrator so that as many people as possible get to work with the site. It is helpful to provide as many roles as possible to get everyone into the action. The actions of the characters must drive the play forward. Everyone knows how it will end, but how they struggled to accomplish the known result creates suspense in the play.

Students became part of Hood's Division when they ran from Devil's Den through the Slaughter Pen to the Valley of Death. Students got to experience the terrain, see the sites, and hear the words of the Civil War participants. The geography of the site formed a natural obstacle course for the students. At various positions along the way, the students viewed Civil War photos (http://memory.loc.gov/ammem/cwphtml/cwphome .html) showing the site then, quotation cards telling what happened there, and what the men who fought actually said at this site. Students needed to feel how big the space was, how tiring it was, and how the elements conspired to slow their advance by running across the site.

Students discovered the thoughts, feelings, hopes, and anguishes of people long silent but now communicated across time. They got an idea of how ideal the ground was for defense. They also understood how hard it was for the soldiers to fight in this area, the scope of the fighting, and what the area looked like then. At Little Round Top students made the Confederate charge up the hill; once they got to the top they performed a play combining role-playing, scripted drama, and teacher narrative. Students went to the site where the men from Maine became the end of the Union line and Chamberlain made them bend on the end of the line before pin-wheeling down the hill in a bayonet charge. Students got to stumble across the same ground making the same charge as the Maine men did on Little Round Top. The students discovered how they picked up speed and overcame inertia as they moved down the slope.

Students found out about a character that grew up in their community, fought at Gettysburg, returned to their community, and died there. At home students got to see where he lived, worked, left for the war, and died. On Meade's right flank students encountered a first-person presentation from the Iron Brigade for the last time. Students used maps, historic photos, and North and South quotation cards to tell the story. Students saw where the character spent the rest of the battle of Gettysburg and what happened to him at this site. Oftentimes historians forget the event at this site even though fierce fighting occurred here. The soldier's personal narrative helped the students see the end of the battle as he left the site to follow the Army of the Potomac and continued to stalk Lee.

Students started at the southern position of Pickett's Charge, where they saw photos of leaders such as Mead, Hancock, Lee, Longstreet, and Pickett. Next, they got to see color transparency overlays on maps of the site with arrows showing beginning positions, movement, and ending positions. Students walked from the Lee statue to the grove of trees and back. At the grove of trees each student drew a straw to figure the odds of whether he or she made it back safely or became a casualty—killed, captured, or wounded. Students read quotations from soldiers written on cards and produced photos and art showing the action.

When students got to the site of the Gettysburg Address in the Gettysburg National Cemetery, the teacher presented a ten-minute lecture about the plan of the cemetery with historic photos of the event. Students saw what the crowd, parade, and platform looked like at the delivery of the Gettysburg Address. Next, students performed a choral reading of the Gettysburg Address in which students read aloud and heard the words spoken long ago on this site. Students pretended to give the Gettysburg

Address, while hearing it at the same time. The students became part of the experience, and students again broke the passive mold and interacted with one another at the historical site.

Students were placed into groups of four in order to pool their information about the Civil War soldiers they had researched. Students gathered information such as fliers, pictures, notes, quotations, programs, exhibits, maps, and books for the Civil War PowerPoint program from the battlefield Visitors' Center. They also gathered resources for the group project while on-site including primary sources, Web sites, music, and artifacts. They found other people who were like their characters, people whom their characters would have met, places where their characters went, what their characters' units did, and who served as their command-

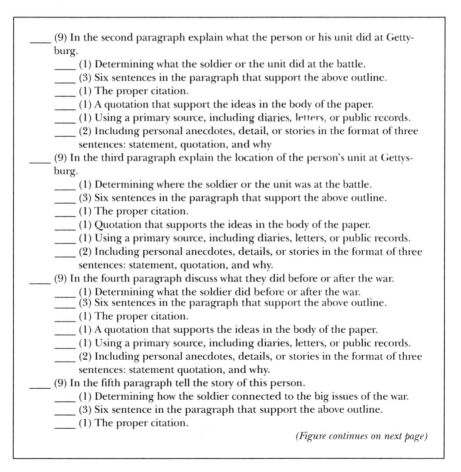

_____ (9) In the second paragraph explain what the person or his unit did at Gettysburg.
_____ (1) Determining what the soldier or the unit did at the battle.
_____ (3) Six sentences in the paragraph that support the above outline.
_____ (1) The proper citation.
_____ (1) A quotation that support the ideas in the body of the paper.
_____ (1) Using a primary source, including diaries, letters, or public records.
_____ (2) Including personal anecdotes, detail, or stories in the format of three sentences: statement, quotation, and why
_____ (9) In the third paragraph explain the location of the person's unit at Gettysburg.
_____ (1) Determining where the soldier or the unit was at the battle.
_____ (3) Six sentences in the paragraph that support the above outline.
_____ (1) The proper citation.
_____ (1) Quotation that supports the ideas in the body of the paper.
_____ (1) Using a primary source, including diaries, letters, or public records.
_____ (2) Including personal anecdotes, details, or stories in the format of three sentences: statement, quotation, and why.
_____ (9) In the fourth paragraph discuss what they did before or after the war.
_____ (1) Determining what the soldier did before or after the war.
_____ (3) Six sentences in the paragraph that support the above outline.
_____ (1) The proper citation.
_____ (1) A quotation that supports the ideas in the body of the paper.
_____ (1) Using a primary source, including diaries, letters, or public records.
_____ (2) Including personal anecdotes, details, or stories in the format of three sentences: statement quotation, and why.
_____ (9) In the fifth paragraph tell the story of this person.
_____ (1) Determining how the soldier connected to the big issues of the war.
_____ (3) Six sentence in the paragraph that support the above outline.
_____ (1) The proper citation.

(Figure continues on next page)

Figure 9.9.   Research project rubric.

_____ (1) A quotation that supports the idea in the body of the paper.
_____ (1) Using a primary source including diaries, letters, or public records.
_____ (2) Including personal anecdotes, details, or stories in the format of three sentence: statement, quotation, and why.
_____ (9) Make a map of the person's life.
_____ (2) Labeling at least three sites connected with the soldier.
_____ (2) An additional site (1) labeled and documented (1) on the map.
_____ (1) Providing documentation for each site proving the solder was there.
_____ (3) Presentation:
_____ (1) Uses clear lettering
_____ (1) Uses color
_____ (1) Easy to read and understand
_____ (54) Total

Figure 9.9.   (Continued).

ers. They compiled all of this information to create a program in which they describe how four people came together at one time on the field of Gettysburg (Figure 9.9).

After the Trip

Students got together in groups to create a Civil War PowerPoint program using the information from the presentation about a Civil War person. The group members formed a script using the information gathered from the trip and their research on their individuals before scanning in original photos, photos from today, historic art, contemporary art, and maps. Students set captions or headings for the images, found appropriate background music for the program, and read their script onto tape. The students reported their experiences and research thus creating an instructional tool for other members of the class. Multiple class members can create a body of knowledge to help future students with their pooled research (Figure 9.10).

Students had an opportunity to evaluate their own participation as well as that of the other group members in the experience (Figure 9.11). Students used criteria on a rubric, evaluated themselves, and evaluated others on the group project. They worked together, used technology, and engaged in historical research. The students produced products that communicated their results with the audience in tangible ways. Students shared products with other audiences beyond their school community, such as service clubs and historic roundtables.

```
____ (4) All group members represent their individual report information
____ (4) Bibliography
____ (3) Clear beginning, middle, and conclusion to the script
____ (4) Connect the individual to major events, themes, or ideas from the time
____ (4) Develop a main point in the script
____ (1) Include contemporary art
____ (1) Include historic art
____ (1) Include a contemporary photo/picture
____ (1) Include historic photography
____ (2) Include a map
____ (4) Include information from each group member's trip notes
____ (1) Use captions to tell their story
____ (1) Use music from the time
____ (31) Total
```

Figure 9.10.   Civil War PowerPoint program assignment.

In the Power Point peer group evaluation, students rank the members of their group and themselves numerically from 5: Excellent, 4: Above Average, 3: Satisfactory, 2: Below Average, to 1: No Contribution. The example scoring guide includes name, a place for a numerical score, and a place to enumerate the contribution made to the group. Of course, other lines could enlarge it to accommodate the size of the group needed.

Name: Numeric Score (1-2-3-4-5)

My contributions were:

Name: Numeric Score (1-2-3-4-5)

What they contributed:

Figure 9.11.   PowerPoint peer group evaluation.

FINAL THOUGHTS

After debriefing from the trip, the students concluded their study by examining the cost of the war and its lingering horror. The students had an opportunity to select content that was important to them. Students also encountered many of the experiences in a playful manner; even though the grim content was cheerless, the students had opportunities that appeared felicitous and engaging. Because of the playful spirit, students had an opportunity to select the additional material that they wished to learn. Teachers need experience planning and executing study travel experiences that help students interact with content (Figures 9.12 and 9.13). In addition teachers need to learn to assess students based on the products they produce in their field research. Teachers also need to learn to help students engage in playful experiences in which they have choices about what they learn. Through these multiple and varied experiences, the teacher can observe how the student fully engages with the site and the content as well as being stimulated to think through this process of playful exploration.

When students learn about the Civil War, they witness the military cost of a political revolution and see the human face of suffering, death, and misery in one day of fighting. Students find the ideas of liberation, equality, and freedom in balance with opportunity cost. When students travel, they focus on the interaction between groups of students and the learning process. Teachers value student travel experiences because they can work with students to explore content in depth. The teacher selected this battle because of the political implications associated with the military event acted upon the field. In traveling teacher and students must work toward coming together for the common good in making their study a success. Teachers participating in these types of experiences witness connections between classrooms and cultural institutions. Moreover, they witness examples of student groups forming affinity with cultural institutions; student voices both reflect and define the interest of their group. In the type of historical context discussed in this chapter, instructors have an example of extreme controversy and ineffectual response to public controversy resulting in a failure of democracy. Teachers find opportunities to teach about controversial issues, and instructors can also help students see the radical changes unleashed by armed struggle rather than by deliberation (Figure 9.13).

Sunday
Nashville, TN
3:00 – 4:30 p.m.   Check in
4:30 p.m.   Introductions
        Assignment
        Schedule
        Trip Jobs
5:30 p.m.   *Dinner $10.00*
6:00 p.m.   Tennessee Campaigns
        Maps
        Readings
7:00 p.m.   *Pool time 615-259-6314 city pools*
10:00 p.m.   On floor
10:15 p.m.   In room
10:30 p.m.   Quiet hours

Monday
6:00 a.m.   Wake up
6:30 a.m.   *Breakfast*
7:00 a.m.   *Bus departs*
8:00 a.m.   Ft. Donaldson National Battlefield Visitor Center exhibits and
        video (931-232-5706)
8:30 a.m.   Battlefield tour with ranger
        Artifacts
        Artillery
        Dover Hotel
        Supply Fort
11:00 a.m.   Depart
11:30 a.m.   Lunch McDonald's $7.00
12:30 p.m.   Travel to Ft. Henry
1:00 p.m.   Depart Ft. Henry site
2:30 p.m.   *Jefferson Davis*
3:00 p.m.   Depart
4:00 p.m.   *South Union*
5:00 p.m.   Depart
6:30 p.m.   *Dinner*
7:30 p.m.   Depart
8:00 p.m.   *Nashville Now*
9:00 p.m.   Depart
10:00 p.m.   On floor
10:15 p.m.   In room
10:30 p.m.   Quiet hours

Tuesday
6:00 a.m.   Wake up
6:30 a.m.   *Breakfast*
7:00 a.m.   Bus departs
8:30 a.m.   Shiloh National Military Park Visitor Center video and museum
        (731-689-5275)
9:30 a.m.   Battlefield tour
11:00 a.m.   *Ranger program*
12:00 p.m.   Depart for Corinth

(Figure continues on next page)

Figure 9.12.   Corinth to Chickamauga.

12:30 p.m.	*Lunch fast food*
1:30 p.m.	Depart
2:00 p.m.	Corinth Civil War Visitor's Center
2:30 p.m.	Depart
3:00 p.m.	Curlee House $2.50 adults $1.50 students (662-287-9501)
4:00 p.m.	Depart
4:30 p.m.	Northeast Mississippi Museum
5:00 p.m.	Depart
5:30 p.m.	Battlefield Tour
	Battery F
	Battery Robinett
	Civil War Earthworks
	Corinth National Cemetery
7:00 p.m.	Depart
7:30 p.m.	*Dinner in Corinth $15.00*
8:30 p.m.	Depart
10:00 p.m.	Arrive and on floor
10:15 p.m.	In room
10:30 p.m.	Quiet hours

Wednesday

6:00 a.m.	Wake up
6:30 a.m.	*Breakfast*
7:00 a.m.	Bus departs
10:00 a.m.	Chickamauga National Military Park Visitor Center Exhibit and Video *$3.00*
11:00 a.m.	*Sack Lunch*
11:30 a.m.	Ranger Tour
12:30 p.m.	Depart for Chattanooga
1:00 p.m.	*Battles for Chattanooga*
1:30 p.m.	Depart
2:00 p.m.	*Point Park Visitor Center painting, exhibits, video, and ranger walk* (423-821-7786 Anton)
3:00 p.m.	Depart
3:30 p.m.	*Cravens House*
4:00 p.m.	Depart
4:30 p.m.	*Missionary Ridge Program* *(meet at Point Park)*
6:30 p.m.	Depart
7:00 p.m.	*Dinner*
8:00 p.m.	Depart
8:30 p.m.	*Check in*
9:00 p.m.	*Pool Time*
10:00 p.m.	On floor
10:15 p.m.	In room
10:30 p.m.	Quiet hours

Thursday

6:00 a.m.	Wake up
6:30 a.m.	*Breakfast*
7:00 a.m.	Bus departs

(Figure continues on next page)

Figure 9.12.   (Continued).

8:00 a.m.	Stones River National Battlefield Visitor Center media program and museum
9:00 a.m.	Battlefield tour with four stops including Stones River National Cemetery
10:00 a.m.	*Ranger walk*
11:00 a.m.	Two non-contiguous sites
11:30 a.m.	Depart
12:00 p.m.	*Lunch fast food $7.00*
1:00 p.m.	Depart for Franklin
1:30 p.m.	The Carter House video and guided tour $4.00 students
2:30 p.m.	Depart
3:00 p.m.	Carnton Plantation $3.25 students
4:00 p.m.	Confederate Cemetery
5:00 p.m.	Depart
5:30 p.m.	*Pizza $9.00*
6:30 p.m.	Depart
7:00 p.m.	*Ice skating*
10:30 p.m.	*On floor*
10:45 p.m.	In room
11:00 p.m.	Quiet hours

Friday

7:00 a.m.	Wake up
7:30 a.m.	*Breakfast $6.00*
8:00 a.m.	Bus departs
9:00 a.m.	Tennessee State Capitol
9:30 a.m.	Depart
10:00 a.m.	Traveler's Rest and the Battle of Peach Orchard Hill $6.00 per person
11:30 a.m.	Depart
12:00 p.m.	*Lunch $8.00*
1:00 p.m.	Depart
1:30 p.m.	Tennessee State Museum
2:30 p.m.	Depart
3:00 p.m.	*Pool time*
5:30 p.m.	Dress for dinner
6:00 p.m.	Depart
6:30 p.m.	*Dinner*
7:30 p.m.	Depart
8:00 p.m.	*Play*
10:15 p.m.	Depart
10:30 p.m.	On floor
10:45 p.m.	In room
11:00 p.m.	Quiet hours

Saturday

6:00 a.m.	Wake up
6:30 a.m.	Pack
7:30 a.m.	*Breakfast $6.00*
9:00 – 10:00 a.m.	Check out

Figure 9.12. (Continued).

Monday

7:30 a.m.	Depart
10:00 a.m.	*South Union*
11:00 a.m.	Depart
12:00 p.m.	*Lunch McDonald's $7.00*
12:30 p.m.	Depart
1:00 p.m.	*Ft. Donaldson National Battlefield Visitor Center exhibits and video (931-232-5706)*
1:30 p.m.	*Battlefield tour with ranger*
	Artifacts
	Artillery
	Dover Hotel
	Supply Fort
4:30 p.m.	*Depart*
5:30 p.m.	Travel to Ft. Henry
6:00 p.m.	Depart Ft. Henry site for Nashville, TN
7:30 p.m.	*Dinner*
8:30 p.m.	Depart
9:00 p.m.	*Check in $25 per person per night*
	Free Time
10:00 p.m.	On floor
10:15 p.m.	In room
10:30 p.m.	Quiet hours

Tuesday

6:00 a.m.	Wake up
6:30 a.m.	*Breakfast*
7:00 a.m.	Bus departs
11:00 a.m.	*Tupelo National Battlefield Site*
11:30 a.m.	Depart
12:00 p.m.	*Lunch*
12:30 p.m.	Depart
1:00 p.m.	*Brice's Crossroads National Battlefield Site*
1:30 p.m.	Depart
2:30 p.m.	*Corinth Civil War Visitor's Center*
3:00 p.m.	Depart
3:30 p.m.	*Curlee House $2.50 adults $1.50 students (662-287-9501)*
4:30 p.m.	Depart
5:00 p.m.	*Northeast Mississippi Museum*
5:30 p.m.	Depart
6:00 p.m.	Dinner $15.00
7:00 p.m.	Depart
7:30 p.m.	Battlefield Tour
	Battery F
	Battery Robinett
	Civil War Earthworks
	Corinth National Cemetery
8:30 p.m	*Check in*
	Pool Time
10:15 p.m.	In room
10:30 p.m.	Quiet hours

(Figure continues on next page)

Figure 9.13.   Tupelo to Chickamauga.

Wednesday

6:00 a.m.	Wake up
6:30 a.m.	*Breakfast*
7:00 a.m.	Walking tour of Corinth
7:30 a.m.	Bus departs
8:00 a.m.	*Shiloh National Military Park Visitor Center video and museum (731-689-5275)*
9:00 a.m.	Battlefield tour
10:00 a.m.	*Ranger program*
11:00 a.m.	*Ranger program*
12:00 p.m.	Depart
12:30 p.m.	*Lunch*
1:00 p.m.	Depart
5:30 p.m.	*Check in*
6:00 p.m.	Depart
6:30 p.m.	*Dinner*
7:30 p.m.	Depart
8:30 p.m.	*Play*
10:30 p.m.	Depart
11:00 p.m.	On floor, in room, and quiet hours

Thursday

6:00 a.m.	Wake up
6:30 a.m.	*Breakfast*
7:00 a.m.	Bus departs
8:00 a.m.	*Spring Hill, Tennessee Aggra Ree Home*
9:00 a.m.	Depart
10:00 a.m.	*The Carter House video and guided tour $4.00 students*
11:00 a.m.	Depart
11:30 a.m.	*Lunch $7.00*
12:00 p.m.	Depart
12:30 p.m.	*Carnton Plantation $3.25 students*
1:30 p.m.	*Confederate Cemetery*
2:30 p.m.	Depart
3:30 p.m.	*Traveler's Rest and the Battle of Peach Orchard Hill $6.00 per person*
5:00 p.m.	Depart
5:30 p.m.	*Dinner*
6:30 p.m.	Depart
7:00 p.m.	*Pool time*
8:00 p.m.	*Meeting*
9:00 p.m.	*Pool time*
10:00 p.m.	On floor
10:15 p.m.	In room
10:30 p.m.	Quiet hours

Friday

6:00 a.m.	Wake up
6:30 a.m.	*Breakfast*
7:00 a.m.	Depart
8:00 a.m.	Stones River National Battlefield Visitor Center
	Media program
	Museum

(Figure continues on next page)

Figure 9.13. (Continued).

9:00 a.m.	Battlefield tour with four stops including Stones River National Cemetery
10:00 a.m.	*Ranger walk*
11:00 a.m.	Two non-contiguous sites
11:30 a.m.	Depart
12:00 a.m.	*Lunch*
12:30 p.m.	Depart
2:30 p.m.	*Point Park Visitor Center painting, exhibits, video, and ranger walk (423-821-7786 Anton)*
3:00 p.m.	Depart
3:30 p.m.	*Cravens House*
4:00 p.m.	Depart
4:30 p.m.	*Battles for Chattanooga*
5:00 p.m.	Depart
5:30 p.m.	*Missionary Ridge Program (meet at Point Park)*
7:30 p.m.	Depart
8:00 p.m.	Dinner
9:00 p.m.	Depart
9:30 p.m.	*Check in*
10:00 p.m.	On floor
10:15 p.m.	In room
10:30 p.m.	Quiet hours
Saturday	
6:00 a.m.	Wake up
6:30 a.m.	Breakfast
7:00 a.m.	Depart
8:00 a.m.	*Chickamauga National Military Park Visitor Center* Exhibit Video $3.00
9:00 a.m.	*Ranger Tour*
10:00 a.m.	Depart
12:30 p.m.	*Lunch*
1:00 p.m.	Depart
1:30 p.m.	*Confederate Memorial Hall*
2:30 p.m.	Depart
5:30 p.m.	*Dinner*
6:30 p.m.	Depart
7:00 p.m.	*Check in*
7:30 p.m.	Depart
8:00 p.m.	*Performance*
10:00 p.m.	Depart
10:30 p.m.	On floor, in room, and quiet hours
Sunday	
6:00 a.m.	Wake up
6:30 a.m.	Breakfast
7:00 a.m.	Bus departs
8:00 a.m.	*Perryville State Historic Site*
8:30 a.m.	*Museum*
9:00 a.m.	Depart
12:00 p.m.	*Return Home*

Figure 9.13. (Continued).

II.	Time, continuity, and change
III.	People, places, and environments
V.	Individuals, groups, and institutions
VI.	Power, authority, and governance
VIII.	Science, technology, and society

Figure 9.14.   NCSS (1994) national standards.

CHAPTER 10

SHARING A
CROSS-CULTURAL EXCHANGE

INTRODUCTION

The members of a self-contained, gifted, fourth-grade class included the study of the Amish community in their social studies curriculum. This is not unusual in areas with large Amish and Mennonite populations, but when an Amish family invited this class of fourth-grade students to visit their farm for a weekend of field-based experience, genuine learning occurred. The Mueller family[1] lived on a farm in an area of the state with a large Amish population. The Amish follow the Anabaptist religious tradition as interpreted by Jacob Amman. The students traveled three hours from their school to the Mueller farm. The English[2] elementary students had a cross-cultural experience in which they interacted with the Amish students of the same grade and age. Very early one Friday morning in spring the English students left their school, immersed themselves in a foreign culture (NCSS, 1994) (Figure 10.1) for two complete days, and returned to their own school on Saturday evening.

BACKGROUND

The Amish are a group that has remained distinct from the common culture for many generations. Their plain dress and unique transportation make them visually distinctive, and they view separation as a calling from

The Field Trip Book: Study Travel Experiences in Social Studies
pp. 159–182
Copyright © 2010 by Information Age Publishing
All rights of reproduction in any form reserved.

I.   Culture
II.   Time, continuity, and change
III.   People, places, and environments
IV.   Individual development and identity
I.   Production, distribution, and consumption
II.   Science, technology, and society

Figure 10.1.   NCSS (1994) national standards.

God based on biblical texts such as "Be not conformed to this world" (Romans 12:2) and "wherefore come out from among them and be ye separate, saith the Lord" (2 Corinthians 6:17) (Kraybill, 1994). Their religious beliefs cause them to reject secondary education, marriage to outsiders, mass media, and electricity. This religious group has received national attention in the popular media for its views, and at times the lifestyle of the Amish puts them in conflict with their non-Amish neighbors, especially when automobile and buggy traffic accidents occur. Often elementary students have seen the Amish through the popular press or at shopping areas, but in this case, because of the teacher's mutual friends, a cross-cultural exchange occurred with this class of elementary students. An Amish family hosted the school children and gave them access to the Amish community including their school and various businesses.

While the Amish remain separate from the world, they cannot absolve themselves from it completely. The Amish have found themselves in conflict with their neighbors many times in the twentieth century over economic, educational, or legal entanglements. "The Amish have enjoyed the tolerance of a political order resting on a constitutional commitment to uphold religious liberty for cultural minorities" (Kraybill, 1994, p. 17; Arons, 1975; Rodgers, 1969). Their character and convictions stand as sentinels of church and state relations. Since they remain separate, the possibility exists for misunderstandings, myths, and falsehoods to cloud their neighbors' eyes. Their neighbors are not always gracious to the Amish in cases of fraud, rape, drug supply, and manslaughter in auto versus buggy road incidents.

While popular culture is filled with misconceptions about the Amish, from the romantic and violent film *Witness* (Feldman & Weir, 1985), to the vulgar music of Electric Amish (http://www.electricamish.com/), or the goofy film *For Richer or Poorer* (Baker & Spicer, 1998), social studies plays a role in correcting misconceptions and illustrates how our diverse neighbors fit into our community through religious acceptance. The popular media conveys misconceptions about the Amish community, while at the same time the Amish do not conduct a vigorous information campaign for obvious reasons (Luthy, 1994). Citizens in a democracy must exhibit some measure of religious toleration (de Tocqueville, 1945). Teaching about the Amish requires a historical context so that the students do not view the Amish as an inconvenient people, but rather view them as a people who draw on the strength of their community to solve problems. Students must transfer this cognitive information into action for democratic participation. Through social studies members of a school community learn important lessons in democratic thought and action.

The Amish reflect modern religious dissension in issues between church and state, individualism and community, as well as consumerism and contentment. The Amish come from a long line of individuals and groups who have exercised their rights of conscience. In America religious freedom grew from widely practiced religious toleration (Hammond, 1998). In their interactions the Amish have tended to present a reactionary position. At every point they have resisted being overwhelmed and absorbed by the majority culture and its demands (Evans, 1997). By rejecting these demands the Amish refuse to move into that culture, thereby preserving their way of life. While the Amish do not feel political or economic discrimination, they do not always enjoy easy relations with their neighbors. Their clothing makes them stand out immediately.

> Because of their distinctive customs, many people deride them for being different. They are often referred to as "backward" or "ignorant".... [A] group of outsiders hit and spat upon a group of Amish men, taking advantage of their nonviolent stance.... [L]ike other minorities, the Amish endure verbal affronts as well. (Locke, 1992, p. 35).

Great citizens cultivate humility when they face clashing values, for they balance their integrity with their respect for others (Carey, 2000). Great citizens do not need to force their views on others, nor do they respond with indifference. The founding fathers talked about the ideal representative as being disinterested or dispassionate, and their statesmanship is required of citizens in order for them to effectively demonstrate religious acceptance. Whether the issue is between church and state, individualism and community, or consumerism and simplicity, citizens need to deal effectively with the plurality. While the Amish may reflect modern religious dissension, they also provide all citizens with opportunities for religious toleration.

Around the world religious toleration is a key issue in maintaining peaceful communities. Another place where misunderstanding, myth, and falsehood have bred generations of violence is between the Jews and the Muslims in the Middle East. Wallach (2000) describes a program in which Arab and Israeli teenage students come together for three weeks of summer camp in Maine and reach an understanding with one another. Some of the results of the camp include the following: They meet "the enemy" as a human being; they become aware of their biased and incomplete knowledge of history; they learn an awareness of stereotypes and prejudice in each community; they learn to distinguish individuals within the nation of the "other side" and they become a community willing to help one another sustain their mission. In comparison the gifted students who visited the Amish were younger; there was a much shorter contact time; and the problem was not as deeply ingrained as that in the Middle East. Yet the encounter between the two groups of Middle Eastern young people—whose families have hated or at least had inadequate information about each other thus creating suspicion of one another for generations—and the encounter of the students with the Amish community had similar results. The prospect of friendship between people of feuding faiths provides hope for a peaceful future.

In a democracy citizens practice religious toleration even if those views, values, and beliefs are foreign, odious, or alien to the rest of the population. The constitution is very clear that government is to neither encourage nor discourage religious practice. Some religious groups are so distinctive in their customs and practices that they stand out in daily life. For people in these groups, their manifestations of differences make them stand open to hazing, misunderstanding, myth, and stereotype. Social educators need to look for ways to help students to understand the customs and practices of these people who are their neighbors in the community. Students from diverse homes are always learning, but they must become resourceful and confident learners (Boyer, 1995).

A citizen in a democracy needs to be able to solve the problems of the society (Rubin & Giarelli, 2007; Sehr, 1997; Engle & Ochoa, 1988). These problems may be conflicts between values, religions, or political philosophies. Students may learn to become democratic citizens by using a variety of methods from field trips to reflective inquiry. In reflective inquiry students move from questioning the familiar to questioning the unknown (Boyer, 1995). When students start learning about a topic in their classroom, they start by formulating questions. When they go on a field trip, they take their questions with them into a new and unknown place. Teachers use primary sources, discovery, and reading packets to help students formulate their own questions. In reflective inquiry students practice some of the skills they will use as an adult when they seek answers to their questions. When students tell their specific concerns, such planning moves the members of the school community to share and learn from unexpected moments of racial or culture tension (Dilg, 1999).

Where does a cross-cultural exchange fit into democratic education? In a democracy citizens live next to a variety of people of differing faiths and political thoughts. To create a democratic classroom requires including all students (Pearl & Knight, 1999). Democratic education is education bound to a vision of a hopeful future. Part of that future is the prospect of many people of different backgrounds and religions living in peace with one another. In a democracy parents, teachers, and members of the community come into conflict over multiple education issues relating to religion and philosophic outlook. Educational "issues of secular humanism, sex education, multiculturalism, and affirmative action" divide the population and parents of children in the public schools (Spring, 1997, p. 20). These issues provide grist for continuing abrasion between parents and members of the public who have differing religious and political views and agendas. Democratic education requires citizens to make compromises to ensure that they acquire knowledge, social skills, attitudes, cognitive competencies, and moral values (Pai & Adler, 2001). In a democracy society expects people to see each other as political equals regardless of religious affiliation. Each person is accorded the same rights and privileges to both freely practice and to not infringe upon the religious rights of their neighbors. Cross-cultural experiences do not necessarily result; many things can go wrong to mar the experience of the participants. Goncu (1999) explores the tension in cross-cultural experiences when the established methods containing a western bias are applied to a culturally diverse population. If the experience is merely a validation of the status quo, the results will be meager. Many religions hold the dream of peace as a virtue. Since the days of Rome, members of society have confronted pacifists. Citizens practice religious acceptance to ensure peace within the democratic community.

Students in elementary school learn about their past and the present reality of community life through experiences involving travel. Elementary students need to learn about social studies, while at the same time establishing meaningful connections with it (Brophy & VanSledright, 1997). The students know not only the place but also the people involved with the topic that they study; they get direct learning experiences and they draw conclusions from their firsthand experiences. The students establish human connections through human interactions in order to form personal connections to the past and the present. The students who visited the Amish community made connections based on their experiences with others in addition to their classroom study.

For the students to have connections required that they work within their community to explore another community. In order for students to learn about others in social studies requires a commitment to a basic democratic ethic (Goncu, 1999; Boyer, 1995); these students learned about democracy within their community (Goodman, 1992). Their classroom community made a commitment to this exploration. The students viewed the Amish community as a valuable part of the greater community that needed exploration to find common ground (Pai & Adler, 1997). With understanding of the broader community, the students grew in demo-cratic thought to see their self interest as including the Amish.

PRACTICE

Unlike many field trips that explore events, places, or sites, the purpose of this field trip was to meet a group of people and examine how they live (Cartwright, 2004; Cartwright, Aronson, Stacey, & Winbush, 2001). The Amish rarely open their homes, schools, or community to such an extent. While many opportunities for cross-cultural interactions are available for middle and high school students, very few such opportunities are avail-able for elementary school students. Students in a fourth-grade self-con-tained classroom went to an Amish school and traveled by horse and buggy to the Amish dry goods store, harness shop, horse breeding farm, auction barn, and saw mill. The students traded songs with the Amish in the evening, and they explored the farm, including the barns and other buildings (Rowell, Hickey, Gecsei & Klein, 2007). The class members, who were evenly divided by gender, reflected the population of a small liberal arts college town in the Midwest. This was Mrs. Grace's first year teach-ing, and she had inherited the project from the former teacher.

For a project such as this to work, there needs to be student interac-tions through both formal and informal events (Schur, 2007; Culling-ford, 2006). Students need common didactic adult and student exchanges such as formal experiences with both adults and students in situations such as in the school classrooms or the Amish harness shop. There also needs to be informal times when students could talk with one another. Informal times would include basketball games in the hayloft of the barn or common meals shared at long tables with benches. Through both formal and informal events, students learned about each other as they mingled.

Prior to Trip

The students spent a week at their school preparing for this enriching learning experience before spending two days visiting the Amish commu-nity and then returning to their school to debrief for a week. Pre-trip preparation provided students with multiple sources of information to educate students about Amish people. The students had these facts as they entered a foreign environment so that they would know what was important, what to look for, and what needed particular attention. These students then spent time as guests of an Amish family who shared their multiple-generation family farm.

Mrs. Grace prepared the English students prior to the trip by helping them learn more about the members of the Amish culture they would meet. She did this by providing the students with a variety of background experiences. Mrs. Grace helped students examine and compare sources of information. She also helped the students make connections between the present day and other topics, about which they had previously learned.

> [The Amish community] show[ed] them in real life some of the things we had learned about in ... [state] history, like the horse drawn plow, as close to real life pioneer living as you can get.... And that was probably the initial reason why this project was done. But other objectives I saw coming out of this was getting to know other people and realizing that they are just people not a lot different than ourselves. (Mrs. Grace, personal communication, August 6, 1998)

Mrs. Grace expected the students to interact with people from the Amish community as they lived together for a weekend. She expected her students to meet the Amish not as representatives of the whole group but as individuals who could share their lives and community with the students. Finally, she expected the students to make comparisons between their lives and that of the Amish as well as between the past and the present.

Mrs. Cummings, a retired fourth-grade teacher, came to visit for a day in character as Mrs. Grabel, one of her Amish neighbors. A first-person historical presentation helped the students to imagine what work she would do, how she organized her life, and what school would be like for her children (Morris, 2009). She used the first-person technique to help the students become familiar with daily life and understand how the community works. She encouraged the students to ask her questions. She also brought her quilts and talked about them; the students then tried their hands at quilting by creating their own squares from colored construction paper. Mrs. Grabel placed her character in context by holding a day of Amish school. She transformed the modern classroom into an Amish school by giving each student an Amish name, having them sit in rows on separate sides of the room, stand to recite their lessons, cipher, learn English and German, hold a spelling bee, memorize history, and recite geography. This gave students some idea of what to expect from Amish life; the students discussed the experiences of the day by debriefing before going home.

To prepare the elementary students for the trip their teacher, Mrs. Grace, served as a curriculum organizer. The teacher gathered a variety of publications from the popular press, and she sorted these into topical files; students and their partners got files to read and report on to the class. These files provided the students with additional information about the topic such as religious beliefs, past religious intolerance, and present day religious intolerance. The students covered a wide spectrum of family, business, community, personal, and religious characteristics with their reading and then reported their findings to the group. As students shared information, they learned about the other students' topics, too. They compared what they had learned with a video about the Amish and a number of books about the Amish as well as some artifacts.

Mrs. Grace helped students read *The Budget* (http://www.thebudget-newspaper.com/), the newspaper of the Amish community. Students used a data retrieval chart to identify facts and relate them to concepts focused on specific elements including: Advertisements, Auctions or Benefits, Baptisms, Church Services, Disaster and Responses, Farm Work, Frolics, Helping Others, Names, References to Horses and Buggies, School News, Size of Families, States Where Amish Live, and Weddings. The students gathered information from looking at concepts that they could compare to customs in their own community. The established criteria allowed students to compare their work with one another and to look at comparable information from their local newspaper. When students used *The Budget*, they got to construct their own ideas about concepts by using the evidence they found.

In the week before the trip the teacher increased the students' awareness of the Amish, their history, customs, and social organization. Students learned large amounts of information to prepare them for this experience (Noel, 2007; Noel & Colopy, 2006; Beglau, 2005). "Before the trip we just give them a background, so they kind of understand some of the things that they can see" (Mrs. Grace, personal communication). Mrs. Grace wanted to heighten the students' awareness so that they would see more in the experience and be able to interpret what they were seeing. Students started a *Know, Want to Know, Learned* chart in class on which they listed a wide variety of things that they knew about the Amish before going on the field trip (Figure 10.2). The students expressed their understanding about the Amish prior to the trip with the following facts:

> They believe in being plain, and not drawing attention to themselves. They usually have large families, and "different" names. They usually only have a few different last names. The Amish can't use electronics, but can use batteries. They ride in carriages. They have an Ordnum (a set of rules). They are

sort of like Mennonites. They can also use gas powered things. (Miriah, survey)

The students defined the Amish by what they are and are not allowed to do; they also defined the Amish by apparel and geography. The students briefly described the beliefs of the Amish, but at this point, there was little interpretation or evaluation by the students.

I know that they live mostly in Indiana, Illinois, Canada, Ohio, and Pennsylvania. They are Anabaptist and don't believe in progress. Married men grow beards, [and] women wear prayer coverings. They are mostly farmers, [and] they live in communities. They don't believe in using certain things like electricity and cars. (José, survey)

After the field trip the students' comments changed from lists of information to descriptors of experiences. The trip allowed students to study the Amish community in-depth, and the students' knowledge became deeper through their experience on the farm. Although the students had a great deal of background information, their early understanding involved simply repeating lists of facts.

On the Trip

Students started to write a journal with the help of guiding questions; each student wrote the first entry on the bus by responding to the following question: "What do you think will happen today?" Mrs. Grace did not limit the students to the topic, but gave them something to start their initial writing. The students accurately anticipated the occurrences over the weekend due to their preparation for the trip. Some of the students expressed some slight anxiety about the experience along with the elation of getting to go on the trip. "I feel good, yet I feel nervous. I think it will be fun, but it will be scary to visit another culture. What if they don't like me? How will I fit in with them" (Evan)? These students looked forward to a good experience, but they also wondered how things would work out between the two groups. They also worried slightly about being personally ostracized. "I hope the kids like us. I wonder if the kids will think we're weirdoes?" (Ann). Most of the students' writing focused, however, on what they expected or on the order of events.

When the English students arrived in the Amish community on Friday morning, they went immediately to the school and filed into the Amish schoolrooms. They entered the dark and absolutely quiet building, sat at the back, and listened to the students of a combined third- and fourth-grade class singing their music lesson and orally reading their lessons.

- What we know:
- Good food.
- Don't eat Cheetos, Fritos, or chips.
- Speak Pennsylvania Dutch, English, and German mix.
- Don't use electricity.
- Anabaptist.
- Bible-based lifestyle.
- Came in 1500s for religious freedom.
- Religion a branch of Christianity.
- Ordnum is a set of rules.
- Leader=Bishop.
- Use fuels, not electricity.
- No cars—horses and buggies.
- Horses and plows.
- Most are farmers or prefer to farm.
- Barn raising.
- Out houses.
- Old fashioned.
- Keep life like ancestors.
- Common people.
- Quilting bees.
- Pretty quilts.
- Get up early.
- Time spent busy with chores.
- Nothing flashy.
- Belief in being humble.
- Hide pride.
- Don't show many emotions.
- Quite bashful.
- Shunning.
- Use batteries.
- No phone in house.
- Very plain clothes.
- Prayer caps and bonnets.
- Aprons.
- Men bearded if married.
- One-room schools.
- School only until eighth grade.
- Live in northern and eastern Indiana or Parke and Davis Counties. (field notes)

Figure 10.2.   Student KWL chart.

When the students met one another, an opportunity for tension existed. "The first thing I recognized was their clothes. I felt sort of embarrassed because of what I was wearing. We lined up against the wall and the teacher introduced us. Then they sang a song for us. They sang a lot different than we do" (Andrew). In an interesting switch of perspective,

Andrew realized that in this community he was out of place and that realization created some anxiety, which the teacher quickly alleviated. In the first- and second-grade class the Amish students recited their numbers and letters in both English and German. "My group visited the first/second grade class room. We felt very awkward, but the teacher spoke to us and the class sang us a song" (Ann). This initial awkwardness passed quickly as the students started meeting the different classes. In the seventh- and eighth-grade class the Amish students stopped their geography lessons and the students from each group asked the other group questions. Students really do feel the disconcertion and disorientation of meeting a foreign culture and visiting an alien situation.

After seeing three of the four multiple-age classrooms, both groups had lunch in the third- and fourth-grade classroom. After a silent prayer at noon all the students produced a packed lunch to eat at their desks. When everyone finished eating, more silent prayer occurred before they dismissed for recess and all rushed out to play on the playground.

The Amish students invited the English students to join games of basketball, swings, softball, volleyball, Andy Over, Duck Duck Goose, and catch. The English girls taught the Amish girls how to make dandelion chains.

> The Amish girls hang back in the classroom while the Amish and English boys start two basketball games roughly divided by age. The swings are available so the English girls go over there. The Amish and English girls come together to play a game of volleyball and then move into the game of Andy Over before moving to Duck Duck Goose. Two softball games between the Amish and the English started, too—one for the girls and one for the boys. The only cross gender interaction on the playground all recess is a female teacher who acts as the pitcher in the boys' softball game. The English girls teach the Amish girls how to make dandelion chain necklaces. (field notes)

This was the first opportunity for students to mix in an unstructured situation. Though hesitant at first, the students very quickly moved into games that they played without interference from adults. They constructed their rules, enforced their rules, played under those rules, and mediated all disputes.

> We got to play basketball. The third [to] fourth [grade students] were the ones that took us on. We won two and lost two. We equals Joel and me. The rest of the boys played against the other three [and] four boys. They lost extremely badly. We played up to 20. They just played. When we heard about the Amish being rough I had a hard time believing it. But now, I realize that the Amish might be the future Michael O'Neals, a mixture between Michael Jordan and Shaqeal O'Neal! (Evan)

These English students got their first opportunity to interact with the Amish in this experience. When English and Amish students played basketball, they both thought that they were doing something that was a part of their culture, and they started to find similarities and differences between their cultures.

The Amish students regrouped for class after a fast trip to the outhouse and each group challenged the other to a spelling bee. The Amish were much less demonstrative and much more deliberative than their English counterparts, but neither side liked to lose when they got a word wrong. The Amish shared a snack of popcorn, chips, and pop with their English visitors and school dismissed for the weekend with students walking, driving a buggy, or riding a school bus home. The Amish hung around after school to play volleyball, catch, basketball, or to talk about books with the English students before the late bus picked them up. "After [school] we played basketball again. This time with two rough eighth graders" (Evan). Many students talked about the Amish students that they met. "We played a basketball game. The teams were an eighth grader named Dave with Joel and Evan and the other team was an eighth grader named Matt with me and Bob. We won big time" (José).

The English students traveled to three community businesses that make shipping pallets. The students watched the logs come into the mill, and they observed as the Amish used machines to saw the logs into pallets right before their eyes. "It was very loud. It is surprising how all of these humongous and noisy machines are run by diesel" (José). The Amish derived all of the energy provided for the mills from the unconventional power source of diesel as opposed to electricity. Students had neither thought of how the Amish interacted within the economy nor how the Amish could provide goods and services outside agricultural pursuits. One student saw all of the machinery and commented on the economic investment that it reflected. "It was a sawdust kingdom!" (Evan). The Amish try to be good stewards of natural resources; therefore the sawdust is marketed as mulch so that there is little waste.

> Then we went to three sawmills. The second and third sawmills were not in operation. The first sawmill was in operation. It was very ... loud. Some girls were working in there. They [wore] earmuff like thing[s] to protect their ears. I don't understand how they can breath[e] in there. The second saw mill was Mr. Mueller's.... [T]he third sawmill was not operation [sic] because it was brand new. At the sawmill we saw an icehouse. [It] was filled with ice chunks bigger than shoeboxes, but they weren't hollow. (Nicole)

One student described the physical sensations of being in a factory, and she also found the ice storage on the farm interesting. The industry of the

Amish and the fact that their community interacts with the economy intrigued the students.

Before leaving for the Muellers' farm, the students saw how the Amish packed the icehouse from floor to ceiling last winter with ice cut from a local lake. The whole family worked on the ice harvest project during the winter. "A girl we had met earlier at the school … [w]ell her and her brothers took us for buggy rides with her pony Jay. The girl's name was Naomi. She is very nice and in fifth grade" (Nan). At the same time that the English students explored the farm through more formal instruction they continued to build relations with their Amish peers. They met the Muellers' grandchildren and cousins at different farms and traveled with them between farms. At this time the Amish and the English started to lose their inhibitions toward one another.

Since the English students live in a small town, the farm was an adventure in itself. "Then the bus driver took us back to the Muellers' house. It is so beautiful and nice. The lawn was mowed, the house was clean, the whole farm was in great shape" (Nan). The most imposing feature of the farm was the great bank barn with a horse and buggy on the first floor and hay and a basketball court on the second floor; chickens and peacocks resided in an adjoining building as did more horses. The simple large white-sided farmhouse held both Mueller families with another adjacent living area for a dining room furniture and handicraft store. Three generations of Muellers lived in the great frame house; these included the grandparents (our hosts), their youngest son's family, and the grandchildren. One of the grandchildren, Naomi, showed the students the trampoline and where to find puppies in the haymow. Ten-year-old Nathan offered pony cart rides before starting a game of basketball in the hayloft with integrated teams of Amish and English children.

Prior to dinner the English students wrote in their journals to reflect upon the activities of the day up to that point responding to the prompt, "What did you do with the Amish children at recess?" When the students responded, they wrote about the order of the school day and their experiences with the Amish children. Students continued to respond in their journals throughout the next day. Students first made entries into this journal the next day before breakfast and then finished their journal entries on the bus as they returned to school.

All the Muellers' children came by buggy from their farms bringing food and assisting in preparing the meal of homemade bread and fresh butter, salad, noodles, mashed potatoes, gravy, grilled chicken, corn, Jell-O, and cinnamon buns. They brought all of the grandchildren, who then got to play with the English. The Mueller family started and ended each meal with prayer in German, and the women served the men, children, and English guests before eating and then clearing the table. The subtle lesson on religious toleration allowed students with many different beliefs to share a meal, play, and enjoy hospitality with people who might otherwise be viewed through eyes that only see diversity. The students easily saw the lesson of "out of many one" in this situation.

All of these experiences gave students opportunities to speak with one another; Rebecca explained the nature of the conversation with her new Amish friend and how they experienced the two days together.

> I really talked to Naomi a bunch because she was our age.... I kind of asked her about what she did on the days she was out of school, what she did in school, and what happened if they got in trouble at school. And what kind of things would happen, and if she's ever thought about us, the way we live.... We went and looked at her horses, and we rode on the buggy together. We really just stayed together. (Rebecca, individual interview)

Multiple grandchildren, nieces, and nephews provided plenty of children for the students to play with at every stop, and Rebecca had made a new friend by the end of the first day. Students and adults rode in buggies driven by the Amish children to other farms in order to formally learn about the community. At every Amish farm Amish children had a pony cart that they could use to give rides, and the Amish children also drove the buggies. Being allowed the responsibility of driving the buggies really impressed the non-Amish students. "They have just the same personalities as us, just different clothes. They do ride school buses to and from school. Amish kids can drive horse and buggies at age six or seven . . . . I had a lot of fun talking with the Amish kids" (Elmo, survey). Students found many similarities with their Amish peers despite the appearance of their dress and conveyance. Students also saw deep differences in how people organized their lives and how they found meaning in their lives. "I think that they have different values than us. Well, we value being on time and getting things done quickly so that we can do what we want to do, but they value being close to the earth and working, worshipping God, and spending time with their family" (Ann, focus group). The students compared their lives through conversations and experiences; they found what was meaningful to each group and they found friendship, too. These students found connections in their two-day adventure that they wished to continue in the future. "I wish I could stay a little longer and get to know everybody better" (Annitta, journal). Students felt included and wanted to further develop their relationships; they had a good experience and wanted to extend it. Students went from Amish business to business listening to the Amish talk about the work they do and their role in the community. Students had experiences in formal and informal situations together, and they could interact to learn about one another.

As dark fell Mrs. Mueller lit the naphthalene light, Amish boys got chairs for Amish adults who held toddlers squirming on their laps, and the Amish families gathered together to share traditional songs and hymns. As the evening closed in on the students they continued to build friendships with those outside their community. "I sat by and made friends with three Amish kids named Vernon, Aaron, and Elmer" (José, journal). The students shared their patriotic, camp, and folksongs with the Amish, too. As the Amish made preparations to go down the dark roads in their black buggies, the English students continued to ask the Amish how to pronounce words in German. English and Amish students shared this time together and enjoyed just being around each other.

The next morning before breakfast the students wrote in their journals, and after breakfast Mrs. Mueller took all of the students to her garden to talk about what she grows, how she tends it, and how she cans or "puts up" food to preserve her own produce for the winter. She does all this without electricity. The students stepped carefully over the hot caps for the tomatoes, parsley, peppermint, potatoes, red pepper, rhubarb, and sweet corn. She pointed out the tobacco dust for insects and the bird-house home for martins that eat mosquitoes. She talked about what she can make from her garden: chili sauce, salsa, ketchup, and pizza sauce from tomatoes; pickles and pickled red beets for her large extended family or church suppers; she no longer cans cabbage or peas. The English students dodged the still-wet low places and the manure used for garden fertilizer.

The English students piled into buggies for a tour of the community. Ruben, my driver, age eleven, had been holding the reins since he was five and could go to the next farm when he was seven. Our first stop was a horse barn. The students got to see the differences between various kinds of horses: Belgians, Arabian, American Saddle Breed, and Standard Breed. The English students learned that they needed to be observant of various things when visiting a farm. First, they discovered that it was necessary to watch where they stepped in a barn lot (especially after one student was not observant of where he stepped). Then Enid suffered from having a horse step on his foot, thus proving that just because horses are fascinating does not mean that one need not pay attention to what one is doing on a farm.

As we rode to the dry goods store, my new driver, thirteen-year-old Elmer, stopped for a train and got out to hold the horse to keep it from getting skittish around the powerful locomotive. Although the store seemed dim on a cloudy day compared to the flood of lights found in city shopping malls, the store interested the students with its modest space and abundance of goods. "The dry goods store had many cool things like little toys, candy bars, Amish hats, and Amish goods. We also bought fab-

ric for a class quilt there.... We stopped back at the dry goods store and
each bought an Amish straw hat" (José). The students selected fabric for a
nine-patch class quilt; they told Mrs. Mueller's sister, the proprietor, what
they wanted and paid for it. After the dry goods store the Amish took us
to a horse-breeding farm where the students got to watch the activity
around a blacksmith, the horses, a horse auction, and a saddle/harness
shop.

> Then he showed us how to put on and take off a horseshoe. He then acted
> like he was auctioning off the horse. Irene won at $10,000. Then for real he
> auctioned off a horseshoe that he [the horse] had worn and then sold it to
> Joel for a $1.50. Joel's dad gave it to him out of his allowance. (Bob)

Students got to see the auction procedure, hear the banter, and bid on
horses. All of this occurred with their new friends. "Naomi rode with me
everywhere" (Irene). The students made friends and spent a lot of time
running around with them. The trip showed that the Amish had significant responsibilities in the community. The students enjoyed each other
and wanted to spend time around each other.

Over lunch Nate and Enid talked to the Amish children, and Nate
spent time lightly teasing his Amish peers. When it was finally time to
leave, the students exchanged addresses with the Amish children. "Also
before I left I exchanged address[es] with Naomi!" (Irene). They waved
goodbye and thanked Mr. Mueller, Evan hugged the little Amish pre-
schoolers, and all waved goodbye to the Mueller family as the bus turned
down the lane towards home.

> I thought that the Amish wouldn't be quite as modern. They had a lot of the
> same things as we have. I never figured out why some women tie their
> prayer caps because little children have theirs tied, and students don't, most
> teachers do, and so do most mothers I saw. (Nicole)

When the English students left the Amish community, they took with
them information about the Amish, an appreciation for them as people,
and some continued asking questions about them. The students successfully experienced a cross-cultural exchange in an Amish world.

Post Trip

When the students returned to their school, they finished the *Learned*
section on the *KWL* chart. Then the students turned to their journals and
started to edit their writing for a memory book about their experience.
Each student got a copy of the memory book from the trip that contained

a copy of each student's story about the trip. Finally, with the assistance of Mrs. Grace, the students started a nine-patch quilt that served as a class souvenir from the trip. The students used symbol systems both in writing and in art to interpret their experience.

After the trip students changed orientations from looking at and listing facts about the Amish to discussing relationships. Students discussed the purpose, merits, and importance of the trip as well as the value in spending time with the Amish. Students talked about the people they met and the experiences they had together; students compared their lives with those of the Amish to find similarities and differences. They found many deep similarities with one another and a few differences; speech patterns tend to both draw people into groups and to exclude people from each other.

The Amish use very little of the world's oil supply; compared to other Americans they practically use no oil for transportation. Students were asked to consider the question, "Should everyone live as the Amish do?" The students wrote their answers to four sets of issues, giving examples and illustrating their consideration of local, regional, national, and global perspectives (Figure 10.3). Then they worked with partners to compare their responses with those of their peers (Figure 10.4). Finally, they conducted survey research to see if people agreed or disagreed with their ideas. In this way, the students determined whether their ideas were shared by members of the community.

Post-Trip Relationships

After the trip students talked about the Amish as people they knew and the relationships that they had experienced (Black, 2000). The teacher encouraged students to develop the idea of religious acceptance for people who live and act differently in the community and to develop an understanding of common interests between the two groups. "[The] objectives I saw coming out of this were getting to know other people and realizing that they are just people not a lot different than ourselves" (Mrs. Grace, personal communication, August 6, 1998). Mrs. Grace sought to foster cross-cultural understanding; she had a definite objective that she was trying to help the students accomplish through the field trip. When the students returned, they were able to define the importance of the project in their own words because they found it meaningful.

José: We could learn about other cultures.
Greg: And how to cope with other people in different situations.
Irene: And to respect other people.

Local
4   Listed a local issue, provided an example, and compared the life of the Amish to the student's life
3   Listed a local issue and provided an example
2   Listed a local issue
1   Did not list an issue

Regional
4   Listed a regional issue, provided an example, and compared the life of the Amish to the student's life
3   Listed a regional issue and provided an example
2   Listed a regional issue
1   Did not list an issue

National
4   Listed a national issue, provided an example, and compared the life of the Amish to the student's life
3   Listed a national issue and provided an example
2   Listed a national issue
1   Did not list an issue

Global
4   Listed a global issue, provided an example, and compared the life of the Amish to the student's life
3   Listed a global issue and provided an example
2   Listed a global issue
1   Did not list an issue

Interactions
4   Listed an interaction between four of the issues
3   Listed an interaction between three of the issues
2   Listed an interaction between two of the issues
1   Listed no interactions between the four issues

If everyone lived as the Amish, would this be good for all people? Would it be good for most of the people? Would it be good for some people?
4   Evaluated all three
3   Evaluated two of the above
2   Evaluated one of the above
1   No evaluation

Figure 10.3.   Memory book rubric.

Bob: And to learn to respect them more.
Evan: And not to laugh at them or make fun of them because they are different.
Greg: Just to cope with differences.
José: So we could realize that most other cultures aren't very different from us. (focus group)

The students reported increased acceptance, flexibility, and connection with the Amish. The students still saw many similarities to their Amish peers. "Most Amish are just like us. The children act like us and play the same games" (Alexia, survey). Students saw common interests in the types of amusements and diversions they experienced together as well as in how they reacted to those kinds of entertainment. They observed their peers in behaviors that they recognized in themselves, and Nan emphasized this point of commonality in the colloquial phrase she overheard. "I have learned that the Amish are not that different from us at all. They talk just about the same way we do. When I was at the Amish house I even heard someone say, 'Weird!'" (Nan, survey). Students identified speech as a way to include or exclude people, and they discovered that the Amish had speech in common with the English students. The language is a defining trait in an area where German speech patterns died out three generations ago and German folk customs have faded. While many of the students have German ancestors, strong German language and culture vanished in the early twentieth century and are not presently a part of the family traditions of the students. Students also saw contrasts when they compared their lives to those of the Amish: "Well, they know about us and we know about them a little, but they just don't dress like us. They don't communicate like us or anything like that" (Rebecca, individual interview). The students observed that the Amish knew more about the English than the English students knew about the Amish. Students saw similarities and differences in the Amish, but they also explained how meaningful these types of experiences were to their lives. Students talked about the Amish people that they knew after the trip and factual lists receded in importance.

Four students provided discrepant cases through expressions of their anxiety in the new situation. Meeting the Amish provided them with enough fear of the unknown that they wrote about it in their journals. "I feel good, yet I feel nervous. I think it will be scary to visit another culture. What if they don't like me? How will I fit in with them" (Evan, journal)? Fears about not fitting into the group, of rejection, or of looking different all haunted the minds of these four students before going into the Amish school. These students never spoke these comments; they only recorded them in their journals before meeting the Amish. After meeting the Amish all thoughts of alienation vanished as if they had never existed in the minds of the students.

REFLECTION

Students may have gone to visit the Amish with some preconceived ideas about the Amish and their culture. Their teacher, Mrs. Grace, commented about how students brought their ideas to the field trip and how the trip changed both the students and their ideas.

> I think they had some preconceptions. Still today [when] we talked there were some variations. They take two or three people in the class that they saw and then try to generalize it for the whole thing.... I think, to a small extent, they learn to look past the clothes. And I think some made some friends. (Mrs. Grace, personal communication, August 6, 1998)

Mrs. Grace mentioned the over-extension of the generalizations by the students, but she also noted that students saw personalities not just habits of dress. Nicole expected more isolation between her world and the world of the Amish; she found that they had more connections to the outside world than she originally imagined. "I thought that the Amish wouldn't be quite as modern. They had a lot of the same things as we have" (Nicole, journal). The students held views that the Amish were more isolated from the outside world and that they rejected all consumer goods as well. Similarly, Andrew had a specific type of public architecture in mind, and he had difficulty at first moving away from that perspective. "When we got to the school, I didn't think that it was the school house because it didn't look a thing like our school" (Andrew, journal). Consolidated schools as a model for education was not easily overcome in the minds of students accustomed to graded schools with indoor plumbing, copious administrators, and staff. The students had to either adjust or discard some of their preconceptions before acquiring information through the experiences that later helped them interpret the Amish culture.

One persistent myth that the students held was about the disposition of the Amish. The students thought that the Amish character would be as plain as the exterior ornamentation on their homes. The students thought that the Amish would be passive, placid, and perfectly peaceful; Elise predicted what she would find in the Amish community and compared it to her life. "I expect when we go to the Amish school, it will be a small school (nothing like ours). They will be studying very quietly (again nothing like us)" (Elise, journal). Students had very clear ideas about what they thought the life in the Amish community would be like. One of those ideas involved how their Amish peers would act when they met together. "Well, I thought they'd just be ... sitting there, ... but they told jokes and stuff.... They talked a lot more than I thought they would" (José, individual interview). José found that the idea that the Amish were a uniformly somber and colorless people was a myth. He was surprised when he encountered Amish boys who were only a little older than himself; instead of being dull, these Amish boys were as full of life as any of the English students' peers.

Anachronisms

Sometimes an anachronism startled the students, surprising them by something that they thought would not be a part of the Amish world or disconfirming what they thought they understood about the Amish. The access to consumer goods surprised the students; brand name shoes on the Amish seemed like a nod to consumerism that the English students would make.

> Well, I didn't think they'd be wearing shoes like Nikes, and I thought they would like be doing a whole bunch of chores.... They don't do as many chores as I thought they would, and I didn't think they'd play baseball. I knew they played basketball.... They ate pizza from Pizza Hut. I didn't think they'd like pizza. (José, individual interview)

The types and variety of food, some of which the students did not think would be available to the Amish, surprised the students. Food preferences and games also surprised the students by their presence; moreover, chores were surprisingly inconspicuous to the students.

> Evan: What surprised me the most w[erc] the lunches. I thought they'd be bringing these metal tin things with last night's chicken and mashed potatoes and stuff, but they had pizza and chips and Bologna sandwiches. And they had all kinds of stuff.
> Bob: That's what surprised me.
> Irene: They had ... lunch boxes ... just like the ones that we use.
> Greg: I saw this one girl had a Barbie one. (focus group)

Seeing lunch boxes similar to the ones the students themselves carried to school surprised the students; further, technology was present on an industrial scale. The students visited three mills, and they had difficulty understanding how the Amish could use technology to operate commercially viable businesses.

> Only one of these sawmills was running at the time, and it was very loud. It is surprising how one of those humongous and noisy machines [is] run by diesel. Next, we went to an icehouse. They get the ice from the pond and store it in there. I was amazed at how crystal clear the ice was. (José, journal)

The students noticed that even in the work place power was derived from a diesel engine rather than from electricity. Modern technology impressed students in a fully automated factory; however, the students also saw technology that was very simple at the icehouse. These anachronisms stood out and surprised the students so much that they stopped to question what they were seeing.

CONCLUSIONS

Elementary students experienced a cross-cultural exchange with their peers by spending two days in an old order Amish community. They experienced religious tolerance via this study travel experience. Students prepared for the experience in their classroom and debriefed from the experience after returning to their school. While on the trip, the students spoke with their Amish peers and Amish adults both on the farm and in the Amish community. After the trip the students referred to the Amish through the relationships and experiences they shared. The students interpreted how they learned about a foreign culture by examining preconceptions, exposing myths, and confronting anachronisms.

This case illustrates a curriculum that used social studies content to examine the experience of the students. Students confronted preconceptions and anachronisms during their study. When the students interacted with the Amish, their responses changed from recitation of lists of information to descriptions of events, experiences, and religious toleration. Students successfully learned about the traditions, culture, and lifestyle of a different group of people. The students' adroit interactions enabled them to socialize and communicate with their peers. Clearly, the implications for the students point to the fact that age ten is not too early for cross-cultural experiences. Indeed, this trip indicated the potential for greater use of these types of experiences with elementary-age students. Students should engage in developmentally appropriate experiences across the curriculum with multiple people and groups.

Teachers who engage in cross-cultural experiences need to exhibit a degree of commitment to the process of learning from study travel experiences to enable them to advocate effectively and gather support for their implementation. They must communicate effectively with administrators, parents, students, and community members and find resources that encourage the long-term support of this endeavor. Teachers need to relate content from classroom work to the field experiences. Highly structured experiences in pre- and post-field activities allow students more freedom in less structured study travel experiences. Teachers use the pre, field, and post experiences as evidence when working with the greater community to show how both students and the community benefit from the experience.

Several implications exist for the field of elementary social studies. Elementary social studies does not need to reserve cross-cultural experiences

Listen to another student explain his or her essay. List the points you agree with and the points with which you disagree. Tell why you agree or disagree.

4 Listed two (2) points he/she agreed with and listed two (2) points with which he/she disagreed, plus documented an opinion of each point

3 Listed one (1) point he/she agreed with and listed one (1) point with which he/she disagreed, plus documented an opinion of each point

2 Listed one (1) point he/she agreed with and listed one (1) point with which he/she disagreed

1 Listed no points

Compare your essay with the other student's essay. Which social issue would be the easiest to change? Which social issue would be the hardest to change? Explain why one would be the easiest and one would be the hardest.

4 Listed both social issues with justifications

3 Listed both social issues

2 Listed one social issue

1 Listed no social issues

Select a social issue from your or the other student's essay. Make a prediction on whether or not people would change. Ask twenty people over the age of eighteen (18) how likely it would be for them to change. Gather the data and the comments of the people surveyed.

4 Reported on the results of the data

3 Interviewed people to gather data and comments

2 Wrote a hypothesis

1 Gathered no data

Figure 10.4.   Follow-up assessment.

for middle- or high-school international travel experiences. Elementary social studies study travel experiences do not need to avoid the topic and experience of religious diversity. The field of elementary social studies does not need to limit study travel experiences to sites of historic, geographic, or economic importance, but can encounter people and their communities (Gutman, 1987). Elementary social studies should use structured study travel experiences frequently as an educational tool to help students learn more about themselves and how they relate to their neighbors.

This experience provides a potential model for elementary students interested in religious toleration, cross-cultural understanding, and prejudice reduction. Students live in a globally interconnected and multicultural world in which religious acceptance has broken down in places such as the Balkans, the Indian Subcontinent, Northern Ireland, the Middle East, and East Timor. In a democracy students need to practice religious toleration.

The Amish continue to be a part of today's world. With the growing Amish population, shrinking acreage available for farming, and the accompanying inflation of farmland prices increased contact between Amish and English will be more and more common.

The class members and the present and former teachers, principal, and curriculum supervisor contributed to and supported the in-depth teaching methods exhibited in this classroom. The support of these people directly contributed to the quality of the exciting educational experience that these students enjoyed. The school and the school district deserve credit for supporting the vision of religious toleration by encouraging individuals to take on this type of project with freedom and flexibility in the classroom, curriculum, and assessment.

ACKNOWLEDGMENT

An earlier draft of this manuscript was published as: Morris, R. V. (2003). Sharing a cross cultural exchange in an Amish world. *Canadian Social Studies, 38*(1). Available from http://www.quasar.ualberta.ca/css/Css_38_1/ARsharing_culture_amish.htm. Reprinted with permission.

NOTES

1. All names have been changed in this chapter.
2. The Amish refer to all non-Amish as the "English."

CHAPTER 11

SCIENCE, TECHNOLOGY, AND SOCIETY

INTRODUCTION

The integration of science and social studies is natural. Many of the global environmental issues the people of the world face today have implications for economic, geographic, and public policy issues. The lives of people changed by the application of technology is certainly history. What did it mean for an Islamic cleric to discover calculus or the ability to bisect an arc? No longer must a sailor hug the coast of the Arabian Sea, hoping against hope that a storm will not blow him off course to be lost forever in the vast ocean. Now by using calculus and the sun and the stars, he can determine his position on the globe and find his way to safety. The consideration of the implications of those technological changes certainly called for decision making on the part of citizens. What does it mean that the highest elevation in the county is the local landfill? Some of the implications of new technology on people in less industrially developed portions of the world call for consideration as to the ethical implications of applying or imposing the technology on different ethnic or regional groups. The resulting social justice considerations certainly merit discussion and further examination.

When students go into the field to determine how minerals are mined and forests are logged, they reach their own conclusions about the wis-

The Field Trip Book: Study Travel Experiences in Social Studies
pp. 183–203
Copyright © 2010 by Information Age Publishing

dom of using these products. They gather data in the field and bring it to the classroom where they can continue their analysis by using print and electronic resources. They discuss what they can do to protect the environment through legislation, cleanup efforts, lobbying, and personal use of resources. They discuss the roles of government, media, and consumer groups in guarding and harvesting natural resources. They also determine the merits of recycling, reducing, and reusing materials made from natural resources.

Students need to explore the closed areas of society in order to understand the impact of technology. Even among themselves, adults do not usually talk about where things go once they enter a sewer; yet this closed and hidden world offers many adventures in discussing public policy. When considering public policy issues, students need to make decisions while considering the needs of society to determine the associated costs of implementing a new technology. Technology is never free; there is always a cost to society in closing as well as opening opportunities for the people who use, do not use, or misuse the technology. When technology speeds up a process or eliminates people from an economic process, the result requires that persons must quickly learn a new way to create income or obtain food, or both.

As students explore the impact of technology, science, and the environment, their explorations can be adventures, challenges, and adversity. All three of these form the foundation of memory. Students find physical experience a form of challenge when they walk distances to explore the site or experience primitive conditions on the site. Students find natural landmarks an adversity when they investigate muddy and slippery slopes when the elements do not cooperate. Students find cultural resource adventures when they find unexpected ideas and surprising sites.

When planning a study travel experience, it is important to remember that natural features help students understand the characteristics of a place (Halocha, 2005; Heines, Piechura-Coulture, Roberts, & Roberts, 2003; Howat, 2007). The story of a place can tie into many aspects of social studies as well as tying individuals to a place or community. These types of adventures with individuals, community members, and natural features allow students to have direct experiences with geography and even get dirty at the bottom of a sinkhole. Students scramble over coal strip-mine spoil looking for evidence of fern leaf fossils in the rock, look for fossils exposed by a road cut, or visit a deep limestone quarry. Unusual adventures such as these really interest students because they like both adversity and challenge. Scrambling down and then back up a steep hill to get to and from the base of a notable rock outcropping, walking into a dark cave at a state park with a flashlight, taking a cave tour when the lights go out, and taking a boat ride into a water-filled cave are all far better adventures than media experiences because they are real. Students store this information as part of their memories of the community (B isbee, Kubina, & Birkenstock, 2000)—memories students later recount with other members of the community who shared the experience as a common bond or connection.

Some aspects of the past, such as the glaciations of an area, cannot be directly witnessed, making it difficult for students to experience these firsthand. The glaciers are gone, but the students use evidence of their presence to find out how glaciers changed the land. Students find out about glacial action by visiting nature preserves, which demonstrate the power of the glaciers to shape the land. If water or mud will be encountered, a change of footwear or boots is needed because student preparation is important in insuring successful and interactive adventures. If students will be in cold or wet weather or will take long walks, proper clothing and footgear is suggested; walking more than a mile especially in warm or cool conditions will seem long to suburban students, who are often not used to walking very far.

Natural landmarks have attracted and fascinated visitors for many years; they have a history all of their own (Aleixandre & Rodriguez, 2001). Meetings for peace or council many times occurred at definable geographic sites that can provide modern visitors space for picnic lunches. The distinctive characteristics of a place that attracted people in the past continue to attract people and will continue to attract people to the site.

Students prepare for the trip by examining newspaper stories about ground water from three different local papers. Students determine what impact agriculture, industry, and residences have on the quality of ground water. Students create a data retrieval chart with agricultural, industrial, and residential impacts listed on one axis and the dangers identified in the newspaper articles on the other axis. These might include runoff of pesticides, animal wastes, herbicides and fertilizers, dumping of heated water, metals, chemical wastes, detergents, sewer, and storm sewer water. They then fill in the cells created by the intersection of these ideas with information found from the newspaper stories.

Students then turn to print and electronic sources to determine what the effects of these pollutants are on humans. They interview environmental protection agents to determine what has been done to limit the dumping of these compounds in the past, and they interview university biologists to determine what more needs to be done. Students talk to a journalist to determine whether the laws are being enforced, and they talk to business people to determine how much it would cost to clean up these problems. Furthermore, they determine whether there is money to be made in the reclamation of discarded products by interviewing an environmental engineer connected with a landfill. Landfills demonstrate that recovering by-products of waste can generate income for the landfill company.

SCIENCE

State parks frequently contain cultural resources that may or may not be interpreted. Oftentimes park officials are conscious of the cultural resources in the park, but for a variety of reasons, including a lack of funds for interpretation or the attempt to protect the site from vandalism, they choose not to interpret a site. Other sites, however, definitely work to interpret their human history. Spring Mill State Park near Mitchell in south central Indiana has tree-covered land with springs, woods, sink holes, hills and valleys; the park also contains a restored village complete with gristmill. Students learn about commercial and social interactions between people from this site. A group of fifth-grade students in Indiana explored the restored pioneer village in Spring Mill State Park. This isolated pioneer village attempted to be self-sufficient, so students made a list of all of the products created within the village (Morrell, 2003; Wolff & Wirmer, 2009). Students went from site to site examining tools and the contents of houses, barns, outbuildings, shops, and businesses to see what pioneer residents created in this community. When they returned to school, they compiled a list of the goods and services created by the community. The students found evidence of some obvious activities such as grinding grain into meal and sawing logs into boards at the mills, but evidence of other kinds of work such as preserving green beans by drying them and making furniture was more difficult to perceive. In this example, the fifth-grade students realized that the commonwealth of the community depended on the contributions of individual members. Natural features found in the park such as the water flowing out of the cave that was harnessed for the grist and lumber mills have significant stories of human interactions. The story of the twentieth century is illustrated in the prior use of the park land as homestead, farm, business, or cemetery. How the park was preserved reflects the ideals of the Progressive Era, and the site of the old Civilian Conservation Corps (CCC) camps illustrates how the Great Depression caused Franklin Delano Roosevelt to create work programs that ameliorated the suffering among unemployed young men.

Students have experiences that remind them of the past in addition to having current experiences (Wolff & Wirmer, 2009; Polette, 2008; James, 2006; Schulte, 2005; Dils, 2000). Students spent the night at the site of an old 1930s CCC camp, and they hiked trails that were laid out in the area of the CCC camp. Even though the students did not stay in real CCC barracks nor live like the CCC, and the trails were neither laid out nor followed by the CCC, by doing similar things to what the CCC did, the students learned, remembered, and commemorated the CCC.

TECHNOLOGY

When traveling to a military base, a space center, or a local space memorial, the teacher produces a first-person presentation to help students learn about lives of the first seven astronauts. The presentation helps students understand the beginnings of the space age. Figure 11.1 is a sample content outline for a first-person program covering Gus Grissom's life, how a multi-stage rocket works, and the Mercury, Gemini, and Apollo projects. Because the teacher is traveling, costuming is kept to a minimum—an old white dinner jacket is the only item required. The outline provides a rough frame for organization and content notes, but elaboration and questions can be fielded from student questions during and after the presentation. The first-person presentation provides another way for students to get a reinforcing experience with the content of the site.

Institutions play an important role in providing services to individuals and groups in communities; one group of institutions that reflects the idea of the connection of science, technology, and environment is medical history museums. Although the scope of their collections interprets the story of how medicine became a science by gathering data, they also provide visitors with interpretation about medical education and mental health care. Students see human specimens and photographic records. Students learn how individuals created institutions to care for people, conducted research, and tried to improve patient care through scientific processes. The story of citizens looking to science to help with medical and psychological problems reflects the practice of institutions trying to create specialized communities to assist with social problems (Bruce & Lin, 2009; Jornell, 2009; Lim, 2008). Students also see that the government can create institutions or agencies to help solve community problems as well.

Many early-elementary-aged classes seem to take field trips to working farms during the course of the year; they look at the animals and plants and find out where the food supply starts. It is a great place to start talking about all of the steps that our food goes through before it appears on our table. A farm is a great place to talk about soil and conservation, suburban sprawl taking over farmland, the economics of farming, and the future of farming. Even the ubiquitous trip to the farm can help students

I. "How does a multiple stage Redstone rocket work"?
    A. Three stages
    B. Nose cone
        1. One person in the tip
        2. Lift off
            a. Shaking
            b. All the rides at an amusement park put together
            c. Pressed into the seat
    C. Each stage falls into the sea
    D. Heat shield
        1. Red hot
            a. Hot gasses glow past window
            b. Hot inside
    E. Parachutes deploy
    F. Capsule splash down in the water of the ocean
    G. Flotation balloons inflate
    H. Capsule picked up by helicopter
        1. Dropped on the aircraft carrier deck
II. Background of Gus Grissom
    A. Born in 1926
    B. Mitchell Public School education
    C. Waterwheel in Spring Mill fascinated him at an early age
III. Flying
    A. He sold his gun for his first airplane ride.
    B. In WWII he was a fighter pilot.
    C. He was a Purdue graduate in aeronautical engineering
    D. In Korea he was a fighter pilot.
    E. After the war, he became a test pilot.
IV. Project Mercury
    A. Original seven astronauts
    B. Purpose: Put man in space and return him safely
    C. Fifteen-minute flight
    D. Hatch
    E. Exploding bolts
    F. Nearly sank in the ocean
V. Gemini Project
    A. Twins: Two people in the capsule
    B. Purpose: Dock in space
    C. Meet in space
    D. Three sub orbits
    E. Unsinkable Molly Brown
VI. Apollo I
    A. Purpose: First man on moon
    B. Oxygen flash fire on the launching pad

Figure 11.1.   Gus Grissom first-person presentation outline.

see the connections between science, technology, and environment in their own world. As students take field trips, they think about issues of sustainability and how they work a planet that is green when they are adults (Knapp & Barrie, 2001).

ENVIRONMENT

In the twenty-first century where technology envelops us, the natural world is divorced from us by contrived ventilation systems and unpleasant sights and smells are removed from our daily experience, it is important to show students where our conveniences originate (Figure 11.2). A favorite field trip is to the water treatment plant; the water flows straight from the reservoir with all of the remains of weekend boaters, swimmers, trash, leaf litter, and bird feathers (Pressick-Kilborn, 2009; Thomas, 2002). As the water passes through screens and then settlement tanks, the material that floats to the top is skimmed off, the material that falls to the bottom is removed, the water is shot into the air, and microbes eat their fill in the

- Airports
- Bird sanctuaries
- Caves
- Coking plants
- Dams
- Electrical plants
- Factories
- Farms
- Food processing plants
- Forests
- Lakes
- Landfills
- Medical history museums
- Military bases
- Mines
- National, state, or community parks
- Natural monuments
- Nature preserves
- Pharmaceutical museums
- Ponds
- Rivers
- Quarries
- Rock formations
- Sewage treatment plants
- Space centers
- Steam plants
- Reservoirs
- Water treatment plants
- Wet lands

Figure 11.2.   Science, technology, and society field trip locations.

agitated water; then the water passes through sand and charcoal, and chlorine is added to the water. The students see all of these steps, including the lab where the tests are done; at the very end there is a drinking fountain. Most people do not feel thirsty at that point, but the teacher knows the students are really thinking about water quality—maybe for the first time in their lives.

The trip to the local landfill is not quite so much fun, but it is interesting to see how everything is sorted. Truck after truck comes in all day bringing waste; the staggering amounts are fascinating, but the amount that can be recycled is also amazing. Every possible effort is made to use all the products of waste. Human interactions with the environment are natural and needed parts of the exploratory nature of study travel experiences. If students take study travel trips to cities, then they need to consider the environmental implications of the site (Figure 11.3).

It is important to consider the costs by working on-site to gather data on the costs, witnessing the impact on the land, and documenting the costs through drawings. For elementary school students drawings serve as a form of note taking while they are learning in field experiences. Students can record their observations, reflections, and recommendations by creating quick pencil sketches of what they are discerning. Through their note taking, they bring ideas and information back to the classroom, where further discussion occurs. Students make detailed drawings about one site or they compare several sites through their drawings.

Students compare sink holes and springs when studying ground water pollution in a karst region. The students hike along the Lost River to record sketches of swallow holes, a karst window, and the rise of the river. The students place captions on their drawings showing the pollutants that impact each of the areas. Back in the classroom the students compile all the different pollutants that flow into the cave system and compare those

I.	Culture
II.	Time, continuity, and change
III.	People, places, and environments
IV.	Individual development and identity
V.	Individuals, groups, and institutions
VI.	Power, authority, and governance
VII.	Production, distribution, and consumption
VIII.	Science, technology, and society
IX.	Global connections
X.	Civic ideals and practices

Figure 11.3.   NCSS (1994) national standards.

Natural Resource Development
4 Documented two (2) achievements and two (2) failures in extracting the natural resource
3 Documented both an achievement and a failure in extracting the natural resource
2 Documented an achievement or a failure in extracting the natural resource
1 Documented no achievements or failures

Community Resource People
4 Quoted two or more resource people showing opposite sides of an issue
3 Quoted two resource people
2 Quoted one resource person
1 Quoted no resource people

Advocacy
4 Asked for the reader to take action
3 Took a position that encourages social justice
2 Identified a position that is socially responsible
1 Took no position

Controversial Issue
4 Described both sides of the issue
3 Identified both sides of the issue
2 Identified a controversial issue
1 Identified no controversial issue

Responsibility
4 Encouraged a balanced and fair accounting of both sides of the issue
3 Respectfully acknowledged differing views on the topic
2 Respectfully illustrated only one side of an issue
1 Took no responsibility

Figure 11.4. Assessment.

pollutants with those found in the local streams. After this they determine whether legislation is needed to protect ground water that is used for public or private drinking supplies. When students return from the field, they need to create newspaper stories for their local newspaper and their school newspaper describing what they found. The results of these news releases also serve as assessments and are graded on a rubric (Figure 11.4).

WORLD CONNECTIONS THROUGH TRANSPORTATION

What is the role of government in encouraging good transportation? The government plays a variety of roles: from regulation of transportation systems, to creating and maintaining them with tax funds, to taxing them for revenue, to ensuring their safety. Citizens need to understand how these transportation networks function and how the government interacts within those systems. Citizens need public policy that encourages transportation and trade while using a responsible balance of producing revenue to pay for government expenditures for transportation systems. Citizens need safe efficient transportation that helps them move goods from one part of the nation to another. Citizens need to understand the role the government plays in keeping them safe on the water, air, and land through vehicle design, regulation, and enforcement.

The continued development of transportation corridors may have included the paths of Native People or the traces of migrating North American bison. These paths such as modern US 150 still function after years of upgrading by pioneers, private toll roads, or state highway workers. The features found along the way include residences, factories, schools, churches, businesses, and courthouses. These sites build on top of previous structures or stand as neighbors to co-existing structures spanning two hundred years of building practices. When they are in the field, students study the built environment, which includes all of these examples along the route.

People have developed a number of ways to connect with other people through trade and communication. At first these methods were slow, but over time they have become faster and more reliable in linking people to their world. Students examine a number of these different methods of communication and transportation then they compare them with the communication and transportation systems with which they are currently familiar (Lybolt, Techmanski, & Gottfred, 2007; Maher, 2004; Alleman & Brophy, 2003A, 2003B).

The people whom students meet when they travel to learn about transportation are often as interesting as the sites the students visit. Students who have played with toy cars, buses, boats, airplanes, and trains such as Thomas the Tank Engine easily assimilate the new information about transportation networks that they learn by taking field trips and apply it to the modern world of distribution systems.

One way to set up a field trip is to organize it around a transportation corridor such as a canal, railroad, river, or road. Each stop along the route can be connected to the history of the corridor, thus giving a theme and coherence to what might otherwise appear be just a jumble of stops. This sort of field trip can provide a theme that easily goes beyond any one time period; students therefore see a variety of sites juxtaposed without a specific historic context. Students experience sites that may not normally be open for tourists; these sites may have little or no cost, but it is not likely that any interpretation will be provided. The transportation corridor is easy for students to map; they chart their way through the field trip both prior to the event and during the event.

Internal Improvements

Students need to create maps of transportation systems prior to field investigation of the transportation systems. Whether these are maps of roads, harbors, canals, rivers, or rails, each transportation system intersects with other forms of transportation. The students examine points of embarkment and disembarkment, towns along the way, and where other transportation systems cross the transportation system. The students find how traffic, trade, and communication get from one community to other points around the nation or the world. Furthermore, students learn about points where cargos are moved from one type of transportation to another.

Students trace the National Road across the capital cities of the then western states of Ohio, Indiana, and Illinois. Running from Cumberland, Maryland, to Vandalia, Illinois, the road was the obvious attempt to connect the western states to the east coast. Immigrants took the road to enter the area, farmers moved their goods to market, travelers carried news and mail, and traders prospered all along its route. It was updated to US 40. All along the route towns sprang up and at places such as the Whitewater River or the Whitewater Canal major communities developed because of the intersection of trade and commerce.

In east central Indiana students follow the National Road (Figures 11.5 and 11.6), which was the first federally funded highway. The National Road was designed to link Cumberland, Maryland, in the east with the west by going through the three state capitals of Columbus, Ohio; Indianapolis, Indiana; and Vandalia, Illinois. One of the best stops along this route is the Huddleston Farm House Museum, which is operated by the Indiana Landmarks. This group is devoted to working for the preservation of historic buildings and regional landscapes, and as part of that mission they have restored and operated the structure as a museum to interpret life on the National Road and the westward migration as well as incorporating the best practices of preservation (Ferretti, MacArthur, & Okolo, 2007; Clark, 2000). The students' next stop is the home of Levi Coffin, the president of the Underground Railroad. This site reflects how the migration of Quakers, who left slave states for reasons of conscience, intersected the National Road and how this promoted the Underground Railroad activity in the area. Students later stop at the junction of the east fork of the Whitewater River. The falling water at this juncture with the National Road provided mechanical energy for the emerging industries.

8:00 a.m.	Depart from school
9:30 a.m.	Gaar House
10:30 a.m.	Depart
11:15 a.m.	Levi Coffin Home
12:15 p.m.	Depart
1:00 p.m.	Lunch
1:30 p.m.	Depart
2:00 p.m.	Wayne County Historical Museum
3:00 p.m.	Depart
3:30 p.m.	Huddleston Home
5:00 p.m.	Depart
6:00 p.m.	Return to school

Figure 11.5.   National road tour.

Gaar House	$2.00 per person
Levi Coffin Home	$.25 child, $1.00 adult
Wayne County Historical Museum	$.75 child, $1.50 adult
Huddleston Home	$1.50 child
Total per child	$4.50

Figure 11.6.   Fees for the national road tour.

The students can see the home of one of the industrial families when they stop at the Gaar Mansion. Their next stop is the Wayne County Historical Museum, where they learn how Mrs. Julia Gaar traveled throughout the world and brought back curiosities to display first in her home and then later placed them in the museum to interpret the world to her neighbors. Her family shipped their products by using transportation networks, and she traveled the world by using transportation networks. Both of these examples help the students to learn about the role of movement in geography and history.

The canal system, which laborers dug in the early 1800s, has been erased from the landscape in many places, but in certain places it can still be seen by careful observation. Students visit Indiana's Canal Park and Interpretive Center at Delphi, Indiana, which affords an interesting interactive history of the Wabash and Erie Canal through the use of working models and recreated canal features. The students also climb into the remains of an old lock, walk in the old canal and beside the restored canal on the tow path, walk under the canal where it crosses local streams, and walk over a river where the canal crossed it. Some of this exploration requires students to go down a muddy bank and get their feet wet as they look for clues of the existence of former canals. On field trips students look for clues and examples of places where the physical landscape changed over time.

The docents of the Howard Steamboat Museum show a different type of transportation system in Jeffersonville, Indiana. The first floor of the museum interprets the life and times of the Howard family when they built boats for the Ohio, Mississippi, and Missouri Rivers; the second floor portrays the history, geography, and economics of the family-owned and operated company and is interpreted with models, artifacts, photographs, and documents. Floating palaces and work horse boats all powered by steam engines were the specialty of the family; in addition to producing a large number of boats, the Howard family produced some of the best known boats on the river system. Their company continued to make boats for World War II, and boats continue to be made at the site where their company once stood. For students who have not grown up on a river, the river itself provides a variety of new sensory experiences to help them think about how the river has been and is presently being used by people.

While students are on the river, they see an international harbor where boats bring in raw materials and pick up agricultural and manufactured products to exchange on a world market. The boats, containers, railroads, cranes, and warehouses are on a super-human scale, and all of these physical symbols of international trade are available for student inspection. Similarly, all of the raw materials of trade are visible on the wharves while being moved to and from warehouses. Usually transportation systems intersect, which mean that railroad corridors, roads, wharves, and air hubs cross one another to provide ways for goods to be transported to the next location. Students see how goods and services travel from one transportation corridor to another, and they learn how raw materials and finished goods move in a world economy.

Students bring notes back from the field by using a sheet of paper and the side of a crayon with the paper removed. By rubbing the side of the crayon over the paper held steady on an incised stone or raised metal plate, students bring images back to the classroom as a form of note taking. Students make rubbings of cast historical markers, information plates on modes of transportation such as trains or steamboats, or they rub informational text from stones. They hang these rubbings on the walls as a reminder of the trip or they use the information found in them to try to acquire more information about individuals, groups, or institutions from the past with the help of additional print or electronic

Careers
4   Identified two transportation related jobs that require a college degree
3   Identified a transportation related job that requires a college degree
2   Identified a transportation related job
1   Identified no job

Sources
4   Used more than one primary and more than one secondary source
3   Used one primary source
2   Used one secondary source
1   Used no sources

Transportation Policy
4   Identified a transportation policy, cited sources to justify it, and discussed its implications
3   Identified a transportation policy and cited sources to justify it
2   Identified a transportation policy and justified it with a rationale
1   Identified no transportation policy

Community
4   Provided more than one primary or secondary source for their peers
3   Provided information for peers
2   Provided information for other students in another room
1   Provided no information

Figure 11.7.   Inforamtion file assessment.

sources. They find primary source documents, illustrations, and photographs to determine what other stories they can find about the site that are not told in the text.

Students determine controversial issues that surrounded the construction or improvements of these transportation routes. Students determine that not everyone thought that they were a good idea and that not everyone approved of them. Some people had their towns bypassed by the transportation routes; others had their farmland crossed, thus losing easy access to their land; still others had their land seized through eminent domain. Students see that people in the past as well as in the present are not usually all of one mind; there was dissent and faction in the past just as there is in the present. Modern infrastructure projects, including roads, light rail, air hub, and harbors, displace and disrupt people in addition to bringing new business and connections to an area.

When using primary sources, students find a variety of information they use to create information files for students in the class next door (Figure 11.7).

EXPLORING DIVERSITY OF THOUGHT AND COMMUNAL GROUPS

The frontier can be misperceived as colorless, genderless, and filled with lusty pioneers, who were all the same and held no beliefs while conquering the wilderness. Excellent teachers help students see diversity in thought, country of origin, color, age, and gender. The people who made up the group called pioneers came from a variety of countries and states. They brought a variety of religions or none, and they had passionate beliefs about how government ought to operate. These are the people who fill the pages of the history books, and they need to have their multiple thoughts represented in social studies classrooms.

Good primary and secondary sources exist to illustrate the diversity of thought represented by these people. Fortunately, there are still some sites that tell the stories of these people. Some of these sites are opened by ecclesiastical hands to visitors, and other sites are opened by educational foundations that are eager to educate visitors. These sites are difficult to interpret because bricks and mortar only tell so much; the unfortunate habit of *presentism* often occurs, whereby visitors think that the people acted in the past with today's motives and conventions. Museum educators need careful interpretation to tell the story of religious dissenters in the face of a romanticized enthusiasm for the past.

Communal societies from both the past and the present are difficult to understand. One of the most difficult parts of telling these stories is that critics and apologists for the groups created primary sources at the time. In their beginnings the groups were controversial, over time they became no less so. Of course fear, disdain, and prejudice of people who were different in very important ways—such as their means of establishing family and community—are still controversial issues. Even the cloistered communities of convents and monasteries are still clouded in jokes and ignorance.

Teachers usually teach the pioneer period as a festival of log cabins, food, split rail fences, and fun, but the frontier had significant diversity of thought and unique groups of people. Teachers help students explore these varying viewpoints by finding discrepancies in the idea that all pioneers were rugged individualists or even that all pioneers lived on farms in the wilderness. At the edge of civilization, some groups of people lived surprisingly comfortable lives in well-established communities. They lived in urban communities with all of the advantages of Europe or Philadelphia within the towns they created in the wilderness. Some of these utopias were religious and others secular, but the members of each group believed that they could create a community for a specific purpose that would change the world forever.

One such group was the celibate, communalistic, and millinenialistic followers of George Rapp of Harmony on the Wabash; the world called these German immigrants The Harmony Society or Harmonists. They carved a quality of life out of the wilderness equal in convenience to living in Philadelphia or Boston and produced manufactured goods equal to those produced in Europe. While the Lincoln family was living in a rough cabin with a dirt floor just a few miles to the west, the Harmonists enjoyed brick buildings with glass windows, musical concerts, and landscaped gardens. This group, like many others such as the Amana, Moravians, Oneida, Shaker, and Zoar, made contributions to the opening of the west from their communities. The contributions and thoughts of these people represent an important alternative path of study about those who settled in the west as pioneers (Peterson, 2004; Levstik & Groth, 2002; McMillan, 2000).

Today, Historic New Harmony is an open-air museum preserving much of the residential portion of the town. As with most open-air museums, there is much that must be left to the imagination that a modern visitor cannot see nor experience. When students visit the town, the most obvious things missing are the two massive churches that dominated the center of town. They must also imagine the dirt streets lined with Lombardy poplar trees, the gardens filled with flowers, and the music that visitors described hearing at a variety of times throughout the day. The extensive fields and herds are difficult for open-air museums to interpret for visitors, and the large factories and keelboat construction at the side of the Wabash River are prohibitively expensive to replicate. Today the steady stream of outsiders, who come to trade and observe contrasts with a time in the past when people knew everybody in the community.

Students who come to Harmony on the Wabash now can try to solve two puzzles. First at Harmony, Pennsylvania, and later at Economy, Pennsylvania, the Harmony Society created large stone sinks that drained water through the wall and out of the building. Why are none of these built in Harmony on the Wabash? The students need to create three hypotheses, determine which one they think is most feasible, and state the reasons they believe this one is correct. The second puzzle is that at both sites in Pennsylvania the Harmony Society had extensive wine cellars, but these do not seem to exist in the Indiana settlement. Once again the students need to determine three hypotheses, determine which one they think is most feasible, and state the reasons they believe it to be correct.

Students can perform structured role-play to simulate life in Harmony. Through this activity the students determine the types of jobs that were available in the town and the beliefs of the Rappites including holding property in common, equality of members, how to settle problems, living in non-violence, and religious beliefs (Figure 11.8). Students take on dif-

I. Jobs
    A. Farmers (*farm symbol*)
    B. Mechanics (*pull lever*)
    C. Traders (*push me pull you*)
II. Build Community
    A. Common
        1. What problems could be caused if everything were owned by the community and not by individuals?
    B. Equal (*balanced hands*)
        1. Free store (*cash register*)
            a. How could you keep people equal if there were a free store?
            b. What would the neighbors think of a free store where they had to pay money to trade?
    C. Harmony
        1. Who would settle problems?
    D. Peace (*sign*)
        1. What would the neighbors think about members of the community not serving in war?
        2. What would the neighbors think about their liking the Indians?
        3. By not serving in war, do you think that the community members were consistent with their beliefs?
    E. Religion
        1. Jesus was coming to Jerusalem
            a. What would you want to do?
        2. The world was going to end
        3. No children (*international sign*)
            a. Why would you not want to have children?
            b. Do you think that the Harmony Society had a good or bad life without children?
    F. After ten years, the Harmony Society left Indiana.
        1. What were their jobs?
        2. Where were their markets?
        3. Would you have liked life in Harmony on the Wabash?

Figure 11.8. Role-playing the history of the Harmony Society on the Wabash.

ferent roles as members of the town, perform physical mnemonics to remember ideas, and engage in open-ended questioning. The different roles help the students to understand the various types of labor conducted in the town, and by being active the students connect the kinesthetic motions with the ideas they need to remember. The open-ended questioning helps the students to understand what motivated the group and how they would need to deal with similar types of situations. The role-play also describes and interprets how these people conducted business and moved goods to markets by making economic decisions while taking geographic locations into account.

I. Gertrude lived in Harmony from age 7 to 17.
    A. Granddaughter of Father Rapp
    B. Much loved by the community
    C. Sick: coughed until she choked
        1. Sang and jumped around
    D. Needlepoint
    E. Flowers and gardens
    F. Learned English from Shakers at West Union
        1. She received letters from Shaker friends
        2. She wrote her grandfather's letters for him in English

---

Figure 11.9.   Gertrude Rapp: Child in Harmony.

Gertrude Rapp lived in the Harmony community as a child from age seven to seventeen. The primary sources of the Rapp community give the best description of her because she was the granddaughter of Father George Rapp (Figure 11.9). Students read these documents when they are on the site to find out what life for one child would have been like in the community. Students learn about health care, leisure activities for children, and the presence of other communal groups on the frontier from these documents. Students also discover how historians learn by using evidence from primary sources. By using the primary sources in the field, students can get a better idea about what happened in the life of people and especially that of children their own age.

Owen and New Harmony

When the Harmony Society left the Wabash and returned to Pennsylvania, they sold their entire community to Scottish textile manufacturer, philanthropist, and social reformer Robert Owen. The utopia he attempted was called New Harmony, and it was based on science and universal education. The group held all property in common, but they were neither religious nor celibate. The members of the community entertained ideas that were very foreign to those of their geographic neighbors including the equality of women and the equality of people regardless of the color of their skin. These ideas allow students to look at intellectual history, see how ideas emerge, evolve, and are tested, accepted, or rejected by society (Haibo, 2009; Milewski, 2008; Sevier, 2002).

Before, during, or after the trip, the students engage in structured role-play to simulate life in New Harmony with the Owenites and compare it with their life. Students take roles, act out physical mnemonics,

I. Jobs
   A. Thinkers (*thinker*)
   B. Scientists (*pour test tubes*)
      1. Geology
      2. Shells
      3. Insects
      4. Books
   C. Educators (*write*)
      1. School all of your life
         a. What jobs do the Owenites not have?
         b. What problem could this cause?
II. Everyone was equal (*balance hands*)
   A. Owned all in common
      1. What problems could this cause?
   B. Fights (*act*)
      1. Who could settle problems?
   C. Split town
   D. Fights (*act*)
   E. Quit common community
   F. People stayed
      1. Why did people stay?
      2. What kind of people occupied New Harmony?
      3. Were the people staying here going to benefit the community or cause a problem for it?

Figure 11.10. Role-playing the history of Robert Owen's New Harmony.

and engage in open-ended questioning. Students consider the jobs of thinkers, scientists, and educators, and the equality of members of the community, and they contemplate why the Owenites were still unable to solve their problems (Figure 11.10). Students examine the reasons the community failed and speculate about the causes for the decline and failure of the community. Students also consider whether there are connections between this event and other events in the present or in the past. When they identify an event, they need to give examples of how it is and is not similar.

Students also learn about the site through a first-person presentation in the character of Joseph Neef, one of the educators who came to the town for the utopia. Children lived in boarding schools, and the stories of students from the past are both compelling and whimsical descriptions. The utopia failed, but the people stayed. Joseph describes the scholars he worked with, the trip to the community on the keel boat filled with so many thinkers and scientists that it was called the boat load of knowledge, how he ran the upper school with his wife and daughters, his career, and

I.   Searching for Victor Collin Duclos
II.   Two French students fell through the ice and nearly drowned when the Philanthropist stopped near Louisville.
III.   Teacher and conducted the upper school with my wife and daughters
  A.   Madame Fretageot has the lower school
  B.   Colleague of Pestalozzi
  C.   Taught for Mr. MaClure in Philadelphia
  D.   Quit teaching and moved to a farm near Louisville
IV.   Fought in the Napoleonic Wars
  A.   Favorite friend of Robert Owen
  B.   Kindly man
    1.   Scared students because he swore
  C.   Education
    1.   School
    2.   Trade
V.   Checked with Mr. Say

Figure 11.11.   Joseph Neef first-person presentation outline.

Social World
4   Compared two communal groups including flaws, strengths, dangers, and promise including a group that still has members in the area
3   Compared two communal groups including flaws, strengths, dangers, and promise
2   Described one communal group including flaws, strengths, dangers, and promise
1   Described no communal groups

Controversy
4   Included cultural similarities and differences
3   Quoted appropriate sources for each group
2   Included two different points of view for each group
1   Included only one point of view

Literature
4   Cited both primary and secondary sources that offer conflicting perspectives about the two groups
3   Cited primary sources that offer conflicting perspectives about the two groups
2   Cited secondary sources that offer conflicting perspectives about the two groups
1   Included only one point of view

Figure 11.12.   Assessment.

how he worked with other members of the community (Figure 11.11). Whether given on-site or prior to going to the site, the first-person presentation helps bring a human dimension to the story (Howes & Cruz,

2009; Morris, 2009: Cruz & Murthy, 2006). Students like to hear about the adventures of their peers even when they are separated by time.

Probably the most sustainable celibate communal religious groups were established by Catholic orders at Ferdinand, Oldenburg, and St. Meinrad, in Indiana. In their prime these groups owned vast tracts of land, large herds, employed many of the surrounding parishioners, practiced large-scale agriculture, engaged in cottage industries, and, despite being mono-sex communities, functioned in a way surprisingly similar to West Union and Harmony on the Wabash. Their tendency to employ parishioners was the largest difference in contrast to other frontier deliberate communities; in this regard, they tended to look like European monasteries and convents. They divested themselves of most of their land in the early twentieth century, but it is still possible to visit the main buildings of each of these cloisters. The brothers and sisters are still there carrying out their holy and secular duties with connections to Europe, the traditions of their respective community, and their history at the site.

The students create an essay comparing communal groups that might include Owenites, Harmonists, Shakers, Benedictine Sisters at Ferdinand, or Benedictine Brothers at St. Meinrad (Figure 11.12).

CHAPTER 12

ARCHITECTURE AND STUDY TRAVEL

INTRODUCTION

On a sunny day in September, the fourth-grade class from Washington Elementary School took a field trip to the Lanier Home. There they learned how the architectural styles in this building represented democratic ideals. Many young people live in communities where historically interesting buildings are present, and tours of these historical sites reveal much about life in the past. Something that students often overlook in the analysis of historic sites is the civic values of the people who lived there. The ideas of architecture cannot be divorced from the people or common ideas of the time; many early American buildings reveal a deep respect for democratic ideals.

Architectural styles in public and private architecture represented civic virtue in the young republic. Before the turn of the century in the United States, the citizens rejected the former Colonial Georgian architecture in a fit of revolutionary fervor in favor of the popular Federal style. The Federal or Adams style consisted of symmetrical buildings with simple lines and little ornamentation. Homes had little or no roof overhang, an odd number of facade openings toward the street, and a fan and sidelights surrounding the main entrance. All of these elements represented democratic simplicity and economy, and the Federal style celebrated the indig-

The Field Trip Book: Study Travel Experiences in Social Studies
pp. 205–217
Copyright © 2010 by Information Age Publishing
All rights of reproduction in any form reserved.

enous folk construction of dwellings found at that time. The structures exemplified the common man and his importance as a citizen, and the Federal style was very adaptable to either rural or urban structures.

When Thomas Jefferson returned from France, he brought with him ideas, books, sketches, and models from his travels to sites built during the time of Roman Gaul. His model for the capitol of Virginia remains on display at the state capitol. Jefferson introduced Greek Revival architecture as a building style for the young republic. Greek architecture typically includes columns, pediments, pilasters, entablatures, symmetry, and heavy window and door headers (Kennedy & Hall, 1989). The people of the United States adopted this as the de facto national building style for public and private structures. People built hundreds of thousands of Greek Revival homes, stores, churches, and civic buildings. Kennedy (1989) views efforts to build in the Greek Revival architectural style as a means of national resolve to show both the strength and maturity of the young republic. Examples of the democratic spirit reminded people of the young republic through examples of architecture reflecting Greek democracy and the Roman republic.

While many people used folk construction patterns such as the center chimney salt box, the single pin log home, or the double pin dog trot log home, the focus of this study remains on formal architectural styles rather than folk or vernacular idioms. At the turn of the century (1799–1800), patriotism was reflected through the built environment; the local community provided these examples. Students use buildings seen on field trips to examine architecture built from 1800–1850 (Shaw, 2002; Peat, 1962). When students learn about these types of buildings, they learn what motivated people at the turn of the century to build their buildings in this pattern. Students increase their knowledge of civics through direct educational experiences that promote engagement and exposure (Ellis-Williams, 2007; Minow, 2006). Individual rights and responsibilities need purposeful planning and execution without counting on accidental exposure.

A STUDENT GUIDE TO LOOKING AT THE BUILT ENVIRONMENT

Madison, Indiana, serves as an example of a place where students examine democratic ideals in the context of the architecture of an early-nineteenth-century town. In other places, students may need to look at civic and governmental structures to find examples of Greek and Roman architecture. Of course, the architectural elements described here continue to be used in modern construction, but the total finished product rarely looks Greek or Roman in the twenty-first century.

Preparation for the Trip

Children learn social studies from a carefully planned and executed study travel experience; when teachers share civic education with children, they begin by selecting a site appropriate for the children. The teacher needs to visit the site beforehand and have questions ready to pose that will help the students interpret the themes of the trip (Figure 12.1). In choosing a site such as the Lanier Home, teachers think about the themes for class exploration (Figure 12.2). What topics exist for discussion, and what are the most important ideas about the site? In choosing the Lanier Home, three ideas emerge: architecture, human environment interaction, and transportation. Think about these questions: What caused Madison, Indiana, to highlight architecture? How did the people interact with the land? How did transportation become the key to Madison's growth, decline, and survival? After developing these themes, preview with the children what they should look for, what will they see, and what they will do at the site. Very important learning starts with the child's previous experience, so ask where the students have been and what they have done. How are these experiences similar and different from the experiences that the students are about to have? The teacher attempts to show students how people built structures for homes, churches, businesses, and civic buildings containing architectural ideas representing democracy. Public buildings as well as middle-class residences show that the idea was important enough for builders to want to remember and display it. Students may find that these representations surround them as almost constant reminders of the virtue of democracy, just as the original builders surrounded themselves with symbols of their faith in the republic. When the teacher picks ideas to explore, he or she can work with the site to tailor the trip around the major ideas he or she wishes to study. While it is problematic to attempt to get the same docent every year, the teacher can have copies of original maps, prints, photos, artwork, or artifacts to help the students interpret the site. Teachers also prepare written assignments or packets to help the students focus on specific content or issues raised on the trip.

What the students do on the site is a key factor to consider. Students must be more than passive spectators on trips to sites; they need to have mental engagement with the site. For students to become more than passive spectators, they must assume the role of a producer of knowledge. The purpose of the trip must be for the students to find out and bring information back from the trip; students may plan this ahead of time during the preparation for the trip. On the trip, the students need an assignment; they may gather data for the completion of the assignment through using technology or using clipboards to take notes, making marker rub-

I. Fences
    A. What do they tell about the community?
    B. What materials did the builder use?
    C. What do they tell us?
    D. Are they original?

II. Water
    A. What is the relationship to water?
    B. Do the homes face or overlook water?
    C. How did developers lay out the streets in relationship to the river?
    D. Is the area flood prone?

III. Public Space
    A. Are there parks or esplanades in the area?
    B. Does the neighborhood look like a park?
    C. What types of vegetation have owners planted?
    D. How well tended are they?
    E. What plan did the original owners have for the vegetation?

IV. Self-Imposed Restrictions
    A. Are there easements in the neighborhood?
    B. What did the original developers plan?
    C. Do or did covenants exist between neighbors?
    D. How did the original neighborhood planners try to protect against unpleasant intrusions?
    E. What is zoning and how does it apply to this neighborhood? What does it exclude or include?
    F. What restrictions do historic preservation organizations impose and what benefits do they provide?

V. Intrusions
    A. What are the relationships to other structures?
    B. How close to roads are the houses?
    C. How close are the houses to a major road?
    D. How do residents restrict traffic in residential areas?
    E. How close is the structure to other houses, other buildings, and out buildings?
    F. What incursions have intruded into the neighborhood, including railroads, airports, power lines, advertising, and pollution?

VI. Neighborhood Health
    A. What is the style of neighboring buildings?
    B. Did the owners build all the structures at the same time, earlier, or later?
    C. Have the neighborhood buildings improved or declined, and has the neighborhood stayed at the same socio/economic level? What caused the change?
    D. What effects have public policy had on the neighborhood?

VII. Individual Structures
    A. Why did the owners use these elements?
    B. Why are false elements like pilasters used?
    C. How did the owner have the exterior match the interior of the home?

VIII. Interior Designs
    A. What styles did owners choose to represent in the home? What might this tell us about the owner?
    B. What decorative motifs seem to be used the most?

Figure 12.1.   Reading a community.

> I. Culture
> II. Time, continuity, and change
> III. People, places, and environments
> VII. Production, distribution, and consumption
> VIII. Science, technology, and society
> X. Civic ideals and practice

Figure 12.2.   NCSS (1994) national standards.

Dear Parent,
The members of our class will travel to Madison on March 20, 20XX. The students will be visiting the J. F. D. Lanier Home, the Shrewsbury Home, the Judge Jeremiah Sullivan Home, Dr. Hutchings' Office, and the Schofield Home. We will leave from school at 7:30 a.m. and return at 3:30 p.m. Lunch will be at a fast food restaurant. A non-refundable $10.00 deposit is needed to reserve a spot on this trip.
Sincerely,

Dr. Ronald Vaughan Morris

--(clip here)-----------------------------------

My child, _____, may go to Madison, Indiana.

_____
Parent signature

PLEASE RETURN THIS FORM AND THE NON-REFUNDABLE DEPOSIT TO
DR. RONALD VAUGHAN MORRIS BY MARCH 5, 20XX.

Figure 12.3.   Permission slip.

bings, or producing drawings. Once students return to school, they need to use the information they have gathered to complete the assignment to inform others of the results of their travels and experiences. This information may take the form of a public display or presentation, but it should have an outside audience.

Before the students move into the field, they need technical instruction, depending on the types of equipment they will use. They may need instruction on a digital camera, camcorder, digital video recorder, or digital audio recorder. The instruction needs to focus on how it works, how to get the best results, and what is the most important information to record. Because students see these as highly coveted jobs, there needs to be a

7:30 a.m.	Depart
8:20 a.m.	Scipio: covered bridge walk
8:25 a.m.	Depart
8:30 a.m.	Vernon: county seat and row houses
	RR tunnel walk
	Morgan Raid sign
8:30 a.m.	Depart
8:35 a.m.	Dupont: Morgan Raid sign
8:40 a.m.	Depart
9:00 a.m.	Madison State Hospital Gate House and Railroad grade
9:15 a.m.	Depart
9:30 a.m.	J. F. D. Lanier Mansion
10:00 a.m.	Depart
10:15 a.m.	Sullivan Home
11:00 a.m.	Depart
11:15 a.m.	Schofield Home
11:45 a.m.	Depart
12:00 p.m.	Lunch/restroom
12:45 p.m.	Depart
1:00 p.m.	Dr. Hutchings' Office
2:00 p.m.	Depart
2:00 p.m.	Shrewsbury Home
2:45 p.m.	Depart
3:00 p.m.	Clifty Falls Nature Center
3:15 p.m.	Depart
3:30 p.m.	Lantern Tour of the railroad tunnel
4:00 p.m.	Depart
4:15 p.m.	Big Clifty Falls
4:30 p.m.	Depart
6:30 p.m.	Arrive at school

Figure 12.4.   Madison itinerary.

J.F.D. Lanier	$1.00 donation
Sullivan House	$1.50 adult
Dr. Hutchings' Office	$1.50 adult
Shrewsbury House	$2.00 adult
Lunch	$5.00
Lanterns	$1.00
Candles	$1.00

Figure 12.5.   Field trip expenses.

rotation of equipment, and the teacher needs to briefly discuss the responsibility and care of the equipment. Students need to see that all of their jobs will contribute information to their projects once they return to their classroom.

Before leaving for the site, help the students think about questions to ask. Students may use questions to develop their own questions for reading their own neighborhoods. What kind of questions do the students want to ask the docent? The students' generation of questions for interpreters reflects student thought and interaction with the site. While at the site, students have an opportunity to work with an expert, and the docent's experiences help to interpret the site and generate more student questions about the site. Oftentimes, students speak to the most knowledgeable person in the state about a specific site. What questions do the students want to ask about Madison, the finishing details surrounding the construction of the Lanier Home, and the people who lived in the home? How does the student find out more about history? Students prepare questions in advance to act as seed questions; this breaks the ice and gets discussion started in a group. This pre-planning and pre-questioning experience encourages students to think about the site and the people they will encounter. Questioning helps students to gather and interpret information about a site before and during the encounter.

What Students Did, Learned, and Saw at the Lanier Home

Students read the community landscape, architecture, interior design, furniture, and decorations.

> A work of art ... can be treated as an artifact, ... as a cultural datum for making inferences about a society.... The point of using art is that works of art possess a content that itself is uniquely informative. To gain access to the context one must have the requisite schemata and refined sensibilities. (Eisner, 1991, p. 553)

Students also use art as a starting point to spark discussion of the qualities of citizenship. Students go to the site to see architecture in context with community along with furniture and decoration in context with interior design. Students read all of these artistic forms to find cultural information about the society that created them.

Students need to read the community to find civic virtue in many small details of city planning and community life. While they are in the field, students look at the streets, sidewalks, and curbs to determine if they think they are original. Students look for the presence of original fences; people erect fences to separate, define, or decorate. Water plays a major role in the orientation of many communities. People build on waterways that serve as transportation corridors for convenience, or because they find them aesthetically pleasing. Next, students also do rubbings with paper and the flat side of a crayon of historical markers to bring notes back to the classroom. Markers tell others how people define an area, how they record the history of an area, and what groups wish to say about an area. The students also look for public lands in the community; some neighborhoods go to great lengths to protect their green space, while others promote public art. Students look at how neighborhoods try to protect their ideas of community. Preservation groups try to maintain the integrity of a home; this often causes controversy between homeowners and community groups. Students also learn about ways they protect communities from intrusions through a variety of processes. Students try to look at the motivation of the planners for establishing a community, and they look at what the planners envisioned as a good community.

Structures and their occupants do not form communities by themselves; they depend on one another for context. Traffic patterns, other structures, and intrusions all intermingle in a community. The effectiveness of community members in detaining community intrusion is a thermometer reading the health of a community. The space relations between roads and other structures also tell the students about the community, how people saw it, and the life people lived in it. The community members must work together if they are to create effective resolutions to incursions such as heavy traffic, pollution, or advertising. Students look around the community to see citizenship related to issues and decisions made in a community through a political process. Boyte (1999) looks at politics and citizenship through civics, community, and commonwealth to examine the moral and religious part of public life, the production of talent and energies, and citizen authority acquired through public creation.

When students look at a building, they must look at the neighboring buildings as well; the students determine the style of the other buildings to determine if all the buildings are contemporary. Students look at the health of a community when they examine the adjacent homes, the care of the property, signs of decay, and accumulations of trash. They need to critically examine the neighborhood for examples of decay or revitalization; students need to find out what causes renewed interest in a community and how a community can redevelop. They also look for signs of an active neighborhood association. Students might find examples of crime watches, posted neighborhood associations, neighborhood meetings, block parties, and historic preservation groups.

When students read the exterior of the building, they determine if the building followed the Federal or the Greek Revival style. While both styles required symmetrical treatment of the building, students pick out a number of differences between the buildings. An odd number of openings across the front, little or no roof overhang, paired chimneys, and little or no window or door frame decoration except for a fan light over the door all indicate the Federal style. Pediments, pilasters, columns, and entablature boards all signal the Greek Revival style. Students look at the house and determine the building style based on the architectural clues.

When students examine the exterior of a building, they look for common elements; the students then continue this process when they examine the interior design of the house. In this field trip example, wide molding inside and outside signaled the classical architecture of the Lanier Home. Builders worked Greek key designs into these moldings; acanthus leaves appear in the corners and the center of these moldings in the Lanier Home. Dentals also commonly cover the moldings of the Lanier Home, and the doorframes in the Lanier home have a dogleg at the top. Interior columns and pilasters grace the Lanier home exterior; interior design elements reflect symbols of authority depicting the new nation. Students examined decorative trim. Teachers ask students to examine interior decorative elements to determine how style affected the way people lived their daily lives. The United States tried to capture the elegance, majesty, and nobility of the other well-known democracy of Greece. Citizens brought representations of democracy to their community and into their drawing rooms. Teachers ask students to look at interior furnishings and decoration to interpret what was important to the resident.

Wheat sheaf candle sconces depict products of the new nation in Judge Jeremiah Sullivan's House, a Federal home. Maps cover the walls at Locust Grove, which was the last home of George Rogers Clark, and pictures of leaders and heroes of democracy cover the walls at Grouseland, the home of William Henry Harrison. Symbols of Greece or Rome remain part of the interior decoration. The Lanier silver contains the acanthus leaf, and prints, art, and wallpaper present classical ruins at Grouseland. The Greek key ornaments silver, but on the interior of these homes there were contrasting influences and competing decorative styles (Reese, 1983; Pilling, 1980). At the time of the Greek Revival style friendship, interest, and enthusiasm for the French republic made anything French fashionable. Napoleonic conquest of Egypt sparked new interest in Egyptian furniture and thus produced a revival of Egyptian style and motif. Hepplewhite from England contributed furniture featuring straight simple lines with contrasting wood inlay. The Sheraton style, also from England, called for artisans to carve and curve wood reeded into spindles. Students looked for these rival decorative influences and evaluated which were most relevant to the site.

At the Lanier Home students listened, explored, questioned, and used cameras, and they later printed photographs to document their experiences. Students documented the trip through photography in order to remember and focus on details and patterns. The trip themes of architecture, human environment interaction, and transportation made excellent questions for the guide. How does the exterior architecture of the Lanier Home carry over into interior decoration? How did the geography of the town influence the house? How did the house influence Madison? How did the people build the house to suit the land? How did transportation influence this particular site? The three trip themes serve as guiding questions for recovering information on hand-held tape recorders that acted as spontaneous journals. These are much more popular with students than writing in journals, and they offer students a way to gather information while on site and relate information to their thoughts, questions, and opinions regarding the site.

Sharing social studies with a child is always an important and exciting endeavor; the Lanier Home is just one of many excellent and interesting places to share with children. Just down the street, the teacher provided other stops that also reflected the ideals of the time. Students consider if other structures in the community confirm or refute their ideas about the primary structure. The Schofield House, a tavern and Masonic hall, interprets the rise of fraternal organizations and how the community now has enough leisure time for social development. The house also served as a business, showing the exchange of goods and services; thus, the teacher was able to help students understand commerce and the exchange of ideas through transportation. Students saw how architecture supported these two endeavors. Furthermore, the churches in Madison strayed from their religious purposes to embrace the ideals of liberty by building their meetinghouses in classical forms.

The personnel of historic sites have long given tours in costume or used first-person presentation to aid interpretation. Teachers should also use this technique to interpret sites that remain difficult for students to explore without help. Through a first-person presentation, the architect of both the J. F. D. Lanier and the Shrewsbury homes, Francis Costigan, addresses the questions of his selection of architectural elements, why he used them, and what he was trying to say. The teacher portrays Mr. Schofield to interpret his business, why he is a committed Mason, and what he thinks Masonry will do for the community. The teacher also portrays Judge Jeremiah Sullivan to bring in ideas of his service as a lawyer, judge, and member of the state legislature. Students question these figures directly about their contributions to the community, why they make these contributions, and how their homes reflect their lives. Students raise questions for these characters rather than only listening. Teachers who use this technique help students interpret sites and events by using the site to enrich student background information before generating questions to interpret the site (Morris, 2009). Student interpretation of sites becomes much more productive when they turn the traditional docent lecture into an interactive event. When traveling, the teacher does not have the time needed to do a full costume change, but if students are familiar with first-person presentation, the teacher quickly steps into character with a few words of introduction and a few simple and easy to carry props such as a hat, vest, or jacket. The teacher will very quickly wish to establish the place and time that the students can see as well as what they cannot see. They need to establish their identity, tell how they connect to this place, and explain how the teacher's objectives connect with the big ideas of the time period. Through taking on the role of a character from another time, teachers help students understand the attitudes of people in another time for the purpose of teaching civics.

After Returning to School

To follow up on the trip the students may organize PowerPoint slides to retell the story of the trip. Students who take photographs may make a scrapbook displaying the images, brochures, and leaflets gathered on the trip. The children read leaflets describing the sites, then organize and arrange their thoughts by using these collected documents. With a copy of a street map of Madison, the students in this chapter's example retraced the route through the city, marking each site visited and making a poster explaining their evidence for each theme. In the slides, scrapbook, and street map of Madison, students included all three areas of architecture, human environment interaction, and transportation in their assessment. Furthermore, they were required to include evidence that they found each of these at each site they documented. Considering the students' prior learning, they were asked what they discovered about the importance of the architecture to the town of Madison. They discussed the people and their relationship to the land in the town of Madison. The students were also asked how transportation changed and how it affected Madison as it changed. After the study travel experience, students planned further trips to Madison to see the Fairplay Fire Company, Judge Jeremiah Sullivan's Home, Shrewsbury Home, Schofield House, Dr. Hutching's Office and Hospital, and the Railroad Station.

CONCLUSIONS

Teachers found this focused field trip important because it helped students learn about democratic ideals and how society interpreted them. The teachers helped students examine people from the past through their possessions and decorative arts. Teachers provided direct, purposeful, and engaging experience based on the roles that individual citizens played. Teachers had opportunities to talk about civics, community, and commonwealth by looking at specific examples of decorative arts. Educators need to devote more attention to explaining the concept relations to representative government and to the role individual citizens play in the system (Fiscus, 2006; O'Brien & Kohlmeier, 2003). Students need to look beyond the mechanics of government to the role of an individual in society, and teachers should plan direct experiences to help students think, experience, and discuss the individual as a citizen.

Students found this information important because they could see the idealism of the young republic carried out in monumental architecture, interior design, and community planning. Many students pass structures from the period every day without recognizing their importance. Students need to see the buildings and their contents both as an art form and as a way to make inferences about society. Students got to experience the aesthetics of the historical structure in an immersion situation, and they recognized the intertwined ideas of civics, community, and commonwealth. Elementary students used the resources of the community to study civic virtue in the young republic, looking at architectural interiors and exteriors to examine the ideals the founders of the new nation were trying to convey through the residences they created for themselves. Students looked at connections between the past and the present and examined how their community intertwines with both. Not only can elementary students look at the built structures in their community to interpret democratic ideals, but these students need to find ways in which to talk about the ideas that accompany the thought that they are citizens in a democracy with rights and responsibilities. Students looked at communities and the exteriors and interiors of historic homes to find ways to talk about democratic ideas. "Civic society is conceived as the realm of organized social life that is voluntary, self-generated, largely self-supporting, autonomous from the state, and bound by a legal order or set of shared rules" (Rubin & Giarelli, 2007, p. 14). The way the families moved civic ideals into their homes gives students some indication of how serious and passionate these people were about their beliefs.

The members of the community find this type of study important because it shows the role of democracy in both community life and the individual spirit of the owner. The members of a civic society show that they enter into the groups freely, and citizen authority emerges from their creative talents and energies. Art reaches the community by making a public statement containing values and pronouncements of ideas important to the owner or creator. The community members must know what they are seeing, why it is important, and how it relates to their lives.

ACKNOWLEDGMENT

An earlier draft of this manuscript was published as: Morris, R. V. (2004). Examples of public and private architecture illustrating civic virtue: Examining local architecture for 1800 to 1850. *The Social Studies, 95*(3), 107–114. Reprinted with permission.

POSTSCRIPT

The Political Act of Teaching

The public observes educators and students when they are on study travel experiences. How the public sees students when they leave the classroom is in some way a political act, because the students and their teachers communicate much about the educational system when they expose the classroom to public scrutiny during a trip. Educators need to take the opportunity of the study travel experience to plan an experience in which students are obviously learning; the public can then see the justification of tax money being spent on public schools that wisely take time to study in alternative learning environments (Yarema, 2002). The obvious implications include the need for university professors to help pre-service teachers see the educative value of study travel experiences. Pre-service teachers need experiences in both planning, perhaps with the use of such resources as Teaching with Historic Places (http://www.nps.gov/history/nr/twhp/state.htm), and participating in educational field trips. Moreover, students need to see learning in alternative settings not as an educational frolic but as a logical extension of the classroom. Students need to see these experiences as opportunities to gather research that is just as necessary to their learning and comprehension as reading or writing. Finally, teachers need to communicate with their students the importance of the objectives they have for learning while also remaining flexible to accept

The Field Trip Book: Study Travel Experiences in Social Studies
pp. 219–220

the serendipitous interactions with the sites where their students learn. Teachers need to make sure the students are both well prepared and adequately debriefed from the experience to make sure students get the full value from the field experience.

Classrooms are like cloisters insofar as they wall out the disturbances in the world and provide time for introspective thought and reflection. The walls also separate students from the pressures of the world, but if teachers hide from the world, teachers deny students real experiences. If teachers give up on the world, pessimism, despair, and cynicism reaches our students. If teachers reject the world, then contentment and narcissism set upon the students. These walls give students security to react to the world, and if teachers use the security of the community to minister to the needs of the community, children learn great lessons of civics, civilization, and civility.

Students need to remember to be gracious and write simple thank you notes to their hosts when they return to school. This does several things: It reminds the site personnel that the students visited, that the students are a good group that the site wants to work with in the future, and that students from the school look forward to visiting again.

Finally, the students carry memories of study travel with them for the rest of their lives, and they talk about these memories long after the fact. Well constructed study travel experiences are those that are well planned, filled with adventures, expect students to participate in the gathering of information from the experience, and have strong educational expectations for learning. The students remember where they went, who they went with, what they did, and what they learned (Bamberger & Tal, 2008, Knapp, 2007; Halocha, 2005; Morell, 2003). The learning the students do in these experiences should be the focus of the school year, and having field experiences at regular intervals will help students learn effectively in the field. The types of field trips discussed in this book are not easy to construct, but they are meaningful to the learners. This is a powerful incitement for teachers to take students on field trips, for educational institutions to encourage field trips, and for parents to demand that their children receive this type of field-based instruction.

REFERENCES

Aleixandre, M. P., & Rodriguez, R. L. (2001). Designing a field code: Environmental values in primary school. *Environmental Education Research*, *7*(1), 5–22.

Alibrandi, M., Beal, C., Thompson, A., & Wilson, A. (2000). Reconstructing a school's past using oral histories and GIS mapping. *Social Education*, *64*(3), 134–140.

Alleman, J., & Brophy, J. (2003A). Comparing transportation units published in 1931 and 2002: What have we learned? *Journal of Curriculum and Supervision*, *19*(1), 5–28.

Alleman, J., & Brophy, J. (2003B). History is alive: Teaching young children about changes over time. *Social Studies*, *94*(3), 107–110.

Alleman, J., Knighton, B., & Brophy, J. (2007). Social studies: Incorporating all children using community and cultural universals as a centerpiece. *Journal of Learning Disabilities*, *40*(2), 166–173.

Allen, R. F. (2000). Civic education and the decision-making process. *Social Studies*, *91*(1), 5–8.

Anesthetics in the Civil War. (2006, October 16). Retrieved from http://www.civilwarhome.com/anaesthetics.htm

Appelbaum, M., & Catanese, J. (2003). *Read-aloud plays: Colonial America: 5 short plays for the classroom with background information, writing prompts, and creative activities.* New York, NY: Scholastic.

Archambault, R. D. (Ed.). (1997). *John Dewey on education: Selected writings.* Chicago, IL: The University of Chicago Press.

Argiro, C. (2004). Teaching with public art. *Art Education*, *57*(4), 25–32.

Arons, S. (1975). Compulsory education: The plain people resist. In A. N. Keim (Ed.), *Compulsory education and the Amish* (pp. 124–135). Boston, MA: Beacon Press.

Arthur, J. (2000). *Schools and community: The communitarian agenda in education.* New York, NY: Falmer.

Arweck, E., & Nesbitt, E. (2008). Peace and non-violence: Sathya Sai Education in human values in British schools. *Journal of Peace Education, 5*(1), 17–32.

Baker, R., & Spicer, B. (1997). *For Richer or Poorer* [Motion picture]. USA: Universal Studios.

Bamberger, Y., & Tal, T. (2008). Multiple outcomes of class visits to natural history museums: The students' view. *Journal of Science Education and Technology, 17*(3), 274–284.

Banks, J. A. (2001). Citizenship education and diversity: Implications for teacher education. *Journal of Teacher Education, 52*(1), 5–16.

Barry'd treasure: Civil war relics. (n.d.) Retrieved from http://www.iglou.com/btreasure/currency.htm

Barton, K. C. (2001). A sociocultural perspective on children's understanding of historical change: Comparative findings from Northern Ireland and the United States. *American Educational Research Journal, 38*(4), 881–913.

Beach, D., & Dovemark, M. (2009). Making "right" choices? An ethnographic account of creativity, performativity and personalized learning policy, concepts and practices. *Oxford Review of Education, 35*(6), 689–704.

Beglau, M. M. (2005). Can technology narrow the Black–White achievement gap? *T.H.E. Journal, 32*(12), 13–17.

Bell, D., & Henning, M. D. (2007). DeKalb County, Illinois: A local history project for second graders. *Social Studies and the Young Learner, 19*(3), 7–11.

Berman, S. H. (2004). Teaching civics: A call to action. *Principal Leadership, 5*(1), 16–20.

Bisbee, G., Kubina, L., & Birkenstock, S. (2000). Create your own field guide. *Science Teacher , 67*(5), 42–43.

Black, M.S. (2000). Using your city as a multicultural classroom. *Teaching Education, 11 (3),* 343–351.

Bobek, D., Zaff, J., Li, Y., & Lerner, R. M. (2009). Cognitive, emotional, and behavioral components of civic action: Towards an integrated measure of civic engagement. *Journal of Applied Developmental Psychology, 30*(5), 615–627.

Boothe, H. (2000). Tools for learning about the past to protect the future: Archeology in the classroom. *Legacy, 11*(1), 10–12, 37.

Boritt, G. S. (Ed.). (1999). *The Gettysburg nobody knows.* New York, NY: Oxford University Press.

Bowdon, S. H. (2006). Here lies.... Cemeteries as historical and artistic lessons for primary-age children: A teacher's K-W-L plan. *Childhood Education, 83*(2), 87–91.

Boyer, E. (1995). *The basic school: A community for learning.* Princeton, NJ: The Carnegie Foundation for the Advancement of Teaching.

Boyte, H. C. (1999). Building the commonwealth: Citizenship as public work. In Stephen L. Elkin and Karol E. Soltan (Eds.), *Citizen competence and democratic institutions,* 259–278. University Park, PA: Pennsylvania State University Press.

Branting, S. D. (2009). Digitizing a heritage of faded memories: A case study on extending historical research capabilities. *History Teacher, 42*(4), 457–475.

Briley, R. (2000). What do you mean you don't do advanced placement? Confessions of an educational heretic. *History Teacher, 33*(4), 527–532.

Brophy, J., & Alleman, J. (2009). Meaningful social studies for elementary students. *Teachers and Teaching: Theory and Practice, 15*(3), 357–376.

Brophy, J., & Alleman, J. (2007). *Powerful social studies for elementary students* (2nd ed.). Belmont, CA: Thomason Wadsworth.

Brophy, J. & Alleman, J. (2006). A reconceptualized rationale for elementary social studies. *Theory and Research in Social Education, 34*(4), 428–454.

Brophy, J., & VanSledright, B. (1997). *Teaching and learning history in elementary schools.* New York, NY: Teachers College Press.

Brosio, R. A. (2000). *Philosophical scaffolding for the construction of critical democratic education.* New York, NY: Peter Lang.

Brouillette, L. (2006). Bringing jazz back to its roots: Inner city students explore their musical heritage. *Teaching Artist Journal, 4*(1), 39–46.

Bruce, B., & Lin, C. C. (2009). Voices of youth: Podcasting as a means for inquiry-based community engagement. *E-Learning, 6*(2), 230–241.

Burch, K. T. (2000). *Eros as the educational principle of democracy.* New York, NY: Peter Lang.

Camicia, S. P. (2009). Teaching the Japanese American internment: A case study of social studies curriculum conflict and change. *Journal of Social Studies Research, 33*(1), 113–132.

Carey, G. (2000). Tolerating religion. In S. Mendus (Ed.), *The politics of toleration in modern life* (pp. 45–65). Durham, NC: Duke University Press.

Cartwright, S. (2004). Young citizens in the making. *Young Children, 59*(5), 108–109.

Cartwright, S, Aronson, S. S., Stacey, S., & Winbush, O. (2001). Field trips. Beginnings workshop. *Child Care Information Exchange, 139*, 39–58.

Catton, B. (1962). *The Army of the Potomac: Mr. Lincoln's army.* Garden City, NY: Doubleday.

Catton, B. (1963a). *The Army of the Potomac: Glory road.* Garden City, NY: Doubleday.

Catton, B. (1963b). *The centennial history of the Civil War: Terrible swift sword.* Garden City, NY: Doubleday.

Catton, B. (1965). *The centennial history of the Civil War: Never call retreat.* Garden City, NY: Doubleday.

The Center for Understanding the Built Environment (CUBE). *Cube.* http://www.cubekc.org/

Chan, E. (2007). Student experiences of a culturally-sensitive curriculum: Ethnic identity development amid conflicting stories to live by. *Journal of Curriculum Studies, 39*(2), 177–194.

Chu, J. M. (2004). The risks and rewards of teaching race. *History Teacher, 37*(4), 484–493.

Clark, A. D. (2000). Living the past at Oak Hill School. *Now & Then, 17*(3), 13–17.

Collins, L., & Redcross, J. (2005). The case of the field trip disaster. *Journal of Cases in Educational Leadership, 8*(1), 35–40.

Coy, M. (2009). Travel blankets. *School Arts: The Art Education Magazine for Teachers, 109*(4), 34–35.

Cruz, B. C., & Murthy, S. A. (2006). Breathing life into history: Using role-playing to engage students. *Social Studies and the Young Learner, 19*(1), 4–8.

Cullingford, C. (2006). Children's own vision of schooling. *Education 3–13, 34*(3), 211–221.

Dallmer, D. (2007). Teaching students about civil rights using print material and photographs. *Social Studies, 98*(4), 153–158.

Dean, E. T. (1999). *Shook over hell: Post-traumatic stress, Vietnam, and the Civil War.* Cambridge, MA: Harvard University Press.

DeSteno, N. (2000). Parent involvement in the classroom: The fine line. *Young Children, 55*(3), 13–17.

de Tocqueville, A. (1945). *Democracy in America.* New York, NY: Vintage Books.

Dewey, J. (1997). The democratic conception in education. In W. C. Parker (Ed.), *Educating the democratic mind* (pp. 25–43). Albany, NY: SUNY.

Dewey, J. (1990). *The school and society—The child and the curriculum.* Chicago, IL: The University of Chicago Press.

Dilg, M. (1999). *Race and culture in the classroom: Teaching and learning through multicultural education.* New York, NY: Teachers College Press.

Dils, A. K. (2000). Using technology in a middle school social studies classroom. *International Journal of Social Education, 15*(1), 102–112.

Dowden, T. (2007). Relevant, challenging, integrative and exploratory curriculum design: Perspectives from theory and practice for middle level schooling in Australia. *Australian Educational Researcher, 34*(2), 51–71.

Duplass, J. A. (2007). Elementary social studies: Trite, disjointed, and in need of reform? *Social Studies, 98*(4), 137–144.

Easley, L. M. (2005). Cemeteries as science labs. *Science Scope, 29*(3), 28–32.

Eisner, E. W. (1991). Art, music, and literature within social studies. In James P. Shaver (Ed.), *Handbook of research on social studies teaching and learning,* 551–558. New York, NY: Macmillan.

Ellis-Williams, A. (2007). Discovering the possibilities: A study of African American youth resistance and activism. *Educational Foundations, 21*(1–2), 107–124.

Elshtain, J. B. (1995). *Democracy on trial.* New York, NY: Basic Books.

Engle, S. H., & Ochoa, A.S. (1988). *Education for democratic citizenship: Decision making in the social studies.* New York, NY: Teachers College Press.

Evans, B. N. (1997). *Interpreting the free exercise of religion: The Constitution and American pluralism.* Chapel Hill, NC: University of North Carolina Press.

Falk, J. H., & Dierking, L. D. (2000). *Learning from museums: Visitor experiences and the making of meaning.* Walnut Creek, CA: AltaMira Press.

Falk, J. H., & Dierking, L. D. (2002). *Lessons without limit: How free-choice learning is transforming education.* Walnut Creek, CA: AltaMira Press.

Fattal, L. F. (2004). Pride of place: Documenting community. *School Arts: The Art Education Magazine for Teachers, 104*(4), 26–27.

Feldman, E. S., & Weir, P. (1985). *Witness* [Motion picture]. USA: Paramount.

Ferretti, R. P., MacArthur, C. A., & Okolo, C. M. (2007). Students' misconceptions about U.S. westward migration. *Journal of Learning Disabilities, 40*(2), 145–153.

Findley, N. (2002). In their own ways. *Educational Leadership, 60*(1), 60–63.

Fink, R. (2009). *The American Revolution: 1763–1789.* Camarillo, CA: Bad Wolf Press.

Fiscus, L. (2006). Learning to lead: Developing young adolescents' skills. *Middle Ground, 10*(2), 17–19.

Foote, S. (1986a). *The Civil War: Fort Sumter to Perryville*. New York, NY: Vintage.

Foote, S. (1986b). *The Civil War: Fredericksburg to Meridian*. New York, NY: Vintage.

Forman, M., & Calvert, R. A. (1993). *Cartooning Texas: One hundred years of cartoon art in the lone star state*. College Station, TX: Texas A & M University Press.

Freeman, D. S. (1995). *Lee's lieutenants: A study in command: Gettysburg to Appomattox*. New York, NY: Touchstone.

Freeman, D. S. (1971). *Lee's lieutenants: A study in command: Cedar Mountain to Chancellorsville*. New York, NY: Scribner Classics.

Gallavan, N. P., & Fabbi, J. L. (2004). Stimulating moral reasoning in children through situational learning and children's literature. *Social Studies and the Young Learner, 16*(3), 17–23.

Giacalone, V. (2003). How to plan, survive, and even enjoy an overnight field trip with 200 students. *Science Scope, 26*(4), 22–26.

Gentry, T. (2002). Documenting the past and the present: Madrid, New Mexico. *OAH Magazine of History, 16*(4), 24–26.

Goncu, A. (1999). *Children's engagement in the world: Sociocultural perspectives*. Cambridge University Press.

Goodman, J. (1992). *Elementary schooling for critical democracy*. Albany, NY: SUNY.

Green, M. (1988). *The dialectic of freedom*. New York, NY: Teachers College Press.

Groce, E. C., Grace, R. D., & Colby, S. (2005). The Big Apple's core: Exploring Manhattan. *Social Studies and the Young Learner, 18*(1), 22–27.

Gutman, A. (1987). *Democratic education*. Princeton, NJ: Princeton University Press.

Haibo, Y. (2009). Naxi intellectuals and ethnic identity. *Diaspora, Indigenous, and Minority Education, 3*(1), 21–31.

Halocha, J. (2005). Developing a research tool to enable children to voice their experiences and learning through fieldwork. *International Research in Geographical and Environmental Education, 14*(4), 348–355.

Hammond, P.E. (1998). *With liberty for all: Freedom of religion in the United States*. Louisville, KY: Westminster John Knox Press.

Heines, E. D., Piechura-Coulture, K., Roberts, D., & Roberts, J. (2003). PARKnerships are for all. *Science and Children, 41*(3), 25–29.

Hess, E. J. (2001). *Pickett's charge: The last attack at Gettysburg*. Chapel Hill, NC: University of North Carolina Press.

Hess, E. J. (1997). *The Union soldier in battle: Enduring the ordeal of combat*. Lawrence, KS: The University Press of Kansas.

Historic Landmarks Foundation of Indiana. (2002). *On the street where you live: Be a building watcher!* Indianapolis, IN: Author. Retrieved from http://www.historiclandmarks.org/sitecollectiondocuments/publication%20pdfs/on%20street%20pdf.pdf.

Holloway, J. E., & Chiodo, J. J. (2009). Social studies is being taught in the elementary school: A contrarian view. *Journal of Social Studies Research, 33*(2), 235–261.

Holman, L. & Sucich, J. (2007). A marvelous journey: Calling from Greece to a U. S. classroom. *Social Studies and the Young Learner, 19*(3), 20–23.

Hopkinson, D., & Farmer, L. S. J. (2001). History must be seen. *Library Talk, 14*(5), 10–12.

Horwitz, T. (1999). *Confederates in the Attic: Dispatches from the Unfinished Civil War.* New York, NY: Vintage.

Howat, C. (2007). Le vieux carré: A field trip to a New Orleans parish. *Social Studies and the Young Learner, 20*(2), 24–29.

Howes, E. V., & Cruz, B. C. (2009). Role-playing in science education: An effective strategy for developing multiple perspectives. *Journal of Elementary Science Education, 21*(3), 33–46.

Hyland, N. E. (2009). One white teacher's struggle for culturally relevant pedagogy: The problem of the community. *New Educator, 5*(2), 95–112.

James, A. (2006). *Preschool success: Everything you need to know to help your child learn.* Indianapolis, IN : Jossey-Bass.

Jimerson, R. C. (1994). *The private Civil War: Popular thought during the sectional conflict.* Baton Rouge, LA: Louisiana State University Press.

Jornell, W. (2009). Using YouTube to teach presidential election propaganda: Twelve representative videos. *Social Education, 73*(7), 325–329, 362–363.

Karner, T. R., Jr., Knapp, C. E., Simmert, R. L., Carlson, P, Criswell, M. R., Arroz, M., et al. (2001). Teaching the 3 R's through the 3 C's: Connecting curriculum and community. *Thresholds in Education, 27*(3–4), 7–30.

Keegan, J. (2000). There's rosemary for remembrance. *American Educator, 24*(1), 34–44.

Kennedy, R. (1989, November–December). A young nation leans on the classics, *Historic Preservation*, 34–39.

Kennedy, R., & Hall, J. M. (1989). *Greek revival America.* New York, NY: Stewart, Tabori and Chang.

Knapp, D. (2007). A longitudinal analysis of an out-of-school science experience. *School Science and Mathematics, 107*(2), 44–51.

Knapp, D. (2000). Memorable experiences of a science field trip. *School Science and Mathematics, 100*(2), 65–72.

Knapp, D., & Barrie, E. (2001). Content evaluation of an environmental science field trip. *Journal of Science Education and Technology, 10*(4), 351–357.

Koetsch, P., D'Acquisto, L, Kurin, A., Juffer, S., & Goldberg L. (2002). Schools into museums. *Educational Leadership, 60*(1), 74–78.

Kornfeld, J., & Leyden, G. (2005). Acting out: Literature, drama, and connecting with history. *Reading Teacher, 59*(3), 230–238.

Kozak, S. & Bretherick, (2002). Visual arts: A vital environmental education program component. *Pathways: The Ontario Journal of Outdoor Education, 14*(2), 25–27.

Kraybill, D. B. (1994). Introduction: The struggle to be separate. In D. B. Kraybill & M. A. Olsaham (Eds.), *The Amish struggle with modernity* (pp. 1–20). Hanover, NH: University Press of New England.

Langhorst, E. (2007). After the bell, beyond the walls. *Educational Leadership, 64*(8), 74–77.

LeCompte, K. N. (2006). Conditions of democracy: Elementary perspectives. *Social Studies and the Young Learner, 19*(1), 28–31.

Levstik, L. S., & Barton, K. C. (2005). *Doing history: Investigating with children in elementary and middle schools* (3rd ed.). Mahwah, NJ: Erlbaum.

Levstik, L. S., & Groth, J. (2002). "Scary thing, being an eighth grader:" Exploring gender and sexuality in a middle school U.S. history unit. *Theory and Research in Social Education, 30*(2), 233–254.

Lim, C. P. (2008). Global citizenship education, school curriculum and games: Learning mathematics, English and science as a global citizen. *Computers & Education, 51*(3), 1073–1093.

Linderman, G. F. (1989). *Embattled courage: The experience of combat in the American Civil War.* New York, NY: Free Press.

Locke, D.C. (1992). *Increasing multicultural understanding: A comprehensive model.* Newbury Park, CA: Sage.

Logan, D. K. (2000). *Information skills toolkit: Collaborative integrated instruction for the middle grades. Professional growth series.* Worthington, OH: Linworth.

Luthy, D. (1994). The origin and growth of Amish tourism. In D. B. Kraybill & M. A. Olshan (Eds.), *The Amish struggle with modernity* (pp. 113–132). Hanover, NH: University of Press of New England.

Lybolt, J., Techmanski, K. E., & Gottfred, C. (2007). *Building language throughout the year: The preschool early literacy curriculum.* Baltimore, MD: Brookes.

Maher, R. (2004). "Workin' on the railroad": African American labor history. *Social Education, 68*(5), S4–S9.

Martin, J. B. (2001). Plug into primary sources. *Library Talk, 14*(5), 10–12.

Mawdsley, R. D. (1999). Legal issues involving field trips. *School Business Affairs, 65*(9), 28–31.

McCall, A. L. (2006). Enriching state studies teaching: Learning from experienced teachers. *Social Studies and the Young Learner, 19*(1), 17–22.

McCall, A. L. (2002). That's not fair! Fourth graders' responses to multicultural state history. *Social Studies, 93*(2), 85–91.

McCall, A. L., & Ristow, T. (2003). *Teaching state history: A guide to developing a multicultural curriculum.* Portsmouth, NH: Heinemann.

McCloskey, P. J. (2004). Hudson River school. *Teacher Magazine, 16*(3), 31–35.

McDermott, J. J. (Ed.). (1981). *The philosophy of John Dewey: Two volumes in one.* Chicago, IL: University Of Chicago Press.

McElmeel, S. L. (2001). Kids search: Social studies research and local resources. *Library Talk, 14*(5), 13–15.

McLellan, A. M., & Martin, J. (2005). Psychology and the education of persons in British Columbia: A critical interpretive investigation. *Canadian Journal of Education, 28*(1–2), 73–91.

McMillan, E. P. (2000). Traveling west in 1845: A first grade project. *Social Studies and the Young Learner, 13*(2), 28–31.

McPherson, J. M. (1988). *Battle cry of freedom: The Civil War era.* New York, NY: Oxford.

McPherson, J. M. (1998). *For cause and comrades: Why men fought in the Civil War.* New York: Oxford University Press.

Michels, B. J., & Maxwell, D. K. (2006). An after-school program for interpreting local history. *TechTrends: Linking Research and Practice to Improve Learning, 50*(2), 62–66.

Milewski, P. (2008). "The little gray book": Pedagogy, discourse and rupture in 1937. *History of Education, 37*(1), 91–111.

Minow, M. (2006). What the rule of law should mean in civics education: From the "following orders" defense to the classroom. *Journal of Moral Education, 35*(2), 137–162.

Misco, T. (2005). The moral nature of elementary social studies methods. *Theory and Research in Social Education, 33*(4), 532–547.

Mislove, R., & Strange, W. (2008). Knowing neighborhoods: Students and teachers as artistic colleague. *Teaching Artist Journal, 6*(4), 259–265

Mitchell, K., & Parker, W. C. (2008). I pledge allegiance to ... flexible citizenship and flexible scales of belonging. *Teachers College Record, 110*(4), 775–804.

Mitchell, R. (2001). *The American Civil War, 1861–1865.* New York, NY: Longman.

Mitchell, R. (1997). *Civil War soldiers.* New York, NY: Penguin USA.

Mitchell, R. (1995). *The vacant chair: The northern soldier leaves home.* New York: Oxford University Press.

Mitoraj, S. O. (2001). A tale of two cemeteries: Gravestones as community artifacts. *English Journal, 90*(5), 82–87.

Morrell, P. D. (2003). Cognitive impact of a grade school field trip. *Journal of Elementary Science Education, 15*(1), 27–36.

Morris, R. V. (2009). *Bringing history to life: First person presentations in elementary and middle school social studies.* New York, NY: Roman & Littlefield.

Morris, R. V. (2006). The clio club: An extra-curricular model for elementary social studies enrichment. *Gifted Child Today, 28*(1), 40–48.

Morris, R. V. (2000A). "Outlines" of history: Measured spaces and kinesthetics. *Social Studies and the Young Learner, 13*(2), 14–16.

Morris, R. V. (2000B). Teaching social studies with artifacts. *Social Studies, 9*(1), 32–37.

Morris, R. V., & Welch, M. (2000). *How to perform acting out history in the classroom to enrich social studies education.* Dubuque, IA: Kendall/Hunt.

National Civil War Association. (2005) *Standard living history association Civil War artillery drill manual.* Wilmington, VT: Author. Retrieved from http://www.livinghistoryassn.org/safety_manuals/CW_Artillery_Safety_Manual.pdf.

National Council for the Social Studies. (1994). *Expectations of excellence: Curriculum standards for social studies (Bulletin 89).* Washington, DC: Author.

National Park Service: National Historic Register. (n.d.) *Choices and commitments: The soldiers at Gettysburg.* Retrieved from http://www.cr.nps.gov/nr/twhp/wwwlps/lessons/44gettys/44gettys.htm

Nespor, J. (2000). School field trips and the curriculum of public spaces. *Journal of Curriculum Studies, 32*(1), 25–43.

Nevins, A. (1992). *Ordeal of the Union 4.* New York, NY: Collier.

Nevins, A. (1960). *The war for the Union: War becomes revolution 1862–1863.* New York, NY: Charles Shribner's Sons.

Noel, A. M. (2007). Elements of a winning field trip. *Kappa Delta Pi Record, 44*(1), 42–44.

Noel, A. M., & Colopy, M. A. (2006). Making field trips meaningful: Teachers' and site educators' perspectives on teaching materials. *Theory and Research in Social Education, 34*(3), 553–568.

Noffke, S. E. (2000). Identity, community, and democracy in the "New Social Order." In D. W. Hursh & E. W. Ross (Eds.), *Democratic social education: Social studies for social change* (pp. 73–83). New York, NY: Falmer.

Nolan, A. (1983). *The iron brigade*. Ann Arbor, MI: Hardscrable.

Obenchain, K. M., & Morris, R. V. (2010). *50 social studies strategies for k–8 classrooms* (3rd ed.). Saddle River, NJ: Person.

O'Brien, J., & Kohlmeier, J. (2003). Leadership: Part of the civic mission of school? *Social Studies, 94*(4), 161–166.

Ohn, J. D., & Wade, R. (2009). Community service-learning as a group inquiry project: Elementary and middle school CiviConnections teachers' practices of integrating historical inquiry in community service-learning. *Social Studies, 100*(5), 200–211.

Olmert, M. (2002). *Official guide to colonial Williamsburg*. Williamsburg, VA: Colonial Williamsburg Foundation.

Overton, D. (2002). Schools and industry get to work. *Education in Science, N198*, 10–11.

Paglin.C. (2002). Taking learning outdoors: A bitter dispute over water in southern Oregon become a first hand lesson in history, ecology, and local culture. *Northwest Education 7*(3), 36–41.

Pai, Y., & Adler, S. (2001). *Cultural foundations of education* (3rd ed.). Upper Saddle River, NY: Prentice Hall.

Parker, (2006). Talk isn't cheap: Practicing deliberation in school. *Social Studies and the Young Learner, 19*(1), 12–15.

Pascal, C., & Bertram, T. (2009). Listening to young citizens: The struggle to make real a participatory paradigm in research with young children. *European Early Childhood Education Research Journal, 17*(2), 249–262.

Patton, J. R. (2006). Family, extended. *Teaching Pre K–8, 37*(3), 42–45.

Pearl, A., & Knight, T. (1999). *The democratic classroom: Theory to inform practice*. Cresskill, NJ: Hampton Press.

Peat, W. D. (1962). *Indiana houses of the nineteenth century*. Indianapolis, IN: Indiana Historical Society.

Peterson, C. (2004). *Jump back in time: A living history resource*. Portsmouth, NH: Teacher Ideas Press.

Pilling, R. W. (1980). John and Hugh Finlay, Baltimore cabinetmakers: Painted and gilt in the most fanciful manner. *Art & Antiques, 3*(5), 86–93.

Polette, N. (2008). *Get up and move with nonfiction*. Portsmouth, NH: Teacher Ideas Press.

Potter, L. A. (2007). The Constitution in action. *Social Education, 71*(5), 224–230.

Pressick-Kilborn, K. (2009). Steps to fostering a learning community in the primary science classroom. *Teaching Science, 55*(1), 27–29.

Quezada, R. L., & Christopherson, R. W. (2005). Adventure-based service learning: University students' self-reflection accounts of service with children. *Journal of Experiential Education, 28*(1), 1–16.

Rabb, T. K. (2007). Those who do not learn history…. *Chronicle of Higher Education, 53*(42), B2.

Ramage, J. A. (1995). *Rebel raider: The life of General John Hunt Morgan*. Lexington, KY: The University Press of Kentucky.

Reese, R. (1983). Richard Dana, Duncan Phyfe and Charles-Honore Lannuier: Cabinetmakers of old New York. *Art and Antiques, 7*(5), 56–61.

Rhodes, J. F. (1999). *A history of the Civil War 1861–1865.* Mineola, NY: Dover.

Rodgers, H. R., Jr., (1969). *Community conflict, public opinion and the law: The Amish dispute in Iowa.* Columbus, OH: Charles E. Merrill.

Rodgers, Y. V., Hawthorne, S., & Wheeler, R. C. (2008). Cross-state variation in economics content standards in the primary grades. *Social Education, 72*(2), 88–94.

Roessing, L. (2007). Making connections: The home front fair. *Middle Level Learning, 10*(4), 32–33.

Rolph, G. V., & Clark, N. (1961). *The Civil War soldier.* Washington, DC: Historical Impressions.

Roser, N. L., & Keehn, S. (2002). Fostering thought, talk, and inquiry: Linking literature and social studies. *Reading Teacher, 55*(5), 416–26.

Rovegno, I., & Gregg, M. (2007). Using folk dance and geography to teach interdisciplinary, multicultural subject matter: A school-based study. *Physical Education and Sport Pedagogy, 12*(3), 205–223.

Rowell, C. G., Hickey, M. G., Gecsei, K., & Klein, S. (2007). A school-wide effort for learning history via a time capsule. *Social Education, 71*(5), 261–266, 271.

Rubin, B. C., & Giarelli, J. M. (Eds.) (2007). *Civic education for diverse citizens in global times: Rethinking theory and practice.* Mahwah, NJ: Erlbaum.

Sandburg, C. (1974). *Abraham Lincoln: The war years: 1861–1864.* New York, NY: Dell.

The Sanitary Commission and other relief agencies. (2002, February 10). Retrieved from http://www.civilwarhome.com/sanitarycommission.htm.

Schelling, G. (2004). 300 years of community history in architecture. *School Arts: The Art Education Magazine for Teachers, 104*(4), 30.

Schuchat, D. (2005). Radio days in the classroom. *Social Education, 69*(4), M4–M9.

Schuitema, J., Veuglelers, W, Rijlaarsdam, G., & ten Darn, G. (2009). Two instructional designs for dilogic citizenship education: An effect study. *British Journal of Educational Psychology, 79*(3), 439–461.

Schulte, P. (2005). Social studies in motion: Learning with the whole person. *Social Studies and the Young Learner, 17*(4), 13–16.

Schur, J. B. (2007). Puritan day: A social science simulation. *Social Education, 71*(7), 348–353.

Schwartz, R. S. (1995). *Texas: A lone star history.* Amawalk, NY: Jackdaws.

Sehr, D. T. (1997). *Education for public democracy.* Albany, NY: State University Press of New York.

Sevier, B. R. (2002). The creation and content of an early "multicultural" social studies textbook: Learning from "people of Denver." *Theory and Research in Social Education, 30*(1), 116–141.

Shaw, B. (2002). *99 Historic homes of Indiana: A look inside.* Bloomington, IN: Indiana University Press.

Spring, J. (1997). *Political agendas for education from the Christian Coalition to the Green Party.* Mahwah, NJ: Erlbaum.

Stevens, R. L. (2001). *Homespun: Teaching Local History in Grades 6–12.* Westport, CT: Heinemann.

Tali Tal, R. (2004). Community-based environmental education—A case study of teacher–parent collaboration. *Environmental Education Research, 10*(4), 523–543.

Tanner, L. N. (1997). *Dewey's laboratory school: Lessons for today.* Albany, NY: SUNY.

Thomas, J. A. (2002). How deep is the water? *Science and Children, 40*(2), 28–32.

Trofanenko, B. M. (2008). More than a single best narrative: Collective history and the transformation of historical consciousness. *Curriculum Inquiry, 38*(5), 579–603.

Van Kannel-Ray, N., & Newlin-Haus, E. (2009). Using media as subject matter to teach thinking. *Middle School Journal, 41*(2), 13–18.

Wallach, J. (2000). *The enemy has a face: The seeds of peace experience.* Washington, DC: The United States Institute of Peace Press.

Warwick, P. (2007). Hearing pupils' voices: Revealing the need for citizenship education within primary schools. *Education 3–13, 35*(3), 261–272.

Wennik, S. (2004). Reporting on the process of legislation: A civics WebQuest. *Social Studies and the Young Learner, 17*(1), 11–14.

Whitmer, S., Luke, J., & Adams, M. (2000). Exploring the potential of museum multiple-visit programs. *Art Education, 53*(5), 46–52.

Wiley, B. (1995). *The life of Billy Yank: The common soldier of the Union.* Baton Rouge, LA: Louisiana State University.

Wiley, B. (1997). *The life of Johnny Reb: The common soldier of the Confederacy.* Baton Rouge, LA: Louisiana State University.

Wolff, A. L., & Wirmer, N. (2009). Shopping for mathematics in consumer town. *Young Children, 64*(3), 34–38.

Wolk, S. (2003). Teaching for critical literacy in social studies. *Social Studies, 94*(3), 101–106.

Yarema, A. (2002). A decade of debate: Improving content and interest in history education, *History Teacher, 35*(3), 389–398.

Yarrington, G. A. (1987). *LBJ political cartoons: The public years.* Austin, TX: The Lyndon Baines Johnson Library and Museum.

ABOUT THE AUTHOR

Ronald Vaughan Morris is a professor of social studies at Ball State University in the Department of History where he teaches elementary social studies methods to graduate and undergraduate students. He leads interdisciplinary teams of students in immersion projects where they work with local history museums and cultural institutions. He received his PhD in curriculum and instruction (social studies) from Purdue University. His research interests include creativity in elementary social studies teaching and learning and elementary history instruction. He has published many journal articles in scholarly journals including *Canadian Social Studies, Gifted Child Today, Social Studies and the Young Learner,* and *The Social Studies.* He is a reviewer for *The International Journal of Social Education* and *The Social Studies.* He is the coauthor of *50 Social Studies Strategies for K-8 Classrooms.* He is the author of *Bringing History to Life: First Person Presentations in Elementary and Middle School Social Studies* and *Drama in Elementary and Middle School Social Studies.* He has produced seven DVDs including one Emmy winner. He has received many grants. Both the American Association of State and Local History and the National Council for the Social Studies have recognized his work.

INDEX

Lightning Source UK Ltd.
Milton Keynes UK
UKOW031329251111

182691UK00001B/36/P